The Emerging Industrial Relations of China

Labour relations are at the heart of China's extraordinary economic rise. This growth, accompanied by internal migration, urbanisation and rising income have brought a dramatic increase in the aspirations of workers, forcing the Chinese government to restructure its relationships with both employers and workers. In order to resolve disputes and manage workplace militancy, the once monolithic official trade union is becoming more flexible, internally. No longer able to rely on government support in dealing with worker unrest, employers are rapidly forming organisations of their own. In this book, a new generation of Chinese scholars provide analyses of six distinct aspects of these developments. They are set in the broader context by the leading authority on Chinese labour law and two western specialists in comparative labour relations. The result is a comprehensive study for scholars and graduate students working in Chinese industrial relations, comparative labour law, human resource management, NGOs and international labour organisations.

William Brown is Emeritus Professor of Industrial Relations and Emeritus Master of Darwin College at the University of Cambridge. He was previously Director of the Industrial Relations Research Unit at the University of Warwick. He is the author and editor of six books on Industrial Relations, including *The Evolution of the Modern Workplace* (2009), also with Cambridge University Press, as well as countless contributions to books and journals.

Chang Kai is Director of the Institute of Industrial Relations and Professor at the School of Labour and Human Resources, Renmin University of China. He is also Adjunct Professor at the Chinese Academy of Governance and at the Capital University of Economics and Business. He is the Chair of the Labour Relations Branch of the China Human Resource Development Association and serves on the Consultative Council of China's Ministry of Human Resources and Social Security.

The Emerging Industrial Relations of China

Edited by

William Brown
University of Cambridge

Chang Kai
Renmin University of China

CAMBRIDGE
UNIVERSITY PRESS

University Printing House, Cambridge CB2 8BS, United Kingdom

One Liberty Plaza, 20th Floor, New York, NY 10006, USA

477 Williamstown Road, Port Melbourne, VIC 3207, Australia

314-321, 3rd Floor, Plot 3, Splendor Forum, Jasola District Centre, New Delhi - 110025, India

79 Anson Road, #06-04/06, Singapore 079906

Cambridge University Press is part of the University of Cambridge.

It furthers the University's mission by disseminating knowledge in the pursuit of education, learning and research at the highest international levels of excellence.

www.cambridge.org
Information on this title: www.cambridge.org/9781107534964
DOI: 10.1017/9781316335222

© Cambridge University Press 2017

First published 2017
First paperback edition 2018

A catalogue record for this publication is available from the British Library

Library of Congress Cataloging in Publication data
Names: Brown, William Arthur, 1945– editor. | Chang, Kai, 1952– editor.
Title: The emerging industrial relations of China / edited by William Brown, University of Cambridge, Chang Kai, Renmin University of China, Beijing.
Description: Hoboken : Cambridge University Press, 2017.
Identifiers: LCCN 2017020506 | ISBN 9781107114418 (hardback)
Subjects: LCSH: Industrial relations – China. | Labor movement – China. | Labor laws and legislation – China. | BISAC: BUSINESS & ECONOMICS / Human Resources & Personnel Management.
Classification: LCC HD8736.5 .E54 2017 | DDC 331.0951–dc23
LC record available at https://lccn.loc.gov/2017020506

ISBN 978-1-107-11441-8 Hardback
ISBN 978-1-107-53496-4 Paperback

Contents

Figures and Tables

Figures

Tables

Contributors

WILLIAM BROWN is Emeritus Professor of Industrial Relations and Emeritus Master of Darwin College at the University of Cambridge. He was previously Director of the Industrial Relations Research Unit at Warwick University. He was a member of the Council of Britain's Advisory, Conciliation and Arbitration Service and a founder member of the Low Pay Commission which fixes the National Minimum Wage.

CHANG KAI is Director of the Institute of Industrial Relations and Professor at the School of Labour and Human Resources at Renmin University of China. Apart from holding other policy-related roles, he is a member of the Consultative Council of China's Ministry of Human Resources and Social Security and a member of the Expert Group of the Financial and Economic Committee of the National Policy Committee.

CHANG CHENG is Lecturer in the Department of Labour Relations in the School of Labour Economics at the Capital University of Economics and Business, Beijing. Her doctoral research was conducted at the University of Cambridge.

WEN XIAOYI teaches at the China Institute of Industrial Relations. His doctorate in economics was received from the Renmin University of China. He has published extensively on Chinese trade unions, collective action and collective bargaining.

TU WEI is Research Associate at China Academy of Labour and Social Security in Beijing. His doctoral research was carried out at Renmin University of China and the Max Planck Institute for the Study of Societies in Cologne.

LEI XIAOTIAN is Lecturer in the Department of Labour Relations, School of Labour Economics, at the Capital University of Economics and Business. Her doctorate was received from the School of Labour and Human Resources of the Renmin University of China.

ZHAN JING is Associate Professor in the School of Labour Economics at the Capital University of Economics and Business, where she studied for her doctorate.

MENG QUAN is Lecturer in the Department of Labour Relations, the School of Labour Economics at the Capital University of Economics and Business, Beijing. He carried out his doctoral research in the School of Labour and Human Resources, Renmin University of China. He is the editor of the *Journal of China Human Resources Development*.

TIM PRINGLE is Senior Lecturer in Labour, Social Movements and Development at the School of Oriental and African Studies of London University. He received his doctorate from Warwick University. He is a co-author of *The Challenge of Transition: Trade Unions in Russia, China and Vietnam* and the author of *Trade Unions in China: The Challenge of Labour Unrest*.

Preface

A profound change is taking place in employment relations in China. The opening up of the economy to both national and international competition is transforming the way in which employers and workers interact. It is also changing the institutions through which they interact and the ways in which the Chinese government is involved. Markets were initially slow to develop after China's post-revolution period as a centrally planned economy and they are still subject to a high level of state regulation. As exposure to market forces has gathered pace, the consequences for workers have often been difficult. The strike wave in the summer of 2010 emphasised the extent to which their response has increasingly been collective rather than individualistic. This has raised industrial relations challenges for China that echo those previously encountered elsewhere in the industrialised world.

In many ways these developments are unique to China, shaped by the country's long and continuous history. The context of employment in China is very different from that of Western countries where industrial relations institutions first evolved. But, under the pressures of market competition, the everyday treatment of workers by employers has increasingly resembled that of employers in market economies elsewhere in the world. The response of the workers has many similarities with that to be found wherever employment is exposed to the uncertainties and pressures of market competition. Governments tackle questions of worker protection and collectivism in different ways, but there are many common underlying issues. Chapter 1 sets out the theoretical framework for what is to follow by discussing the general characteristics of industrial relations systems in industrialised countries with mixed economies. It focusses on the power relationships that are endemic to employment. They are shaped by worker organisations and employer strategies, both of which are strongly influenced by state intervention. This is important in China despite the fact that it has a single legally authorised trade union and no clear legal provision of a right to strike.

Chapter 2 discusses the background to the transition that has been taking place in China over the past decade from individualistic to more collective industrial relations. It describes the development of government policy towards individual rights and the challenge of increased collective worker behaviour, culminating in the strikes of 2010. Chapter 3 picks up the story with an account of more recent developments. It analyses the divide that has been emerging between the official labour movement and grass-roots activism. Chapter 4 describes the structure and distinctive function of the Chinese trade unions and considers how they are adapting to a market economy.

The extraordinary rapid growth of the market sector in China has brought a varied galaxy of private sector employers into view. Chapter 5 discusses the strategies they have been developing both individually and through employer organisations, at a time when the state is increasing legal constraints on them but is less willing to become directly involved in dispute resolution. The increasing impact of market forces is also affecting the role played by the state in China. Chapter 6 argues that government policy towards labour relations has evolved largely by a series of cautious and pragmatic steps. Having established individual employment rights, the government is increasingly forcing employers to take responsibility for collective issues.

The next three chapters are concerned with relations between employers and employees. Chapter 7 describes the development of collective consultation, a more appropriate term in the Chinese context than collective bargaining, which is now central to government policy. Chapter 8 considers how long-established institutions of worker participation, once the bedrock of the centrally planned economy, are being introduced and adapted in the private sector in response to official guidance. Chapter 9 discusses what happens when labour relations break down in strike action. An account of how the character of strikes has been changing is followed by a discussion of the debate over more explicit legal rights to strike. To provide an international perspective, Chapter 10 compares how greater market exposure has altered the regulation of employment in China, Russia and Vietnam. All three countries have been replacing a centrally planned economy with one dominated by competitive markets over much the same period, but their approaches to labour relations have been very different. We conclude with a brief summary of some of the implications of the findings presented in these chapters.

Most of this book has been researched and written by the younger generation of Chinese scholars now studying labour relations in their country. They have little tradition of empirical work on which they can build. Whatever their research methods – statistical surveys, field-work interviews or documentary analysis – they are all fairly exploratory. There has been little independently gathered data on the rapidly changing scene of Chinese labour over the past 20 or 30 years with which they can make comparisons. The subject is, however, commanding considerable attention from this new generation of scholars and there can be no doubt that a solid body of research is beginning to emerge. Each chapter is the independent work of its named author. The role of the editors has been to ensure that they complement each other and are written in English in a style appropriate for publication. The support of The Leverhulme Trust is gratefully acknowledged.

Abbreviations

ACFIC	All-China Federation of Industry & Commerce
ACFTU	All-China Federation of Trade Unions
CEC	China Enterprise Confederation
CEC/CEDA	China Enterprise Confederation/China Enterprise Directors Association
CLA	Collective Labour Agreement (Russia)
CLB	China Labour Bulletin
CPC	Communist Party of China
CPCCC	Communist Party of China Central Committee
FDI	Foreign direct investment
FIE	Foreign invested enterprise
FNPR	Federation of Independent Trade Unions of Russia
FPAD	Federation of Air Traffic Controllers' Unions (Russia)
FTU	Federation of Trade Unions
IEO	International Organisation of Employers
ILO	International Labour Organisation
KTR	Confederation of Labour of Russia
MHRSS	Ministry of Human Resources and Social Security
MOLISA	Ministry of Labour and Social Security (Vietnam)
MPRA	Inter-regional Trade Union of Motor Industry Workers (Russia)
NGO	Non-governmental organisation
NPC	National People's Congress
NPG	National Independent Miners Union (Russia)
NWC	National Wage Council (Vietnam)
PRC	People's Republic of China
RMB	Renminbi
SOE	State-owned enterprise
TPP	Trans-Pacific Partnership

VCA	Vietnam Cooperative Alliance
VCCI	Vietnam Chamber of Commerce and Industry
VCP	Vietnamese Communist Party
VGCL	Vietnam Confederation of Labour
VTsSPS	All Union Central Council of Trade Unions (Russia)

1 What Should We Be Looking for in Industrial Relations in China?

William Brown

Managing work is never easy. Worker discontent can arise over pay, effort levels, job control and much else. Both employers and employees devote considerable effort to stabilising their relationship, and they are generally successful. But when worker discontent is co-ordinated, it can lead to work stoppages and costly disruption. This in turn can have expensive consequences for the wider society. Most countries have experienced periods of turbulent relations between employers and workers. Governments feel obliged to intervene, not only to limit the damaging repercussions of worker action but also to prevent employers from treating their workers in ways that are socially unacceptable.

The result is a complex structure of agreements, laws, procedures and informal rules, applied at any level from the international sphere to the whole nation, and all the way down to the individual place of work. These cover the substantive details of the terms on which workers are employed. They also provide the *procedural rules* by which those details are fixed and challenged and changed. These procedural rules provide an essential scaffolding of legitimacy to relations between employers and workers. They include, for example, whether workers should be dealt with individually or as a group, and on which issues they should be consulted or have the right to negotiate. They set out what to do in the event of a dispute and at what organisational level agreements should be reached. They also specify whether, and how far, such rules should be influenced by the government.

The way in which employers, workers and the state interact to shape these rules is the subject matter of industrial relations. To some extent the term 'industrial relations' can be used interchangeably with 'employment relations' and 'labour relations'. Industrial relations will be used in this chapter because it reflects a particular intellectual tradition which has focussed on the policy implications of different institutional

The author is grateful for the comments of Chang Kai, Paul Marginson, Jackie Scott and Chris Wright, and for the support of the Leverhulme Trust.

arrangements. Fundamental to industrial relations are the power relationships between employers, workers and the state. Within countries,
these vary between firms and between sectors. They vary over time, as
market circumstances and political regimes change. The power relationships also differ between countries, each reflecting the character of its
country's distinctive political and economic history and its legal and
institutional traditions.

What should we be looking for in describing the emerging industrial
relations of China? In particular, what sort of industrial relations is evolving in China's growing market sector? What clues might there be in the
changing ways in which Chinese employment is being managed as
employers respond to the growing pressures of competitive markets?
We should not be searching for replicas of the institutions of the
Western developed world. The growth of the modern Chinese economy
has been so recent, and so rapid, and from so unique a cultural, political
and legal past, whatever is emerging there will be unlike anywhere else.
We can, however, look for some underlying features that might constrain
and shape the power relationships that are implicit in employment in
market economies. The purpose of this chapter is to discuss what these
features are as background to the account of China that follows.

The Inherently Collective Nature of Employment

For employers, work is difficult to buy. Simply hiring workers does not get
work done. They then have to be trained, equipped, managed, monitored
and motivated to work with the required skill, effort and care.
The employment contract is often described as 'open ended' because of
this. The productivity of workers depends to a great extent not on them as
individuals, but on how well or how badly their employer manages them.
The implicit contract of employment is also open ended in the sense that,
for anything other than short-term employment, what is expected of the
worker alters in unpredictable ways as time passes. The technologies
used, the consumers' demands and the skills required are all subject to
change, and the worker will be expected to adapt to these.

Another reason why work is difficult to buy is that its content is usually
difficult to specify. There is no objective measure of 'hard work' in terms
of worker input. Even if one could measure it, other than by the number of
hours worked, workers differ in what they personally find difficult,
tedious, fulfilling or stressful. There is usually no objective measure in
terms of outputs either. The management techniques of 'work study' or
'industrial engineering' were developed in the early twentieth century to
enable the monitoring of workers' inputs by measuring their outputs.

The main challenge was how to be consistent in measuring outputs from the very different sorts of work that are typically being carried out within the same premises. How do you compare how hard people are working when they are engaged in diverse tasks? While these techniques approach the measurement of job performance systematically, their assessment of what is a 'standard effort' and their scaling around that are essentially normative and a matter of judgement. In the end, the appropriate level of effort and quality of work are what the worker's supervisor or, increasingly, highly automated surveillance says they are. That, in turn, depends upon what the targets set by the higher management require, subtly modified by the prevailing norms of the workplace in question.

Setting aside this elusive nature of the content of work, its price – the wage paid – is also notoriously difficult to determine. Labour markets provide very imprecise price mechanisms. For varied reasons, there is typically a substantial dispersion of wages paid within the same small geographical area by different employers for duties with apparently the same job description. But if labour market mechanisms are relatively forgiving, individual workers are not. Besides workers' concern with the extent to which their pay meets their basic material needs, they also tend to be acutely sensitive to what they see as unjustified differences in pay for comparable duties. The closer the source of comparison, socially as well as spatially, the more anxiously it is watched. Workers have no sense of what they are 'worth', whatever that might mean, in any general market sense. How could they? But they have an acute sensitivity to what they consider to be 'fair' in terms of their immediate social environment. This is partly because, for all of us, so much of our own self-esteem is tied up with our concern about how our peers and colleagues perceive us. For better or worse, paid work for most people is a central source of their self-esteem. As individuals, we take very seriously what we are paid relative to those around us, simply because it is a uniquely concrete indicator of how our own very particular social world values us.

This has important implications for the productivity of workers. It is often said that pay provides a valuable method of motivating employees to work harder. There is a lot of uninformed enthusiasm for performance-related pay and other payment by results. In practice, however, the effective use of variable payments of this sort is very difficult. They are appropriate to a rather limited range of production technologies. Indeed, for most managers the dominant aspect of pay is not its potential as a motivator, but concern that it can unintentionally be a powerful de-motivator of workers. A manager's constant anxiety is that something untoward might disrupt the established pay differentials between jobs, the differentials that their workers have come to perceive to be 'fair'. A similar nagging anxiety is that inter-personal differences in payments reflecting different individual performance may be thought unjustified by the workers concerned. Such adverse responses can sour relations and undermine the sort of co-operative behaviour that is usually essential for productive working. Experienced managers have good reason to be extremely cautious in using any discretion they have over pay (Brown and Walsh, 1994).

It is the unavoidably normative aspect of both the content of work and of its payment that makes work so hard to buy. Notions of 'fairness' are never far away. They are inherently based on social comparison, and usually on comparison using limited and flawed information. This complicates the immediate social interaction aspect of employment, whether or not trade unions are present. However much employers try to treat their workers as individuals, those workers are irretrievably locked into comparisons with their work-mates. Furthermore, because workers interact socially at work, many of their attitudes and expectations are collectively formed. It means that a critical aspect of work management is the legitimacy, in the workers' eyes, of the process that determines what they do and what they are paid for doing it. It has to be got right if workers are to be motivated to work hard. To this process we now turn.

The Power Relationship Between Employer and Employee

The social aspect of work matters because workers interact so much. Rumours, grumbles, gossip and jesting about work are unavoidable and inevitably shape workers' attitudes. This becomes much more significant if workers get themselves organised, whether as informal groups or, even more, as trade unions. Such organisation is likely to harden attitudes and reinforce expectations. It also raises the possibility that workers might take concerted action to strengthen their position with their employer, for example, by them all threatening to cease work. Strike action is an important part of the history of organised labour in all countries.

Fundamental to industrial relations analysis is that it is concerned with power. The employment relationship unavoidably involves a power relationship. All social and economic activities are, of course, criss-crossed by power relationships. We experience them, for example, within our families and in our local communities, quite apart from at higher levels. They are usually tacit, and rarely exposed by open conflict. We manage them through unremarkable everyday routines of negotiation, avoidance, guidance, custom and law. But they are particularly important in industrial relations because the way in which the power relationship between employer and worker is shaped, mediated and regulated has a profound impact on the terms on which workers are employed. It is a major determinant, for example, of what they are paid, whether they are trained and how they are treated at work.

There is no shortage of historical evidence on how employers can treat workers when they have unlimited power over them. In Europe, within living memory, hundreds of thousands of workers were deliberately worked to death in forced labour camps. There are many reports in our contemporary world of circumstances where workers, who have no alternative way of earning a living and no prospect of escape, are employed under conditions that are widely seen to be harsh and degrading. These are extreme cases. But because some employers might exploit their power in ways that are generally unacceptable, most countries have laws setting out minimum standards for employment. One reason for these statutory minimum standards is that poor employment conditions impose external costs on the wider society. For example, they may result in occupational ill health and they may lead to the adverse consequences of workers' children growing up in extreme poverty. Another reason for governments' seeking to enforce minimum labour standards is, perhaps paradoxically, pressure from employers themselves. Most employers wish to be seen as 'good' employers, offering rates of pay and employment practices that are considered 'decent', which is difficult if other, 'bad' employers are able to outcompete them by cutting costs as a result of harsh labour practices.

Historically, it was the rise of trade unions which did most to redress some of the imbalance in the workers' power relationship with their employers. Initially, in the nineteenth century, it was workers with a common skill, working within a particular locality, who were most successful at organising themselves. Their employers were obliged to reach agreement with them because there was nowhere else to turn for that skill. Trade unions were later to use a variety of ways of increasing their bargaining strength, including organising workers at strategic bottlenecks in the production process and broadening their worker coalitions with other occupations. Perhaps their most effective strategy was mobilising political power through the electoral votes of their members. In this way they could help the introduction of legislation which gave them rights to organise and take action. By the mid-twentieth century, in most Western industrialised countries, trade unions were largely accepted as an integral part of a democratic society, with a range of rights enabling them to organise workers and to negotiate with employers as a routine process. Strike action, although important as a last resort, was generally rare.

Different Views of the Employment Power Relationship

The power relationship between employers and workers can be viewed in different ways, which imply different policy responses by government. The oldest perspective historically is that employers have an unchallengeable right to manage their workers as they see fit. This was asserted because employers own the place of work and supply the equipment used. They also hire and pay the workers, who can leave if they are dissatisfied. Underlying the implied moral authority of the employers is an assumption that the well-being of workers is aligned with the success of the enterprise for which they work. The implication drawn was that employers and employees have, in this respect, the same interests. This perspective, commonly referred to as *'unitarist'*, allows no role for trade unions and no opportunity to question managerial authority (Fox, 1974).

A contrary perspective, referred to as *pluralist,* views society as a patchwork of groups with often conflicting interests, and it considers that social stability requires them to reach compromises. The interests of workers and of the enterprise that employs them do overlap, but they are definitely not the same, according to this perspective. A weaker implication, which is essentially pragmatic, is that if their workers are organised in trade unions, employers will not be able to run the enterprise satisfactorily unless they are willing to negotiate with them. A stronger, normative version is that, by virtue of the contribution that workers make to the enterprise, they have an implicit moral right to be represented and to bargain. For both versions it follows that a pluralist employer expects there to be a two-way traffic within the employment relationship, accommodating shifts in relative power, and that the employer will provide workers with the rights and procedures that will facilitate this with minimum overt conflict (Flanders, 1970).

The distinction between unitarist and pluralist perspectives is useful in understanding different theoretical views of the employment relationship. Let us compare the implications of three ideologies which have been particularly influential in recent decades, those of free market economics, of Marxism and of pluralism. With the warning that brevity necessitates oversimplification, how do they differ in the way in which they deal with power at the workplace?

At the heart of economic analysis is the idea of markets, which use price mechanisms to maintain a balance between the supply of and demand for goods and services. The analysis of markets has opened up a range of powerful understandings which have contributed greatly to improved living standards worldwide. But there is a normative aspect that is often associated with narrow interpretations of the central body of economic theory, which we can refer to as *free market* economics. This is that the unimpeded working of markets produces outcomes that are not only optimal in efficiency terms but also, in the longer run, optimal in social welfare terms. The distribution of income (or value added) as between profits and wages between the employers and the employed is therefore best left to market forces. Government intervention is only justified, in the free market view, when markets fail to operate, for example, in cases of monopoly suppliers.

The default implication of this view of economics is that whatever impedes a free market is likely to reduce economic growth and social welfare. It implies not only that the organisation of workers in trade unions but also that the collusion of employers in employer associations are anticompetitive and consequently to be discouraged. In contemporary political debate it is associated with hostility to institutions that are perceived to introduce labour market rigidities, such as collective agreements and statutory labour standards. It implies the unitarist assumption that employers should be free to manage workers as markets require, rather than the pluralist assumption that procedures should be made available to enable workers to voice and protect their own interests. The unitarist perspective is sometimes loosely associated with the use of 'human resource management', but that is mistaken. Human resource management techniques are fully compatible with a pluralist approach to employment relations, insofar as they do not prohibit negotiation with employees.

Marxist analysis of market economies starts with some features of the pluralist perspective. In a market economy, described as 'capitalist', the interests of employers and workers necessarily differ. In particular their interests differ over how profits should be divided between them. In practice, this distribution is determined by their power relationship, which will reflect worker organisation, market forces and state intervention. Where Marxism is distinctive from pluralism is that it embodies particular theories both of the relationship between employers and workers in a market economy and of how that relationship might be changed. A fundamental division in capitalist societies is seen to be between the owners of enterprises and those who work in them. The dynamic for change is theorised to be a unified working class replacing the owners and the governmental system they support, and in the process ending the market economy. The outcome, by implication, would be a new form of economy in which employment relationships are essentially unitarist because the workers would have replaced the managers and taken over the government, and would have done so without losing their allegiance to their class. The Marxist approach has a more qualified view of trade unionism than pluralism; unless trade unions increase working-class consciousness and revolutionary potential, they are seen as compromising with capitalism and delaying its overthrow.

The *pluralist* approach is concerned with understanding how a market economy is managed and reformed rather than with how it might be overthrown. It can encompass a range of political views which are anything from conservative to socialist in terms of their aspirations for the distribution of income and wealth. The central focus is on providing different interest groups with some sort of representative voice, and with establishing procedures, accepted by all concerned, through which power can be channelled and compromises achieved. In pluralism, unlike in the free market and Marxist approaches, market mechanisms are of secondary significance. They provide the context, within which pluralist institutions such as trade unions operate, rather than the forces that should either dominate economic life or be overthrown to create a better society. The pluralist attitude towards markets is cautious and critical (Heery, 2016). For pluralists, in certain circumstances, markets may further the efficient allocation of resources. But supposedly freer markets may not necessarily be in the interest of the society as a whole, not least because markets can be shaped by particular interest groups. That is why all contemporary economies are, to a greater or lesser extent, 'mixed' economies, with varying degrees of state ownership and regulation. As we shall see, state (sometimes called 'public') sectors and market (sometimes called 'private') sectors make very different demands of pluralist approaches to the employment relationship.

Institutionalising the Power Relationship through Collective Bargaining

Arrangements that involve trade unions in the management of the employment relationship are generally called *collective bargaining*. They arise when an employer manages aspects of the employment relationship by engaging with employees not as individuals, but as a group that is organised with some degree of independence of the employer. By dealing formally with the trade union, the employer grants it *recognition*. Collective bargaining covers a spectrum of engagement. At the lighter touch end is consultation on employment matters, which involves no more than the exchange of information and views and the discussion of options. The outcome may or may not result in the employer's altering their intended actions. *Collective consultation* does not necessarily involve any formal agreement, written or otherwise. It will be argued in Chapter 7 that this is the predominant form in China. At the more formal end of the collective bargaining spectrum, the employer makes proposals, the workers' side makes counterproposals and a negotiation takes place to achieve a mutually acceptable compromise. This is then recorded in a *collective agreement*, which is mutually binding until both sides are persuaded that there should be a renegotiation. In practice, collective bargaining usually involves a mixture of consultation and negotiation, depending upon the issues (Kochan, 1980).

An important decision for the employer, historically, was whether they should engage in collective bargaining on their own or whether they should coordinate their bargaining activities with other employers. In the early years there was little option. Whether or not trade unions were a threat, employers who were in competition with each other in a local market for a product often saw advantage in adopting a common front to 'take wages out of competition' by colluding on labour issues. Their incentive to do this was greatly increased when labour began to be organised in trade unions. In an economy of small firms in competition with each other, it made no sense for a trade union to organise workers in just one firm. Anything the union won for their members in that one firm might jeopardise their jobs by weakening the firm's chances of competitive survival. Consequently, the objective for unions was to organise the workers at all the firms in competition with each other, which further encouraged the employers to form a united front. They would unite in an *employer association* which ideally included all the firms competing in that particular product market in their geographical area. This employer association would negotiate with the trade union to achieve a collective agreement that would set out common terms on key issues such as wage rates and hours of work, covering all their employees in those groups represented by the union.

These *sectoral* collective bargaining arrangements, sometimes called *multi-employer* arrangements, proved to be very robust. The same agreements would cover many employers within specific industries, within specific regions. They became the main form of collective bargaining in Western Europe in the twentieth century. As markets were extended geographically by improved transport, in most countries they became national arrangements. From the employers' perspective, if trade unions could not be avoided, this was a good way of restricting their influence. Sectoral collective bargaining frustrated the union strategy of using strikes selectively to pick off weaker firms. It provided common pay scales, which reduced the scope for employees to complain about unfair pay comparisons. It provided a solid basis for encouraging all firms to provide uniform skills training to their workers. Often the agreement would be linked to a *dispute resolution procedure*, whereby irresolvable disagreements between the management and the union within a firm could be conciliated by knowledgeable people at the higher, sectoral level. Perhaps most important of all, by focussing the trade union's attention on concluding agreements that covered a whole sector, it meant that the union's influence within the workplace would be reduced. Sectoral agreements protected the employers' day-to-day freedom to manage their workers.

There were also advantages to the trade union. Because employers were committed to granting recognition to the union for sectoral bargaining purposes, it improved the recruitment and retention of union members and enhanced union legitimacy at the workplace. There was pressure for any employer who refused union recognition to follow the rates and conditions set out in the relevant collective agreement, even if they were not formally linked to it. Union leaders could live with a lesser role for workplace union activists if this was accompanied by an enhanced role for themselves and more centralised union discipline (Clegg, 1976). There was also a deeper benefit in terms of sharing the profits. Insofar as there was imperfect competition in the sectoral product market, the sectoral agreement made the union in effect complicit, to the benefit of its members' pay, in sharing with the employer any excess profits that could be extracted from customers.

Last but not least, there were also advantages for the state. These include securing social peace and, in effect, depoliticising industrial relations by delegating regulation to private actors in a way which secured comprehensive regulation of the labour market. The continuing resilience of sectoral collective bargaining in continental western and Nordic Europe over many decades owes much to the legal support that has been provided by their governments, to which we shall turn shortly.

Despite these benefits, in some countries there were particular circumstances under which employers felt that, if they had to deal with trade unions, they would prefer to do so on their own. Rather than join with other employers in sectoral bargaining, they chose to engage independently in what is usually called *enterprise* bargaining. By contrast with multi-employer bargaining, it is sometimes referred to as *single-employer* bargaining. This enterprise bargaining was an early feature of some unionised industries of Japan and of the United States, for example. They were dominated by comparatively few very large enterprises, which saw little benefit to be gained from colluding with their smaller competitors to influence the labour market.

For some countries, a decline in sectoral bargaining has been quite recent. In Britain, in the later twentieth century, enterprise bargaining became dominant over sectoral bargaining in the market sector because sectoral agreements were weak and increasingly loosely followed, and trade unions were strong at workplace level. Enterprise-based bargaining gave employers the freedom to regain control of the management of labour at the workplace. Because of this, and because of the tougher competitive pressures that lay behind it, strike action in the market sector declined so much as to become a rarity. Enterprise bargaining for many firms turned out to be, by the twentieth century's end, a transitional stage to their complete withdrawal from bargaining with trade unions. The firms that abandoned bargaining first were those whose profits were squeezed the hardest by competitive pressures (Brown *et al.*, 2009).

Where trade union organisation continued in the market sector, it tended to become effectively centred on the enterprise and was highly dependent upon the employer for recognition and organising facilities. In these circumstances, the agenda of collective bargaining tended to become more concerned with co-operation with employers in the pursuit of competitiveness, and less with any form of confrontation over the distribution of profits. Britain was not alone. With the end of the twentieth century, a similar story of collective bargaining both shrinking in coverage and withering in impact in their market sectors could be told of, for example, the United States, Canada, Australia and New Zealand.

The rise and, to some extent, the fall of collective bargaining in the Western world has had a profound impact on the development of its economies and societies. Most evident had been the contribution of its rise to reducing the inequality of income distribution within countries, from the middle until the late twentieth century. By internalising and institutionalising conflict over income within enterprises, within sectors and within nations, collective bargaining had provided a pyramid of negotiation by which workers' incomes had, more or less, kept pace with the productivity consequences of technological change. In the process, this encouraged the development of labour-replacing technology and thereby increased labour productivity. The subsequent weakening of collective bargaining has contributed to the more recent failure to stimulate labour productivity in some countries. It has also contributed to the recent decline in the redistribution of the financial gains from productivity improvements to the lower paid and has consequently led to increasing income inequality within many countries (Atkinson, 2014).

The Part Played by Government in Collective Bargaining

Governments have no choice about managing employment relations for their own employees working in state sectors. In practice, governments also cannot avoid becoming involved to some degree in market sectors. Employment relations play too important an economic and political role to be treated as a private matter between employer and employee. Even if trade unions are not present, the wider costs to society arising from irresponsible employment practices are so severe that governments generally have to establish some minimum labour standards by legislation. If trade unions are present, then government involvement in the regulation of collective bargaining is unavoidable. The wider costs of disruptive strike activity are too great. For some countries a crisis provoked by strikes has had enduring consequences for their labour legislation. For Canada and Australia, for example, transport strikes that paralysed their national economies at the start of the twentieth century led to laws being introduced which lasted for decades, providing a central role for state-supported conciliation and arbitration.

The labour laws on collective bargaining of different countries vary greatly. There are many reasons for this. Some are political. For example, the occupying powers immediately after victory in the Second World War were determined to establish a secure legal position for trade unions in Germany and Japan; this was partly because of the unions' impressive pre-War record of resisting the rise of militarism. For some countries their colonial inheritance has played a key part. It has been suggested that the different legal traditions of common law in the Anglophone world and of civil law on the continent of Europe have influenced their contrasting perspectives on the role of the state. The Anglophone perspective tends to see the state playing a role only when labour problems arise, whereas, by contrast, the continental European perspective assumes that the state has a responsibility to establish initial order. In the European Union, there is an additional layer of co-ordination between unions and employers at the national level in some countries, which has resulted in social pacts which address labour market issues and social welfare reforms. As was mentioned earlier, the legal support underpinning collective bargaining tends to be greater in countries where trade unions have been able at some time to influence a ruling political party.

In what ways do governments shape collective bargaining in market economies? One important area is in the support they provide for trade unions in terms of their *rights to strike* and *to organise* workers, free from legal penalties or employer harassment. Having said that, it is the detail of those rights which is important. They may in practice be highly constraining in terms of the procedures that have to be followed for legal strike action, and they may leave much to the discretion of the law courts. Furthermore, as with individual employment rights, collective rights count for little if enforcement by the state is poor or if the costs to employees and unions of achieving enforcement are prohibitive.

The high potential cost to the public of employment disputes has encouraged governments of countries with collective bargaining to facilitate peaceful dispute resolution. These countries typically have an agency that offers to *mediate* disputes, offering expert *conciliators* and, if necessary, *arbitration*. So long as they are seen to be independent, these services generally work well and greatly reduce the chance of disputes either turning into strike action or ending up in the law courts. In most countries which have them, these agencies have in recent years increased their emphasis on preventing disputes from occurring and escalating. They have done this by offering training to employers to help them to improve their *internal disputes procedures* and employment practices (Brown, 2014).

It is common for governments to provide legal procedures whereby workers who can demonstrate sufficient support can win recognition for their union from their employers. It is a rather different matter whether they can then persuade the employer to engage in effective negotiation. At the softer end of the spectrum of collective bargaining, many countries have laws that facilitate consultation arrangements with worker representatives. These may take various forms – for example, work councils, consultation committees and representatives on supervisory boards. They often take the form of hybrid arrangements, with some representatives coming through trade union channels and others being elected by non-unionised workers (Hall and Purcell, 2012).

Another important area of government involvement concerns sectoral bargaining. Some governments are unsympathetic to employers who form employer associations for collective bargaining purposes. They disapprove of it, seeing it as a restriction on competition. Other governments, by contrast, value and encourage sectoral bargaining as providing an important basis for labour market stability and skill acquisition. In many continental Western European countries, where this latter view is dominant, four legal provisions are important. The first is that sectoral collective agreements are considered by the courts to be compulsory contracts. In effect this so-called 'peace clause' means that if either side breaks the agreement, through a strike or lock-out, they can be sued for damages in court. The second provision is that sectoral agreements are considered to be legally enforceable, so that all members of the relevant employer association have to offer terms to their employees at least as good as in the agreement. A third provision, the 'favourability principle', is that employees at the enterprise level may be allowed to improve on the terms of the sectoral agreement through an additional collective bargain with their employer. The fourth provision is that the terms of sectoral agreements can be 'extended' by legal action to apply to any employer in the sector, even if they are not a member of the employer association. They become, in effect, legally enforceable sectoral minimum wages and conditions, but fixed by collective bargaining and thus reflecting the economic circumstances of the sector.

It was noted earlier that many sector-based systems of collective bargaining have proved to be robust. It is notable that, following the financial crisis of 2008 and the subsequent crises in the Eurozone, the majority of European countries with sectoral bargaining have retained it. In the minority of countries where it has been weakened, the main reason has been that, as these were debtor countries, the weakening of sectoral bargaining had been a condition placed on loan packages by the international financial institutions, which tend to have a 'free market' view of economic life. Elsewhere, sectoral bargaining has adjusted to the adverse economic environment by allowing more discretion for enterprise bargaining, within clearly specified 'articulation' provisions governing the relationship between the two levels. As mentioned earlier, governments in countries with strong sectoral bargaining tend to use the sectoral employer and trade union organisations as 'social partners' in a wider pluralist process of political consultation in dealing, for example, with employment problems arising from industrial decline. To that extent, collective bargaining in these countries extends up to the national level and covers the wider economic context (Marginson and Sisson, 2006).

It will be apparent that governments play a fundamentally important role in determining the extent and the nature of collective bargaining in the market sector of their countries. In a past world, where markets were largely confined within national frontiers, trade unions in most western countries were permitted to bargain on behalf of workers in an orderly way and to build institutions with employers. Governments generally saw advantage in providing legal support for this. But in the late twentieth century, sharper competition, and especially greater international competition and more international enterprise ownership, changed all this. On the one hand, trade unions in the market sector have become more dependent upon the legislative support of governments; on the other hand, under less bargaining pressure from trade unions, governments are increasingly unwilling to provide such support (Gumbrell-McCormick and Hyman, 2013). National governments show similar contrasting extremes in their treatment of trade unions in their own state sectors. To this we now turn.

Governments as Employers

At the start of the twentieth century, the great majority of trade union membership in Western countries was in their market sectors. The great majority of strikes at that time, expressed as a percentage of working days lost, also occurred in their market sectors. By the start of the twenty-first century that had been largely reversed. Currently, to varying extents in different countries, trade unionism is mainly a feature of state sectors. It has diminished, sometimes very substantially, in market sectors. Although strike activity has declined across all Western countries in the past couple of decades, where it does occur it is generally largely confined, in terms of percentage of working days lost, to their state sectors. Market sector strikes have become, in historical perspective, rare. Why is the state sector so different?

Employment by governments, in their countries' state sectors, raises very different issues for collective bargaining compared with market sectors. So far this discussion has been primarily concerned with enterprises in the market sector. There the driving force is one of competition – in the product market over goods and services, in the capital market for investment, and in the labour market. Increasingly that competition is international. In sharp contrast, state sector enterprises face little direct competition for their services and they face no international competition. In the labour market, they are typically themselves the main sources of training in the specialist skills they need, and they are also the main users of those skills. There are far higher levels of both monopoly and monopsony power than in the market sector. It is not markets which constrain what terms of employment are affordable, but the government, which indirectly is itself the employer. There are no profits to be bargained over – just the tax-payers' money. To add to this contrast, there is an inherently political aspect to what is considered to be an adequate service in, say, education, government, health, armed forces, prisons, postal service or the police. There is no market to help define standards, and the concept of labour productivity in public services is unavoidably controversial. For example, does reducing the number of nurses in a hospital, or of teachers in a school, or of police on the street, increase or decrease those service's productivity?

These distinctive economic features of state sector employment have shaped their employment relations. Lacking severe market constraints, Western governments in the twentieth century tended to adopt a fairly protective stance towards their own employees in order to maintain their compliance. State sector pay, for example, was generally kept roughly in line with market sector pay in most Western countries. The problem of productivity was partly managed by giving substantial authority to the employees with the key professional skills – the doctors, the army officers, the university professors, the senior civil servants and so on – who largely controlled the professional standards, organisation and training of their respective services. In most countries this was combined with what became high levels of trade union organisation. It suited the unions to work closely with their respective public service professional managers in a collaborative way. In some countries it was accompanied by fairly comprehensive collective bargaining. Elsewhere, favourable employment conditions were a trade-off for a prohibition on strike action. State sector collective bargaining, at any rate for the major public services, was in most countries characterised by detailed collective agreements, substantial trade union influence at all levels, and relatively little overt conflict.

The wider context was that, at least until the final quarter of the twentieth century, employment in state sectors had increased as a proportion of the labour force in most Western countries. Partly because of wartime experience, more demands were being made on services by the public. Many countries saw benefits in state ownership of public utilities such as energy, water, posts, telecoms, transport, and health. The faltering of the post-War economic boom in the 1970s challenged all this. Governments were forced to press harder for the financial efficiency of services while dealing with trade unions which historically had strongly defended the perceived interests of their state sector members.

How can a state services monopoly, committed to a pluralist approach to its workers, also respond to the wider public interest, when that demands substantial changes in working practices? There are countries, for example in north-western Europe, where the experience is that, with far-sighted and politically engaged trade union leadership, this can be successfully negotiated through collective bargaining. But, in other countries, a common government response has been to sell off these services to the private sector, wholly or in part. Unable to impose financial discipline comparable to that of markets, the state has simply given up being the employer. The consequence for the newly marketised services has typically been that collective bargaining has been stopped, or its influence has been greatly diminished. For the services remaining in state ownership, the influence of collective bargaining has often diminished also. For them, to the threat of being sold off has been added the reality of many activities being outsourced to market-sector sub-contractors using non-unionised labour. Many governments in countries with pluralist traditions have not yet achieved a settled form of collective bargaining for their own employees.

The Principal Underlying Features of Industrial Relations

As background to considering the emerging institutions in China, this discussion has looked at issues that generally arise in the employment relationship in mixed economies when employees have a collective response to their employers. It will be apparent that different countries have developed different forms of collective bargaining and collective consultation to deal with this. It will also be apparent that collective bargaining in all countries has undergone repeated change. There was never a 'golden age' of collective bargaining. There is no perfect model to be copied. It has been adapted, country by country, with varying degrees of success, as their economic circumstances have changed.

Would it have helped for this discussion to have focussed less on Western economies, and to have given more attention to the developing world? Probably not. The experience of building industrial relations institutions in the developing world is extremely varied. For many developing countries it has been shaped, for better or worse, by inheritances from a past colonial period or from traumatic liberation experience. It is currently often externally influenced by self-interested pressures from foreign direct investors or dominant trading partners as well as by international institutions such as the World Bank. In many developing countries some of the state sectors have a substantial trade union presence. But in their market sectors any trade unions are typically highly fragmented, with sometimes only sporadic concentrations of strength amid an otherwise very small and often declining percentage membership (Van Klaveren *et al.*, 2015). In the developing world the challenges that trade unions face in terms of getting employers and governments to support collective bargaining are usually far more extreme than in the developed world. Despite this, the institutions they aspire to build usually have the same underlying features. For almost a century the International Labour Organization (ILO) has endeavoured to nurture them.

In describing the emerging industrial relations of China, what should we be looking for? Some issues relate to rights provided by national law. For the worker, a fundamental question is the status of their individual contract of employment. How specific does the law require it to be? In countries where the law provides workers with little support, what the employee is expected to do and when they must do it is effectively at the discretion of the employer. A growing feature of contemporary employment for many employees almost everywhere has been a weakening of the traditional relationship with the employer as a result of increased use of out-sourcing of work and of agency or dispatched workers.

What protections are provided by law? A related issue is the support offered to the employee by the state if the employer breaks the contract or breaches other legal protections by, for example, not paying employees, dismissing them illegitimately, or employing them in illegally unhealthy conditions. It then matters, not just in formal terms, but in reality, how accessible and affordable the courts are to aggrieved workers, how independent of the employer they are, and how speedy and full their remedies are. Although these are related to individual rights, they matter in terms of collective behaviour because an important part of a trade union's role is commonly one of ensuring that their members can implement their legal individual rights.

Important aspects of collective legal rights are set out in ILO conventions. These include rights to organise trade unions, the protection of activists from victimisation by employers, rights to strike, and the right to engage in collective bargaining. One set of questions concerns how far national laws provide these rights, and what constraints they impose on them. Another, that is equally important, concerns how far they are implemented and enforced in practice. The earlier discussion has emphasised the importance of the legal support provided for collective bargaining. The means to enforce collective agreements is important to both sides. But it will be clear that a profoundly important aspect of law for most Western European countries has been the law relating to sectoral bargaining: the legal status of agreements, their enforcement, the scope for individual employers to add to them and the extension of their terms across their sector. This has provided a basis of collective bargaining for many countries which has given stability for decades and has adapted to changing circumstances. It has facilitated job training, dispute avoidance, and the responsible linking of worker pay to productivity improvements, as well as, in many cases, the wider involvement of the social partners in the government of employment.

The behaviour of employers is central to the conduct of industrial relations, quite apart from what the law requires of them. How far do they manage employment autocratically or, alternatively, how far is their approach more pluralist? Do they have relations with a trade union, and in what ways? Do they encourage their workforce to have a representative voice, through the union or otherwise, or to be involved in any routine consultative procedures? Do negotiations ever take place within the enterprise that result in a written agreement? There is also the inter-employer aspect of sectoral bargaining. Do employers discuss employment policy with other employers in their local labour market, or in their product market? Are they members of an employer association, and does it have consultative or negotiating relationships with a union? Is it involved in discussions with the government at any level? In what ways are employers in the state sector different in their dealings with their employees from those in the market sector?

Although the ILO conventions require trade unions to be 'independent' in financial terms, this is a vague concept in practice. Many market sector unions depend heavily on employers for resources and facilities at sectoral, enterprise and workplace levels. They depend on employers granting recognition rights to represent the members and they also often depend on employers collecting their members' subscriptions for them. In state sectors, where most trade union members in most countries are now situated, the trade unions are unavoidably close to both the employers of the state enterprises in which their members work and to the governments on whom their funding ultimately depends. But some degree of independence from employers is essential. One aspect of this is that unions should have discretion over use of the finance that comes from their members' subscriptions. This is necessary if union officials are to be perceived by members to be independent of employers. More important, however, if they are to retain the support of their members, is that unions provide a voting system whereby those members can have some influence over the choice and dismissal of their representatives and of the policies they adopt. An important role of trade unions lies in building realistic expectations and consensus among their members, and for this the members' perception that they are independent and representative is essential.

A crucial aspect of any mature industrial relations system is the processes of resolving conflict. If the power relationships implicit in employment are to be moderated in an orderly way, it is necessary to have clearly defined procedures for resolving both individual and collective grievances and for facilitating, usually incremental, change. These set out, for example, how contentious issues can be introduced for resolution, which representatives of employers and workers should be involved, in what sequence discussions progress, and what time constraints are appropriate. They provide a structure within which grievances can be discussed in a timely and rational way by representatives who can speak with authority for each side.

Procedural rules, as was observed at the start of this chapter, provide a scaffolding of legitimacy for relations between employers and workers. They are essential for orderly industrial relations. But there is always the possibility that, despite the internal procedure, finding a compromise is too difficult for those immediately involved. To deal with this, most procedures have an additional option of bringing in an independent conciliator from outside who can broker a settlement. Should this fail, most also provide for a final arbitration stage to provide a mutually binding settlement. It is a feature of pluralist systems that they seek to internalise the resolution of conflict within the most appropriate unit, whether it is the workplace, the enterprise, or the sector. Achieving this depends upon following clear, integrated and internally consistent procedures. A surer sign of a mature industrial relations system than procedures for settling disputes once they have arisen is the existence of procedures for consultation and negotiation that prevent them from arising at all.

References

Atkinson, A. B. (2014), *Inequality: What Can Be Done?*, Harvard: Harvard University Press.

Brown, W. and Walsh, J. (1994), 'Managing pay in Britain', in Sisson, K. (ed.), *Personnel Management*, Oxford: Blackwell, 437–464.

Brown, W., Bryson, A., Forth, J. and Whitfield, K. (2009), *The Evolution of the Modern Workplace*, Cambridge: Cambridge University Press.

Brown, W. (2014), 'Third-party processes in employment disputes', in Roche, W. K., Teague, P. and Colvin, A. J. S. (eds.), *The Oxford Handbook of Conflict Management in Organisations*, Oxford: Oxford University Press, 135–149.

Clegg, H. A. (1976), *Trade Unionism Under Collective Bargaining*, Oxford: Blackwell.

Flanders, A. (1970), *Management and Unions*, London: Faber and Faber.

Fox, A. (1974), *Beyond Contract: Work, Power and Trust Relations*, London: Faber and Faber.

Gumbrell-McCormick, R. and Hyman, R. (2013), *Trade Unions in Western Europe: Hard Times, Hard Choices*, Oxford: Oxford University Press.

Hall, M. and Purcell, J. (2012), *Consultation at Work: Regulation and Practice*, Oxford: Oxford University Press.

Heery, E. (2016), 'British industrial relations pluralism in the era of neoliberalism', *Journal of Industrial Relations*, 58(1), 3–24.

Kochan, T. (1980), *Collective Bargaining and Industrial Relations*, Homewood: Richard Irwin Inc.

Marginson, P. and Sisson, K. (2006), *European Integration and Industrial Relations*, Basingstoke: Palgrave Macmillan.

Van Klaveren, M., Gregory, D. and Schulten, T. (2015), *Minimum Wages, Collective Bargaining and Economic Development in Asia and Europe*, Basingstoke: Palgrave Macmillan.

2   The Transition to Collective Labour Relations

Chang Kai and William Brown

A transition from individual to collective labour relations is taking place in China. It is a consequence of employment becoming increasingly market-oriented. Although its most conspicuous sign has been rising levels of industrial unrest, this is just a symptom of a broader change. Labour relations are the social and economic relations generated by the transactions between workers, labour users and their associated organisations. The exposure of these to the vagaries of market forces is profoundly destabilising. It sharpens the unavoidable tensions and conflicts of interest that are already implicit in employment. It increases the need to manage and regulate employment if relations are to be both stable and responsive to change. This has always been a fundamental challenge for countries with market economies.

This chapter considers the institutional and legal support that is needed in China to ease the adjustment. It starts by describing China's transition to a market economy. It then discusses the debate around the emergence of the radical Labour Contract Law that came into force in 2008. There is an analysis of the increased unrest that followed. The chapter draws on *ad hoc* interviews and involvement in mediation by the first author in over twenty enterprises which experienced disputes at that time. The next chapter will discuss more recent developments and the tensions currently evident within the trade union organisation.

The Marketisation of Labour Relations

China's market-oriented labour relations have not come from a normal process of gradual economic development. It was a result of deliberate governmental action driving the transition from a planned economy. This was seen to be crucial to the restructuring of the economy. It required the establishment of two fundamental legal principles: first, explicit property

This chapter draws on 'The transition from individual to collective labour relations in China', *Industrial Relations Journal*, 44:2, 2013, by the present authors.

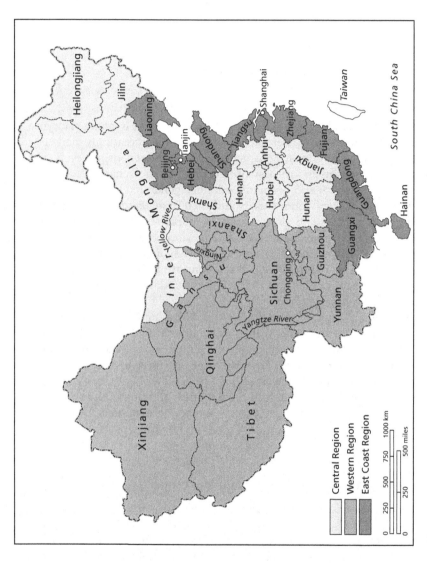

Figure 2.1 The Provinces of China
Tian: Managing International Business in China (Cambridge University Press, 2016).

rights and, second, independent agency for enterprises. As a result, labour has shifted from conceptually being 'owned by all the people' in a planned economy, to become 'free' labour provided by individual workers in the setting of a labour market. The prime objective of the reforms has been to establish a freely flowing labour market.

The establishment of market-oriented labour relations has been an extended process. The first stage, from the mid-1980s to the early 1990s, was one of experimentation with the state-owned enterprises, when the government initiated explicit labour contracts between workers and management. In the second phase of reform, from the early 1990s to the beginning of the twenty-first century, coordinated reforms were pushed forward to establish the modern enterprise system. The workers in state-owned enterprises saw their status transformed from having high status in a planned economy to becoming simply the employees of a market economy. This was achieved under a succession of changes, including efficiency-related cuts in the state-owned enterprises, widespread worker layoffs, and what amounted to an enforced change of the workers' sense of identity. Meanwhile, hundreds of millions of farmers were leaving the land and were joining the modern industries with no more than the identity of migrant workers. They became purely market-oriented wage earners.

The industrial army of ex-state-owned enterprise employees and rural migrants has become the new Chinese labour force. The ex-managers of the state-owned enterprises, and the owners and executives of private enterprises, have become the new employers. Market exposure of both workers and employers has posed the enormous challenge of developing a new form of labour relations. The third stage of reform, from the beginning of the new century to the introduction of the Labour Contract Law in 2008, was mainly concerned with consolidating the achievements of the labour market reforms and with providing this new style of labour relations with appropriate legal arrangements.

These initial steps are not yet sufficient for a full market-oriented transition. Even the rights provided by the Labour Contract Law are still based on individual labour relations, lacking the attention to collective issues necessary for Western-style market-based employment relationships. Just what sort of collective labour law will be appropriate to complete the transition depends on the nature of the market conditions that are emerging in China.

Individual labour relations are concerned with the relationship between individual workers and their employers. The respective rights and obligations are defined and regulated through both written and oral contracts. Although these individual labour relations contracts may superficially seem to be even-handed, they are based on an uneven power relationship – what Marx referred to as the 'formal affiliation and actual subordination of labour to capital' (Marx, 1985). This subordination of labour is the central characteristic of individual labour relations. In a different intellectual tradition, it also underlies the pluralist theoretical view of labour relations that has been developed in mature market economies (Dunlop, 1958; Fox, 1971).

Collective labour relations refer to the social relationships generated through processes of consultation and negotiation, over working conditions, labour standards, and other employment issues, between, on the one hand, the workers' collective or their representatives and, on the other, the employers or employers' organisation. It encompasses collective bargaining, collective disputes, collective consultation and employee participation in management. Such collective relationships might be conducted at different organisational levels, from industrial sector, or corporate headquarters, down to the workplace. The development of collective labour relations is likely to lead to a more tractable power relationship because the key actors involved, management and worker representatives, are given procedural rights. In contrast with the essentially subordinate nature of individual relations, collective labour relations permit more effective negotiation and consultation and better expression of workers' collective views and preferences (Chang, 2004).

The regulation of collective relations in market economies has historically been the focus of labour legislation. Without pressure to do otherwise, employers generally prefer to deal with individual workers rather than with combinations of them because of the advantage of gaining greater control of the labour process (Burawoy, 1979). They are predisposed to resist expressions of solidarity by workers, in order to inhibit the development of collective labour relations (Chang, 2000). Quite apart from employers, the governments of different countries in different historical periods have had very varied views about collective labour policy. The major capitalist countries have mostly experienced phases in which governments have first prohibited, then restricted and then recognised rights to association for workers. Not until the periods around the World Wars, in which trade union movements played a central role in the war economies of democratic countries, was the establishment of workers' rights as a basis for collective labour relations generally acknowledged worldwide (Chang and Zhang, 1993). More recently, with changing economic and political circumstances, many countries have seen their governments curtail these rights.

The transition from individual to collective labour relations in the developed world did not happen spontaneously. It has been the result of a process of compromise. The main driving force has been the threat of organised industrial conflict. Governments, faced with the disruption caused by recurrent strikes, have come to believe that institutions for collective labour relations are necessary to make economic and social development sustainable. Likewise, employers, also with varying degrees of reluctance, have come to appreciate that the use of orderly collective bargaining may be a necessary price to pay. There is ample evidence that it may lead to improved worker co-operation (Kochan *et al.*, 1986).

The main objective of the reform of China's employment policy has been the opening up of labour markets with the intention to increase efficiency and worker productivity. This has been achieved through top-down administrative action. The objective has been similar for China's newly emerging employers, both the corporate leaders of previously state-owned enterprises and the indigenous private enterprise owners. The initial character of this emerging labour relations has been over-whelmingly individual rather than collective. As a result, underlying the Labour Contract Law has been the default assumption that the relationship between individual employers and workers will be based upon subordination, and consequently without means of correction.

The designers of employment reform were aware of the need to take collective labour relations into consideration. This was reflected in both the Trade Union Law as amended in 1992 and the Labour Law passed in 1994. The 1992 Trade Union Law had specific provisions on the nature of trade union organisation, on the rights and obligations of trade unions and of their members. But the 1992 Law did not provide what was later to be added in the 2001 Trade Union Act Amendment; that is, that 'safeguarding the legitimate rights and interests of workers is the basic duty of the trade unions' under the conditions of the market economy.

The reason for this omission was that the liberalisation of the labour market had not yet progressed far in the 1990s. Labour conflict had not become an issue. The workers had little experience of collective consciousness or of their potential collective strength. Any awareness that their position in the new market economy might have changed was still in a process of germination. The state-owned enterprise workers, who had been thrown onto the labour market, acted as if they were still sentimentally attached to the idea that they had some part in the ownership of their enterprises. Migrant workers were not integrated into the industrial work force in terms of their social awareness. What has been called the period of 'collective unconsciousness' or 'collective inaction' in the transformation of the state-owned enterprises during the 1990s has been an important preliminary to workers forming a new awareness (Ching, 1998; Liu, 2003). As a consequence of this 'unconsciousness', the emergence of collective labour relations has been slow. Despite widely publicised incidents of collective action, and despite public concern about the deficiencies of

collective contracts, there had not yet been sufficient shift in worker attitudes to provide the impetus for the reform of collective labour law.

The Enactment and Impact of the Labour Contract Law

The implementation of the Labour Contract Law in 2008 was an important event. It clearly signalled that, with the reform of individual labour
relations, a preliminary phase in the reform of employment law had been
completed. It was also a starting point for the development of a legal basis
for regulating collective aspects of labour relations.

One indication of whether an adequate market-oriented form of labour
relations is developing is whether protections for workers are emerging
that are appropriate and effective. The labour contract system is important, but it is only a legal provision for individual labour relations and,
indeed, it is the only legal provision. The 2007 Labour Contract Law
(Article 1) stipulates at the outset that 'this law is formulated in order to
improve the labour contract system; to clarify the rights and obligations of
the concerned parties to the labour contract; to protect the legitimate
rights and interests of workers; and to build up and develop harmonious
and stable labour relations'. That is, it applies to individual employees
and employers, who are the parties to the contract.

The labour contract system had started with a pilot experiment in the
1980s. It was formally launched as the central part of the reform of the
labour system after the introduction of the Labour Law in 1995. Even
after ten years' experience of it, the results were far from perfect.
In August 2005, He Luli, the Vice Chairman of the Standing
Committee of the National People's Congress, pointed out that:

research showed that the proportion of small and medium-sized private enterprises
which had achieved labour contracts was less than 20 per cent, and for individual
businesses it was a lower percentage. In order to avoid their legal obligations, some
employers are reluctant to sign long-term contracts with employees. The terms of
labour contracts are mostly less than one year, and a tendency towards more short-
term labour contracts is clear. Some employers have abused the probationary
period of labour contracts. After a worker's probationary period was complete,
such employers ceased to employ them. As a result such workers were exploited,
especially those who were migrant workers. Many labour contracts which should
have set out the terms of payment, did not specify the amount. Some specified only
the obligations of workers and only the rights of employers. Furthermore, some
employers signed labour contracts without consultation with the workers, and some
even had the workers sign blank contracts. (He, 2005)

This report was a major driving force behind the labour contract legislation. The legislative process started in 2005, and it brought into play many

different parties with different interests. The workers hoped to improve the protection of their employment rights. The employers opposed any restrictions on their discretion over employment and anything that might increase labour costs. The government hoped to find a balance between the needs of enterprises and the protections for workers.

The proposed legislation affected almost all occupations, and it aroused considerable concern in the wider society. It provoked a fierce debate in the academic community. In March 2006 the draft legislation was released for one month for public consultation. There were a remarkable 191,849 responses. The academic debate revealed serious disagreements. The present first author, as the representative of the 'Beijing School', supported the draft's intention to provide a means to counter the current weak position of workers. In direct contradiction, Dong Baohua, as the representative of the 'Shanghai School', argued that the draft provided 'excessive' protection for workers. He argued that it was out of touch with reality and consequently could be counterproductive. This so-called 'North-South' academic dispute continued up to the publication of the Law (Chang, 2009a, 2009b; Dong, 2011).

The legislators balanced the differing opinions of all parties, taking account of the realities of labour relations and the essential requirements of the legislation. They aimed to protect the workers, while at the same time taking into account the legitimate rights and interests of employers, many of whom were vociferously opposed. The Labour Contract Law, after prolonged debate, was eventually passed overwhelmingly by the 10th National People's Congress (NPC) Standing Committee at the 28th meeting on June 30, 2007. Xin Chunying, as Deputy Director of the Legislative Affairs Commission of the NPC Standing Committee, considered that this indicated a high degree of consensus on the legislative principles of the Law.

The Labour Contract Law and, in particular, its setting of legal liabilities and fines for illegal activities, provided a major stimulus to the further development of the labour contract system. The rate of adoption of labour contracts, on the face of it, increased substantially. According to Xin the proportion of enterprises with over 1000 workers which had signed labour contracts appeared to have risen from under 20 per cent to 93 per cent between January and September in 2008[1]. By the end of 2010, the Ministry of Human Resources and Social Security estimated that the coverage of labour contracts signed by larger enterprises had reached 97 per cent and that the coverage was 65 per cent for small enterprises[2]. A Peking University survey of the cities of Beijing, Shanghai,

---

[1] http://politics.people.com.cn/GB/1026/8932537.html.
[2] www.cq.xinhuanet.com/news/2011–01/04/content_21781409.html.

Shenzhen, Quanzhou, Ningbo, Shaoxing and Henan suggested that the coverage of labour contracts was at about 72 per cent. At the same time, the renewal rate of labour contracts also increased. According to the statistics for Beijing, 11 months after the implementation of Labour Contract Law, the labour contract renewal rate reached 94 per cent (Wu, 2008).

Evidence suggests that the legislation has been effective in curbing the previous trend towards more short-term labour contracts. According to a report by the People's Congress (Hua, 2011) the term of labour contracts was typically three years after the implementation of the new law. In addition, it found that the correct rights were specified for workers in labour contracts, on matters such as wages, working hours, social security payments, rest periods, vacations and occupational safety. Particularly notable was that the provision of social insurance contributions was greatly improved.

Despite this apparent progress, however, new problems have emerged in the implementation of the Labour Contract Law (Cooke, 2011). Some enterprises had avoided its provisions by, for example, extensive use of agency or dispatched workers, and by the use of informal employment to replace formal employment. These evasions have to some extent undermined it. The Law's initial effectiveness as a protection for workers was also weakened by its coincidence with the 2008 international financial crisis, which triggered a sharp economic downturn in China, with many factories being shut down and jobs being cut.

A wave of labour disputes followed the Labour Contract Law. There had already been a rising trend of disputes going to the courts from the late 1990s. Between 1996 and 2007 their number was rising by roughly 20 per cent per year (Elfstrom and Kuruvilla, 2012; Cooke, 2013). But, in the year 2008, the number effectively doubled to more than 690,000 (China Labour Statistical Yearbook, 2009). Supreme Court statistics record that there were 280,000 labour dispute cases concluded in 2008, which was a 94 per cent increase over the previous year. This rise continued in 2009. The courts accepted nearly 170,000 labour dispute cases nationally during the first half of 2009, an increase of more than 30 per cent year-on-year. Some regions experienced a particularly sharp rise; there was an increase year-on-year in Guangdong, Jiangsu and Zhejiang in the first quarter of 2009 of, respectively, 42 per cent, 50 per cent and 160 per cent (Wang and Liu, 2010).

Some commentators have suggested that this surge of labour disputes was caused by government intervention in the labour market and by excessive protection of workers. They proposed that the law should be amended in response (Liang, 2009). As one of those involved in the legislation, the present first author argued that the disputes were a consequence of the extent of illegality rather than of the implementation of the Labour Contract Law. The strike wave could be attributed to the unruly labour relations of the past. On this argument, the resolution of the problem did not lie in deregulation. On the contrary, it lay in the enhancement of the law, in order to ensure proper implementation of individual labour law. It was necessary to stick to the Labour Contract Law, and on this basis to improve the Labour Standards Act and Collective Contract Law. As a general rule, labour relations regulation is an essential component of any policy that aims at tackling the employment relations problems that arise from economic development (Mali, 2009).

The main effect of the Labour Contract Law is to protect the rights of individual workers while restricting those of employers. Its purpose is to shift the status of individual employment away from the characterisation of 'strong capital but weak labour'. But there are limits to what this can achieve. It will not substantially correct the fundamental imbalance of power in Chinese labour relations. It is only the collective strength of workers that can be expected to enhance the relative power of labour.

Legislation can influence labour relations by two distinct but complementary routes. The first is by directly regulating the employers' obligations to their employees. This is done by establishing substantive labour standards and thereby creating rights that can be enforced under government supervision. The second route comes through workers organising through trade unions in order to engage in collective bargaining with employers. This enables them not only to implement the rights and obligations that are provided by the law, but also, under the guidance of the state, to enhance them (Wang, 1988).

The first route is public support while the second route is self-help. Public support is mainly concerned with the regulation of individual labour relations, while self-help mostly regulates by means of collective labour relations. Generally speaking, the former provides the substantive minima, while the latter provides the procedural means for their protection and improvement. Only the combination of adjustments to both individual labour relations and collective labour relations can achieve a functionally balanced mechanism of regulation. Such a combination is the tried and tested way of building institutions which can both resist the employers use of arbitrary power, and also adjust labour relations in line with changing economic and social circumstances (Morgan, 1984).

The recent Chinese legislation is best seen as the start of a process. The implementation of the Labour Contract Law has provided a foundation on which to build collective relations at the institutional level. The evidence suggests that it has extended the implementation of labour contracts, increased their duration and improved their specific details. Along with better protection of individual labour rights has come the enhanced symbolic importance attributed to the labour contract as an institution. The law already includes some provisions regarding collective contracts, in preparation for the next stage of adjustment of collective labour relations. But rather than introduce them simultaneously with the labour contract legislation, the chapter of 'special provisions' in the Labour Contract Law specifically chose to set up a 'collective contract' section. This sequential approach was felt to help the settling in of individual labour legislation and to improve prospects for the development of collective labour legislation.

A second aspect of the process which the legislation has initiated is the enhancement of the concept of legality for society as a whole. The Labour Contract Law initiated a huge debate across Chinese society. It was an unprecedented event in public education with regard to the role of law. It popularised the idea that, whether you support this law or not, you must implement it. Otherwise, you will pay the cost of acting illegally. This has strengthened public awareness of the 'soft law' aspect of labour law. It is gradually strengthening awareness of the importance of employers' abiding by corporate law. In the first year after the implementation of the Labour Contract Law, the number of labour dispute cases in Shanghai increased by 199 per cent year-on-year. It is significant that, of those cases which have been concluded, 17 per cent have been decided in favour of the employer, increasing 5 per cent year-on-year. This was the first time the employers' success rates in lawsuits have been on a rising trend since the statistics have become available (Shanghai Municipal Human Resources and Social Security Bureau, 2008). It suggests that the employment behaviour of employers is improving, and that they may be starting to change from habitually operating outside the law to abiding by it (Chang and Qiu, 2011).

A third important consequence has been that the Labour Contract Law has enhanced workers' awareness of their rights and thereby of their shared collective interests. Its impact on workers' consciousness is reflected in both expectations and aspirations. On the one hand, the popularisation of the Labour Contract Law has made many workers understand legal provisions regarding their own rights. It has helped them to appreciate that those rights can in principle be safeguarded through legal means. Evidence comes from research by the Shanghai Federation of Trade Unions in 2008: 82 per cent of employees were aware that the Labour Contract Law had come into force; 87 per cent were aware that changes in labour contract conditions should be subject to the mutual agreement of both sides; 74 per cent believe that the full implementation of the Labour Contract Law is conducive to safeguarding the legitimate rights and interests of employees; and 94 per cent of employees expressed themselves willing to safeguard their legitimate rights through the approved procedural channels when faced by a labour dispute (Shanghai Federation of Trade Unions, 2008).

On the other hand, Chinese labour law is still far from perfect, and the rights that are specified by the Labour Contract Law are still quite remote from day-to-day practice. This remoteness encourages workers to consider taking action themselves, especially where the government's supervision of employment is seen to be weak and the official trade unions appear to be ineffective. A natural consequence is that workers are encouraged to unite to build their collective power. The present first author carried out relatively unstructured investigation in twenty enterprises with collective disputes, primarily in Guangdong, Shanghai and Liaoning, in 2009 and 2010, sometimes as an unofficial mediator. It was evident that 'worker unity' (*gongrenmen tuanjie qilai*) had become the favourite slogan in these disputes. One of the important topics in worker discussion groups that he attended was how to achieve and maintain their solidarity. The development of workers' awareness with growing collective consciousness is likely to be a powerful driving force as labour relations become more collectivised.

The Move Towards Collective Labour Relations

The move towards collective labour relations is being driven by both the government and workers. The market-oriented transition of employment has been promoted by government, and workers have been placed on the resulting labour markets. Two sources of power and two approaches are evident in this. One approach is a top-down process of institution building which is led by the government, and the other is a bottom-up process which is promoted by workers themselves.

A key government objective has been that trade unions should adapt to the market economy. According to the Trade Union Law, 'Defending the legal rights of workers is the basic function of the trade union. The trade union delegates and safeguards the legal rights of workers, as well as safeguards the overall benefit of the people nationally' (Section 6, Ch. 1). This is called the 'Two Safeguards' principle. Under it, the trade union is expected to encourage responsiveness in labour relations by nurturing the workforce as a community. It should do this by promoting democratic management, and by facilitating transparency in workplace affairs. It is also expected to help vulnerable workers make use of labour legislation, to take advantage of legal aid, to promote tripartite consultation mechanisms, to uphold worker rights, to found new trade union branches where needed and to carry out collective bargaining.

Since the implementation of the Labour Contract Law, the All-China Federation of Trade Unions (ACFTU) has placed increased emphasis on strengthening collective arrangements. This involves the building up of trade unions within enterprises, and the implementation of collective bargaining. In 2010 they announced the 'two universals', aimed at establishing trade unions in enterprises and promoting collective bargaining within them (Wang, 2010). A substantial increase in both trade union membership and of collective contracts has followed. By September 2010, the number of ACFTU members had reached 239 million, and this number had increased by 13.613 million over the previous year, 8.398 million of whom were migrant workers. There were 1.408 million collective contracts, covering 2.439 million enterprises and 185 million workers (Yue, 2011). By the end of 2011, 1.789 million collective contracts had been signed, involving 3.601 million enterprises and 223 million workers (ACFTU, 2012). These achievements of the ACFTU have established the basic architecture of collective labour relations in China. Growth has increased the social influence of trade unions, and will have helped workers to protect their rights.

This promotion of union organisation and collective bargaining by the Party and government has, however, also brought problems. One is that, because employers control union recognition and effectively control enterprise-level union organisation, many new enterprise trade unions are no more than nominal or 'empty-shell' trade unions. More seriously, some are, in effect, 'bosses' unions' because they are so closely controlled by employers. When there are labour disputes, they tend to take the employers' side. As the Trade Union Chair of Guangdong Province, Deng Weilong, put it: 'Many enterprise trade unions are merely bosses' subsidiary institutions. They help workers who have difficulties, they organise social activities and contests, and they seek to raise morale, so that the workers can create value for bosses. However, when labour conflict becomes severe, these trade unions then represent the bosses' interests' (Zhang, 2010: A02).

The formal position can be very misleading. Since the Party and government administration both attach high priority to extending collective bargaining, and include it in their performance evaluation standards, the number of collective contracts and their apparent coverage could be ostensibly 'improved', with little underlying reality. By emphasising the formal position but neglecting the content of it, by emphasising quantity but neglecting quality, by emphasising political achievements but neglecting actual performance, the collective contract system can stray seriously from the original purpose of safeguarding workers' rights and improving labour relations. It is liable to become purely cosmetic.

The key indicators of collective relations are usually taken to be trade union density and the coverage of collective contracts. But in China we cannot judge it by these. It depends critically upon whether the unions in question can represent workers on a genuine basis of unconditional support. Equally important is whether the ostensible collective contracts have been achieved through collective bargaining, with generally applicable substantive contents which can be implemented effectively. If trade unions and collective contracts exist in name only, and if there is no underlying workers' solidarity and no worker participation in making the trade unions truly representative in their enterprises, there cannot be genuine collective labour relations. Thus, although China has the highest number of union members and of collective contracts in the world, the situation of labour relations in Chinese enterprises, especially in privately owned enterprises is still generally fragmented and atomised. That is, each individual employer is dealing with a group of workers as individuals, through what are, in effect, still individual labour relations.

A fundamental requirement of effective collective labour relations is some basis in workers' wishes and actions. This requires the direct participation of workers. The close connection between collective labour relations and workers' own direct interests means they must also be able to draw on their own collective power and be able to take action to develop collective relations. Just as the government's intervention is the external driving force, so the workers' actions can be seen as the internal stimulus. Such action is subject to the development of collective consciousness, because as long as workers are content to tolerate the conditions of individual labour relations, the transition towards collective labour relations cannot be made. The recognition by a workforce that conflicts of interest might arise on an issue, and that it is potentially negotiable, has been called 'bargaining awareness' (Brown, 1973: 142). Only when workers are aware of the potential of a bargaining situation, and of the need to stay united for collective action, can they genuinely take part in collective labour relations.

The collective consciousness of Chinese workers has begun to emerge during the process of market reform. During the early development of markets, the period from 1980s to 2000, there were some cases of collective action arising from the privatising of state-owned enterprises and from their downsizing (Chang, 1988). At that time, workers generally still believed themselves to be the 'owners' of the enterprises in a planned economy. They had not yet formed the distinctive labour consciousness of a market economy. The core of this labour consciousness is labour rights (Chang, 1995). The introduction of the Labour Contract Law effectively acknowledged that urban workers had completed the transformation of their roles from being the owners to being employees, and that rural workers have finished the transition from migrant workers to employees.

This spontaneously generated labour consciousness is quite different from Marxist 'class consciousness'. One scholar describes it as 'class struggle without class organisation' (Chang, 2010: 16). It reflects the reformist tendency of trade unionism, which Marx deplored, in that it focusses on economic rather than political outcomes. It arises from the psychology of group consciousness, in that it remains at the stage of organising for existing partial interests rather than arising from consciousness of class historical status (Lukács, 1999:136). Chinese workers have recently tended to develop the sort of labour consciousness characteristic of a market economy, which is trade unionism in its essence, as first described by the Webbs and explored more recently by Flanders and by Kochan (Webb and Webb, 1920; Flanders, 1970; Kochan, 1980).

Experience of Collective Action after 2008

The main focus of worker demands in recent collective action in China is for more equitable treatment under the current system. This is a typical trade union demand in Western countries. During the Chinese revolutionary period, reformist trade unionism was officially characterised as backward and reactionary. But in the current market-driven era it is widely thought to be both legal and reasonable for trade unions to campaign for their members' economic interests using worker solidarity and bargaining. Workers can now request to establish trade unions, to bargain with employers and to press for supportive laws. Such requests are supported by Chinese law and are promoting the collectivisation of labour relations.

There was, as has been noted, a surge of what proved to be significant episodes of collective action following the implementation of the Labour Contract Law. Particularly notable were episodes of collective action at state-owned enterprises such as Tonghua Iron & Steel Company and Linzhou Iron & Steel Company in the summer of 2009, and also the foreign-owned company 'strike wave' starting at Honda Nanhai in the summer of 2010 (Chang, 2009c; Yang, 2009; Yi and Xu, 2010). These became symbols of the spontaneous collectivisation of labour relations.

The episodes shared some significant characteristics. First, they were essentially economic disputes, focussed on the enterprises' management. In each case the workers hoped that the government would step in to resolve their problems. But, second, an important new characteristic of the disputes had also emerged. This is that they had changed from being disputes of right to being disputes of interest. Collective disputes in China previously were mostly rights disputes, resulting from the infringement of some established labour right. Recent collective disputes have been basically disputes of interest, usually characterised by a request for higher payment and for better and fairer treatment. Disputes of interest generally do not arise until workers are able to develop some awareness of their collective strength. This change from disputes of right to disputes of interest is consequently an important feature of current labour relations (Elfstrom and Kuruvilla, 2012).

The mobilisation of these events is also notable. Recent collective action in China has typically been spontaneously organised by workers. It has been triggered fortuitously rather than planned. Both their leadership and workers' willingness to take action emerged during the course of the action. But the workers' impromptu solidarity was only temporary and it tended to evaporate once their leaders had achieved their goal with the resolution of the immediate problem. It is significant, however, that the scale and scope of these spontaneous actions has tended to expand. Episodes of collective action within an enterprise often set off a chain reaction beyond it, and spread to industries or areas outside. This happened without any organised alliance or premeditation, which suggests that the workers' awareness of solidarity has spread through a wider social process rather than being just confined within the enterprise.

Recent episodes of collective action and of bargaining have mostly been conducted in a relatively calm and rational way. Collective action has typically taken the form of the temporary cessation of work at the workplace, rather than aggressive behaviour such as demonstrations, road blockades or vandalism. Most collective disputes have been solved through negotiation. As the *People's Daily* reported in its assessment of the Honda Nanhai event: 'the whole process of negotiation between employers and employees is being conducted in a rational and peaceful way. Despite thousands of workers having participated in the work stoppage and expressed their demands, the factory is in a good order and there has been no extreme and irrational behaviour between labour and capital' (Li, 2010). The law abiding and rational behaviour of workers has been widely noted.

In popular opinion, the use of strikes is often seen to be a 'normal' feature of collective bargaining in a market economy, a necessary part of resolving conflicts between labour and capital. But this is not the case. Strikes are far from everyday behaviour. It is the possibility rather than the occurrence of such action that plays a part in conflict resolution. Recurrent strikes in a workplace or a region would normally indicate that there are defects in its conflict resolution mechanisms. They would be failing to deal with some underlying problem. The sharp increase in collective action in China in recent years may have arisen from a period of relatively low wages combined with inadequate procedures with which to pursue remedies.

A strike is a crisis in the management of an enterprise. It may, for example, reflect what is perceived to be unfair pay distribution, managerial incompetence, or the failure of the consultation mechanism. Workers' spontaneous collective action reflects a failure in the way work is managed. It also indicates a failure of the local trade union organisation to represent the workers, and a failure of the collective contract to play its procedural role of resolving associated disputes. The first author investigated more than 20 enterprises in which collective disputes had occurred during 2009–2011. These enterprises all had trade unions and they had all signed collective contracts. The fact that workers at them frequently demanded trade union reorganisation indicates the seriousness of the underlying problem. That is, that when labour relations is managed from the top down, this does not on its own achieve effective collective reform. The 'Two Universals' are often little more than a formality, and this can itself provoke spontaneous action.

In response to these challenges, the government has taken an approach which it describes as 'rational treatment and resolution by means of labour law'. This has given two characteristics to the government's response to recent collective action. First, it has been based on a more accurate assessment of the nature of workers' action than in the past. They have increasingly been judged to be economic disputes, rather than political events which might threaten social stability. For example, the official view reported in the *People's Daily* was that the Nanhai Honda action arose because of low pay levels, and that it was resolved by negotiation. This was confirmed by the first author when he witnessed the political leadership of Guangdong province visiting the Nanhai Honda factory during the strike. Diagnosing it to be an economic dispute, they proposed that, rather than intervene directly, the government should facilitate an agreement between labour and management, which is what then happened.

The second recent characteristic of the government's response has been that collective disputes should be resolved according to the law. The Trade Union Law specifies that, if an enterprise or public institution experiences a work stoppage or slowdown, the trade union should represent the employees in relevant negotiations. The trade union is required to respond to the employees' requests, and to propose how the dispute might be resolved. The law requires that the enterprise shall meet any reasonable requests raised by the employees. It requires the union to assist the enterprise so as to ensure that normal production can be resumed as quickly as possible (Article 27, Ch. 3). When a collective dispute occurs the government should not try to force workers to return to work, nor should it compel the enterprise to increase their pay, but it should play a role as a third party to create suitable conditions for collective bargaining.

Again, the 2010 Nanhai Honda dispute provides a clear example. The first author, acting as a legal advisor for the workers, took part in the negotiation that resolved the Nanhai Honda incident. Under the authority of the official labour department of the Nanhai District, negotiations continued for more than six hours. They finally ended the 17 days of collective action with a 34 per cent wage increase. This success in resolving the dispute led to it becoming the model for handling collective disputes all over the country. Most of the later work stoppages of that year ended with agreements involving a 20–30 per cent wage increase. Many enterprises which foresaw the risk of a stoppage pre-empted it by engaging in collective bargaining and awarding an increase. Imitation of this good practice contributed to the widespread legal resolution of other collective disputes in 2010.

This experience of dispute resolution encouraged better co-ordination of union channels both outside and inside the enterprise. This had both substantive and procedural consequences. The first consequence was that there was a widespread improvement in substantive conditions of employment. The settlement of the Nanhai Honda dispute effectively triggered collective bargaining elsewhere. Collective action in Western market economies usually occurs after the breakdown of collective bargaining procedures. In recent experience in China, by contrast, collective bargaining on disputes of interest only became possible after the outbreak of collective action. Unlike under previous more formal collective contracts with 'empty-shell' trade unions, this new sort of collective bargaining, with the workers being directly involved, was notable because it had a distinctly market economy appearance. This was true of all the collective bargaining associated with strikes in 2010. It not only achieved increases in the pay levels of specific enterprises and industries, but also directly affected the official minimum wage. In 2011, 24 of China's 31 provinces adjusted their Minimum Wage Standard, with an average increase of 22 per cent (*Beijing News*, 2011). There have been comparable increases in subsequent years. This increase of the minimum wage was the highest in China's history, an achievement to which the recent experience of collective bargaining must have contributed.

There were also important procedural consequences of the 2010 disputes. They have encouraged democratic reforms of trade union organisation, and have strengthened the relationship between unions and workers. The ACFTU's official view is that the strike is a 'radical' action of which it disapproves. As a senior official said: 'using radical means to solve labour disputes neither corresponds with the national conditions in China, nor accords with the present stage of our labour relations and the fundamental interests of the workers' (Guo, 2011). As a result, none of the 2010 strikes were organised officially by the trade unions; they were unofficially organised by the workers themselves. The role played by the union, and particularly the local union, was that it became involved only once the strike had taken place. Its role then was typically to represent and organise the workers in order to negotiate with the employers, thereby changing the workers' action from disorder into order and resolving the incident in a legal way.

The success of this spontaneously initiated collective bargaining was directly related to the way the strikers involved the trade unions. The chances of a positive response from the official union organisation were greatly helped by the fact that the workers' demand was typically to shake up the existing union rather than to organise an alternative union. For example, the Guangdong union accepted the Nanhai Honda workers' request to reorganise their trade union. After the strike was over, new elections were held in the Nanhai Honda enterprise union. The new union committee, which commanded the support of the workers, negotiated with the employers for the second time in 2012, and won a wage increase of RMB 611. This far exceeded the wage rise that had resulted from the negotiation following the strike of the previous year (Huang, 2011). The collective action directly contributed to improving worker organisation. It also enhanced the popularity of unions with workers.

These spontaneous actions to some extent compensated for shortcomings of government and the official union organisation. They also won public support for a more collective approach to labour. The consequent momentum associated with collective action has moved the transition of labour relations into a new phase. But, given there were high economic and social costs associated with the disruption, as well as positive benefits, there were negative consequences which ideally would have been avoided. The challenge has now become one of how to deal with the problems of reform by refining the government's labour policies. How can the transition be made more orderly, and how can it avoid provoking more social conflict?

The Refinement of Labour Policy

There will need to be further adjustments if government policy is to help the transition towards collective labour relations. In a market economy such policy encompasses a range of social issues, concerned with the interests of the waged worker and with the resolution of associated labour problems. It is concerned with the rights and obligations of each party to the employment relationship, as well as with the regulation of labour relations and of dispute resolution. Within the Chinese government's policy framework, however, labour policy has not so far had an independent identity. It has been seen as secondary, dependent upon broader economic reforms. This arose from the government's long-standing view of economic development as the paramount objective. A consequence has been that problems have tended to accumulate gradually, unintentionally snowballing into what has become one of the greatest challenges to development. Responding to this, the central government made a strategic adjustment in the 12th Five-Year Plan that began in 2011, with the result that improving people's livelihood and industrial relations were introduced as major tasks.

The transition from individual to collective labour relations has consequently become a major responsibility for government. It has been argued that, in order to improve labour relations, China needs to establish more appropriate labour laws, with the implementation of collective contracts, the provision of rights to trade unions and the improvement of employment relations at enterprise level. The objective of such a policy would be the gradual realisation of greater labour autonomy under the government's coordination (Chang, 2009a).

Strong collective labour laws must be the foundation for this. Although China has formed a basic framework of labour policy under the market economy, it is neither perfect nor complete. There have so far been nine major laws passed by the National People's Congress:

- Trade Union Law (1992, 2001)
- Labour Law (1994)
- Law on Mine Safety (1994)
- Law on Occupational Disease Prevention (2001)
- Production Safety Law (2002)
- Labour Contract Law (2007)
- Employment Promotion Law (2007)
- Law of Labour Dispute Mediation and Arbitration (2007)
- Law of Social Insurance (2011)

But, with the exception of the Trade Union Law and minor provisions in some others, all these laws are essentially concerned with individual labour relations. There is no provision for the regulation of collective labour relations as such. Government policy is still narrowly focussed on individual rights.

Experience in other countries suggests that, after the establishment of a free labour market, legal regulation of collective relations becomes the key issue. In Europe and America, the meaning of 'labour law' or 'industrial law' is primarily collective labour relations; by contrast with the regulation of individual labour relations, which is often called 'employment law'. Some of the most critical problems facing collective labour relations in China lack any specific treatment by the law. Examples are the boundary between workers' and employers' organising rights, the limits placed on workers' collective action, the procedures governing the initiation and conduct of collective action, and the responsibilities and obligations of trade unions in disputes. The absence of any rules is an important reason why many labour conflicts are not prevented, and are sometimes unnecessarily exacerbated. Putting collective labour relations on the agenda has become a concern of the national legislature. In February 2010, at a meeting of the legal committee of the National People's Congress, a proposal to speed up the introduction of collective labour relations legislation received considerable attention, with the initiation of a consultation and research process. But there has been no further action on this to date.

Collective rights are central to labour policy. According to ILO Conventions 87 and 98, legislation should provide specific safeguards for the three basic labour rights: workers' rights to organise; collective bargaining rights; and collective dispute rights. The purpose of such regulation is to permit the two sides to deal with labour issues through effective organisation and procedures. Providing workers with these rights allows them to develop the organisational strength with which to stand up to management. Just as, in regulating individual labour relations, the main role of government is one of safeguarding the individual worker's rights, so its main function in collective labour relations should be worker empowerment. In collective labour relations, the workers are not just the people who are being represented and protected; they are also the agents who will make use of collective rights. In circumstances when labour and management are not in a mature relationship, government needs to focus on creating an environment of legality, cultivating relationships between labour and management, and gradually expanding the extent of labour autonomy.

Chinese law does not prohibit workers' associations. The official position is that workers do have the right of association. But they are not permitted to establish workers' associations as alternatives to the official trade union. In the fourth article of the Trade Union Law of 1950 it was set out that all associations and organisations that are not organised according to the provisions of article 3 shall not be called trade unions, and should not enjoy the rights stipulated in the act. This is the only legal provision regarding the association other than the trade union.

Similarly, collective action, including striking, is not contrary to the law in China (Chang, 2010). In practice, however, workers' unauthorised collective actions have in the past tended to be officially characterised as uncontrollable. As a result, the authorities consider it necessary to guide and regulate such action, with political vigilance, in the interests of social stability. But the perverse consequence of the categorisation of spontaneous collective labour action as a form of political opposition tends to be the unnecessary provocation of negative official reactions. If political pressure is used to suppress grass-roots collective action, it can increase the problems, thereby exacerbating social conflict.

A central issue is how to deal with the relationship between union organisation and workers. A recurrent difficulty with the present relationship between the unions and workers in China, as has been mentioned, arises from divided sources of labour power. One of these is the officially authorised instrument of trade union power, which is represented by the ACFTU within the established system; the other is the spontaneous power arising from actions of workers outside the system. The first consists of activities promoted by trade unions in an administrative hierarchy, with authority going from the top to the bottom. This includes the development of union organisation, the establishing of collective contracts and the conduct of labour elections. The second consists of what is going on outside the authorised system, expressed by informal collective action through the grass-roots initiatives of workers, from the bottom to the top, through actions such as strikes and protests.

There is, in effect, a split in organised labour. In a legal sense, the workers are the responsive aspect of labour, while the union is its authorised aspect. Trade unions and workers together form so-called 'organised labour' (Chang and Zhang, 1993). But in more practical terms, the problem of the unions losing touch with the workers is becoming increasingly serious because of workers' alienation from what they see as the 'local administration's union', or even the 'boss's union'. If trade unions inside the system effectively fail to represent the interests and safeguard the rights of the workers, those workers will naturally turn to self-help. Some market economies have experienced this tendency at times in the past when their informal workplace trade union organisations were strong. For example, in Britain in the 1960s and 1970s there were frequent conflicts over the legitimacy of action between official national union organisation and the unofficial 'shop steward' organisations at the workplace. In time representative structures were developed which removed such conflicts (Boraston, Clegg and Rimmer, 1975; Brown, 2013). The fact that the Chinese government is heavily involved in trade unions in China provides a unique context for this tension between top-down and bottom-up collective organisation. This will be addressed in the next chapter.

Conclusion

The reform of labour policy can be usefully informed by some basic theoretical considerations. In China's emerging market economy, as in mature market economies, there is a tension between unitarist and pluralist approaches to the employment relationship. The unitarist assumption that management and workers have largely common interests may be serviceable in situations where there are high levels of trust between them, or where workers have no collective power whatsoever (Fox, 1974). It was reflected in the Chinese government's promotion of the example of the Zhejiang Transfar Group, where it was claimed that an enlightened management had acted on its own initiative to respect the interests of workers, improving their working and living conditions (Transfar Group, 2011). This is the implicit unitarist assumption of some human resources management theory. But it would be a mistake to ignore circumstances where managements are able, and choose, to neglect workers' interests and needs. Such circumstances, where employers seek only to maximise profits, are commonplace in competitive markets. Where there are low-trust employment relationships, and where workers are able to mobilise collective strength against employers, a unitarist analysis provides a poor guide to policy. It will not help to dispel worker discontents.

A pluralist approach to labour is far more serviceable in those circumstances where workers can mobilise collective strength. It assumes that the interests of workers and of enterprises are not necessarily the same. It suggests that there should be institutions through which compromises can be negotiated (Dunlop, 1958; Fox, 1971). The implication is that both labour and management have their own rights and that there should be procedural rules to channel their negotiation of compromise and agreement. In this way, conflicts of interest, and the potential of each side to inflict damage on the other, can be peacefully reconciled in ways that recognise the interests common to both sides. In choosing the appropriate model for labour relations reform, it is the accommodation of conflicting interests that is the basic goal. But it is only a goal. The potential for conflict arising from divergent interests in labour relations is normal and unavoidable under market conditions. If handled by appropriate procedures, the resolution of these conflicts is likely to promote the healthy development of labour relations. Indeed, a feature of mature collective bargaining has been the development of 'positive sum' co-operative relationships in which worker representatives are able to build sufficient trust to win worker consent to the negotiation of radical change (Kochan et al., 2009; Oxenbridge and Brown, 2004).

It is in the nature of competitive markets that they create tensions between employers and workers. Such tensions are already evident as the Chinese economy becomes more market-oriented. But, as the following chapters suggest, there is a real possibility that, with legislation to provide procedures and with rights that will accommodate collective bargaining and the resolution of conflict, such tensions can be managed so as to achieve harmonious labour relations.

References

All China Federation of Trade Unions (2012), *Chinese Trade Unions*, September, Beijing: ACFTU.

Beijing News (2011), '24 ge shengfen niannei tiaozheng zuidi gongzi' [24 provinces will adjust the Minimum Wage Standard within this year], Xinjingbao.

Boraston, I, Clegg H. A. and Rimmer, M. (1975), *Workplace and Union*, London: Heinemann.

Brown, W. A. (1973), *Piecework Bargaining*, London: Heinemann.

Brown, W. A. (2013), 'The ending of unauthorized strikes in the West: some policy implications for China', *The International Journal of Comparative Labour Law and Industrial Relations*, 29:2, 185–198.

Burawoy, M. (1979), *Manufacturing Consent: Changes in the Labour Process under Monopoly Capitalism*, Chicago: The Commercial Press.

Chang, K. (1988), 'Gongchaowenti de diaocha yu fenxi' [The Survey and Analysis of Strikes], Issue 1, Dangdai gonghui (*Contemporary Trade Unions*), Beijing: Worker Press.

Chang, K. and Zhang, D. (1993), *Gonghui fa tonglun* [General Theory of Trade Union Law], Beijing: Central Party School Press.

Chang K. (1995), 'Lun laodongzhe wenhua' [The culture of labour], *Gongyun yanjiu* [Research on the Labour Movement], 2.

Chang, K.(2000), 'Lun budang laodong xingwei lifa' [An argument about unfair labour practice legislation], *Zhongguo shehui kexue* [Social Sciences in China].

Chang K. (2004), *Laoquanlun dangdai zhongguo laodong guanxi de falv tiaozheng yanjiu* [Theory of workers' rights research on the legal regulation of labour relations in contemporary China], Beijing: China Labour and Social Security Publishing House.

Chang K. (2009a), 'Laoquan baozhang yu laozi shuangying–laodong hetong fa lun' [The protection of labour rights and the win-win situation between employer and employees], *Labour Contract Law Theory*, China Labour Press.

Chang, K. (2009b), 'Guoqi gaizhi dang yifa jixing—bu guifan gaizhi shi yinfa gongren jiti xingdong de zhijie yuanyin' [The reform of state-owned enterprise should be carried out in accordance with the law – nonstandard reform is the immediate cause of workers' collective action], *Journal of Banyue tan* (internal edition), 9.

Chang, K.(2009c), *Zhongguo laodong guanxi baogao, [Report on China's labour relations]*. Beijing: China Labour and Social Security Press.

Chang, K. (2010), 'Guanyu bagong hefaxing de falv fenxi–yi Nanhai bentian bagong wei anli de yanjiu' [The legal analysis of the legality of strikes – a case study of the Nanhai Honda Strike], *Zhanlue yu Guanli*, [Strategy and Management].

Chang, K. and Qiu, J. (2011), 'Zhonguo laodong guanxi zhuanxing yu laodong fazhi zhongdian–cong laodong hetong fa shishi san zhounian tanqi' [The transformation of China's labour relations and the key points of the rule of the labour law – a talk at the three years anniversary after the implementation of Labour Contract Law], *Tansuo yu zhengming*.

Ching, K. L. (1998), 'The labour politics of market socialism: collective inaction and class experiences among state workers in Guangzhou', *Modern China*, 24 (1), 3–33.

'Cooke, F. L. (2011), 'The enactment of three new labour laws in China: Unintended consequences and the emergence of "new" actors in employment relations', in Lee, S. and McCann, D (eds.), *Regulating for Decent Work: new directions in labour market regulation*, Basingstoke: Palgrave Macmillan and Geneva: International Labour Organization, pp.180–205.

Cooke, F. L. (2013), 'New dynamics of industrial conflicts in China: Causes, expressions and resolution alternatives', in Gall, G. (ed.), *New Forms and Expressions of Conflict at Work*, Basingstoke: Palgrave Macmillan, pp.108–129.

Dong B. H. (2011), *Laodong hetong fa de zhengming yu sikao*, [Debate and thinking of the labour contract legislation], Shanghai People's Publishing House.

Dunlop, J. T. (1958), *Industrial Relations Systems*, Carbondale: Southern Illinois University Press.

Elfstrom, M. and Kuruvilla, S. (2012), 'The changing nature of labor unrest in China', *Proceedings*, International Labour and Employment Relations Research Association Conference, Philadelphia, July.

Flanders, A. (1970), *Management and Unions*, London: Faber.

Fox, A. (1971), *A Sociology of Work in Industry*, London: Collier-Macmillan

Fox, A. (1974), *Beyond Contract: Work, Power and Trust Relations*, London: Faber.

Guo, J. (2011), *Li Binsheng: Caiyong guoji shouduan jiejue laodong guanxi maodun bufuhe zhongguo guoqing.* [Using radical means to solve labour disputes does not correspond with the national conditions in China], www.people.com.cn.

He, L. (2005), *Quanguo renda changweihui zhifazu guanyu jiancha zhonghua renmin gongheguo laodongfa shishiqingkuang de baogao* [Report on the implementation of Labour Law of the People's Republic of China by the law enforcement inspection group of the Standing Committee of the National People's Congress].

Hua, J. M. (2011), 'Report by the Implementation Inspection Team of the All-China People's Congress Standing Committee on the inspection of the implementation situation of the Labour Contract Law of the People's Republic of China', internet source:www.npc.gov.cn/wxzl/gongbao/2011–12/30/content_1686393.htm, accessed on 10th March 2012.

Huang, Y. (2011), 'Nanhai bentian laozi tanpan Jinnian gongzi zaizhang 611 yuan', [Nanhai Honda negotiation increased the salary of 611 yuan this year], *Southern Metropolis Daily*.

Kochan, T. (1980), *Collective Bargaining and Industrial Relations*, Homewood: Irwin.

Kochan, T. A., Katz, H. C., McKersie, R. B.(1986), *The Transformation of American Industrial Relations*, New York: Basic Books.

Kochan, T. A., Eaton, A. E., McKersie, R. B. and Adler, P. S. (2009), *Healing Together*, Ithaca: Cornell University Press.

Li, G. (2010), 'Bentian nanhai lingbujian chang yin laozi jiufen tinggong' [Workers of Honda Nanhai automotive components plant stop work due to industrial conflict], *People's Daily*, 28 May.

Liang, H. (2009), 'Laodong hetongfa bixu yao dagai' [A big amendment of Labour Contract Law is needed), *Chengdu Business Daily*, 10 March.

Liu A. (2003), 'Workers' options for action in the process of institutional transformation of state-owned enterprises – an empirical study on collective inaction', *Sociological Research*, 6.

Lukács, G. (1999), *History and Class Consciousness*. Beijing: The Commercial Press, pp. 136.

Mali (2009), 'Changkai: Laodong guanxi bixu yifaweijian' [Changkai: Labour Relations should be based on the Law], *Faren Magazine*.

Marx, K. (1985), Economic Manuscript in *Collected Works of K. Marx and F. Engels*, vol. 48, Beijing: People's Press, pp. 3–35.

Morgan, C. A. (1984), *Labour Economics* (Chinese Version), Beijing: Gongrenchubanshe (Workers Press).

Oxenbridge, S. and Brown, W. (2004), 'Achieving a new equilibrium? The stability of co-operative employer-union relationships', *Industrial Relations Journal*, 35:5, 388–402.

Shanghai Federation of Trade Unions (2008), 'Guanyu laodong hetong fa shishi qingkuang de diaocha baogao' [Research report on the implementation of the Labour Contract Law].

Shanghai Municipal Human Resources and Social Security Bureau (2008), '2008 nian laodong zhengyi qingkuang fenxi' [Analysis of the labour disputes status in 2008], www.12333sh.gov.cn/2007sxy/2007news/2007xwzt/200902/t2009022 3_1061830.shtml.

Transfar Group Co. (2011), 'Chuanhua jituan goujian hexie laodong guanxi de shijian he zuofa' [Practice of the Transfar group in establishing harmonious labour relations].

Wang, J. and Liu, M. (2010), 'Laohefa shishi liangnian laodongzhengyi jinpen', [The outbreak of labour disputes after two years of the enactment of Labour Contract Law], *China Youth Daily*, 19 January.

Wang, Z. (1988), *Minfa xueshuo yu panli yanjiu*, [Civil law theory and case studies], Beijing: China University of Politic Science and Law Press.

Wang, Z. (2010), 'Zai zhonghua quanguo zonggonghui shiwujie sici zhiwei huiyi shang de jianghua' [Speech at the 4th Session of the 15th Executive Committee Conference], 26 July.

Webb, S. and Webb, B. (1920), *History of Trade Unionism*, London: Longmans Green.

Wu, S. X. (2008), 'Report on the implementation situation of The Labour Contract Law of the People's Republic of China', www.bjrd.gov.cn/sy/jdzh/2 00902/t20090209_49265.html.

Yi, F. and Xu, D. (2010), 'Qinli yici bagong tanpan' [Experience a strike personally], *Xinmin Weekly*, (31).

Yue, P. (2011), 'Quanguo gonghui huiyuan da 2.39yi ren Gonghui jiada tuijin "Liangge pubian"' [The number of trade union members reaches 239 million; trade union promotes 'two generalizations'], *Peoples Daily*.

Zhang, X. L. (2010), 'Guangdongsheng zonggonghui zhuxi: qiye gonghui zhuxi duo bushi minzhu xuanju' [Chair of trade unions of Guangdong Province: many chairs of trade unions are not elected democratically], *Yangcheng Evening News*, 3 July.

3   The Two Forms of Labour Movement

Chang Kai

Three decades have passed since China started its economic reforms. The introduction of the Labour Contract Law in 2008 not only marked the establishment of a basic legal system for individual labour relations; it also provided the foundation for the regulation of collective labour relations. The strike wave in the summer of 2010 indicated that labour relations in China had entered a new phase, marking the start of its transition from individual towards collective labour relations (Chang, 2013). The regulation of individual contracts was no longer sufficient to resolve conflict and maintain stable labour relations. But a consequence of the shift towards a collective labour relations system has been that two distinct labour movements have emerged. One is government-led, top-down and within the official system; the other is spontaneous worker-led and bottom-up. This chapter discusses the development and characteristics of these two labour movements.

Collective Labour Relations and the Chinese Labour Movement

The change from individual to collective labour relations is unavoidable in a market economy. But such a change cannot take place spontaneously. It is the outcome of interactions amongst the parties involved. The main driving force comes from the workers' demand for rights of self-protection. But government will only respond effectively when it judges that a proper basis of collective labour relations will contribute to more stable and sustainable economic and social development. It also has to be confident that this will enable employers to achieve productivity improvements to compensate for the rising wages that will result from collective bargaining. Only then will the construction of a working collective labour relations system become a prime focus of government policy. Individual labour relations imply a differentiated relationship between individual workers and their employers. Collective labour relations imply that social relations are constructed by negotiation between the workers as a group (usually represented by trade unions) and employers or employer organisations. Individual labour relations embody, for the worker, a subordinate and unequal employment relationship. Collective labour relations provide some redress from the inequality of individual labour relations because their collective nature provides more balanced power.

Workers' solidarity and organisation are necessary conditions for collective labour relations. Their basic requirements are the direct involvement and participation of workers. An effective labour movement is one in which the workers participate to defend and advance their rights and interests. A labour movement is the internal driving force for the establishment of collective labour relations. Until 2010, the structure and basis of regulation of Chinese labour relations was highly individualistic. Workers had not mobilised their collective potential. Despite the formal existence of trade unions, they by and large failed to represent the workers effectively, and consequently failed to embody any effective labour solidarity. Workers were generally fragmented and unorganised. This situation was directly related to a longer history of division and dispersal of labour movements in China.

The Communist Party of China had its historical origins in the labour movement. This provided the Party's working-class foundations. Most of its early leaders had led or participated in the workers' movement. After the establishment of the All-China Federation of Trade Unions (ACFTU) in 1925, the union movement, led by the Party, became an important part of the revolutionary struggle. This is important to an understanding of Chinese trade unions today; political activities have been the main purpose of the ACFTU from its birth. In clear contrast with trade unions in most other countries, even with the arrival of the market economy, the ACFTU has rarely been directly involved in collective bargaining or in economic strikes.

After the Party came to power in 1949, it introduced the Trade Union Law, in 1950, making the ACFTU China's sole legal trade union. The Party defined three functions of the union based on Lenin's thoughts: to serve as the basis of the dictatorship of the proletariat; to act as a bridge between the Party and the mass of workers; and to be the school for workers' education. Since then, the concept of 'the workers' movement' was gradually diluted and dissolved into one of 'trade union work'. This is because the Party does not need the ACFTU to organise workers into social movements to fight for workers' rights and interests. Instead, what the union is required to do is to fulfil its tasks of facilitating production, improving workers' lives, and furthering their education, in a top-down approach under the leadership of the Party.

Another motive for diluting the union movement was to prevent the trade union from detaching itself from the Party as an active workers' movement, and becoming an opposition force. Following the Party's criticism of the then ACFTU chairman Li Lisan's idea of 'union independence' in 1950, and the criticism of the then ACFTU chairman Lai Ruoyu's 'syndicalism' in 1958, the idea of a 'labour movement' in China has become a purely historical notion, and only 'trade union work' exists in reality. In 2003, the union cadres' school known as the 'China Labour Movement College', sponsored by the ACFTU, officially changed its name to the 'China Institute of Industrial Relations'. This symbolised the fact that 'labour movement' as a historical concept had been deliberately detached from the ACFTU.

During the period of the state-planned economy, Chinese society was under the total control of the government. The workers' well-being was seen to be fully addressed by this arrangement. Without the need for the formation of a labour movement, the mass of workers could be seen as simply the nuts and bolts of the state apparatus. Under a market economy, however, the interests of the state, capital and labour have necessarily diverged. The concept of a labour movement as a social movement for workers to fight for their rights and independence becomes historically unavoidable. As the subordinate party in the employment relationship, workers need solidarity to mobilise the organised power necessary to maintain and fight for their own interests. Only by doing so can workers develop a power base that is more comparable with that of capital.

The market economy has revived China's labour movement as an issue for debate and it is now emerging as a social movement. Rapid economic development had initially encouraged the view that the most important condition for competitiveness was low labour costs. China's extraordinary economic growth was achieved at the expense of the rights and interests of the workers. More than 30 million workers were laid off from the state-owned enterprises, and more than 200 million rural migrant workers are now struggling at the bottom of the new industrial society. These workers have made a great contribution to the Chinese economy, but they have not received a fair share of its fruits. Inequitable redistribution and the associated lack of protection for workers' rights have been the underlying economic and social causes of workers' protests and movements.

Starting from the mid-1980s, following the reform and opening up of the economy, work stoppages and strikes have been frequent in China. In the state-owned enterprises, strikes were provoked by the sacrifice of workers' interests. In private enterprises, workers went on strike in protest at the violation of their rights and terms of employment. Strikes initially were sporadic, uncoordinated and lacked collective consciousness. They were simply a reaction, but had not yet developed to have the consciousness, organisation and strategies that are typical of collective action under a mature market economy. Strikes were usually isolated incidents within individual enterprises. They did not trigger repercussions through wider regional or industrial action.

Since the 2000s, however, with the completion of the reform of both state-owned enterprises and of the labour market, workers' awareness both of the nature of markets and of their own rights has gradually been taking shape. Strikes became the main form of collective action. A pivotal event was the strike of over two months long staged by more than 20,000 workers in the Dalian Development Zone in September 2005. As a result of the persistence of the striking workers, their demands were more or less met. After talking with those involved, the author commented at the time that the Dalian strike was a landmark event, signalling the awaking of workers' awareness of their collective rights and collective actions.

Not all action was as successful. Strikes in four Taiwanese-owned shoe factories in Guangdong province that took place at much the same time ended in complete failure. At Stella International several thousand workers took part in a spontaneous strike because of dissatisfaction with their employment terms and conditions. The strike went out of control due to the lack of organisation, leading to vandalism and riots which destroyed production equipment and public property. As a result of these extreme actions nearly one thousand workers were dismissed or resigned, and nearly 100 workers were investigated by the police. A few dozen were arrested and detained for crimes of 'assembling a crowd to disturb social order' and 'inciting trouble'. Ten workers were prosecuted on suspicion of 'intentional destruction of property' (Tang, 2004). As Tang observed, in this disorder the workers had no leader, no representatives, no organisation and no specific demands. Nor did they receive any collective commitment. They formed like a mob and disbanded like a mob on the spur of the moment. It was a collective irrational vent of frustration. Although there were glimpses of workers' collective consciousness and collective action, they were inchoate and naïve.

With the creation of markets and the emergence of labour conflict since the late 1970s, features of a labour movement have re-emerged. Having become hired labour in the market economy, laid-off state-owned enterprise workers and farmers previously in production brigades appear to have developed vague new conceptions about their changed position and rights. Ex-state-owned enterprise workers who were thrown onto the labour market became nostalgic for their past identity under state-planning. The labour movement that had dissolved following the founding of socialist China began to reappear informally. This embryonic labour movement can be seen as a rehearsal and prelude to a broader transition towards collective labour relations.

The Strike Wave of 2010 – The Emergence of a Bottom-Up Labour Movement

The strike wave of 2010 marked the emergence of the Chinese labour movement in market conditions. It demonstrated the bottom-up organising power of the workers and became a driving force behind the transition towards collective labour relations. It is likely to leave a substantial legacy in the history of the development of Chinese labour relations.

The strike wave started in the Suzhou Industrial Park in February. Five relatively large strikes took place there, involving more than 10,000 workers. The strike centre shifted from the Yangtze River Delta in Jiangsu to the Pearl River Delta in Guangdong where, in May 2010, the Nanhai Honda strike broke out. This attracted worldwide attention with intensive media coverage and became the symbolic event of 2010. A chain of strikes soon followed in more than a hundred enterprises, mostly in the Japanese-owned auto-parts industry, in nearby cities, including Zhongshan, Foshan, Shenzhen, Huizhou and Zhuhai. In July 2010, the Dalian Development Zone in Liaoning became the centre of strikes; it was the third strike wave in the Zone since its establishment. Over 70,000 workers took part and 73 enterprises were affected, including 48 Japanese-owned enterprises. In addition, multiple strike actions broke out in Shanghai, Beijing, and Jiangsu, Shandong and other places (Lu, 2015). On a conservative estimate, some 300,000 workers participated in the 2010 strike wave.

Compared with the strikes of the mid-1990s, the consciousness and capacity for collective action of the workers had significantly improved. Nanhai Honda demonstrated this. After the strike started, more than a thousand workers, led by representatives elected by the workers, showed great self-discipline. They stopped work but protected the production equipment and the factory. They won the understanding and support of the public and they negotiated with the management in a calm, factual and reasonable way. The strike was a success, with the workers being awarded a 34 per cent pay rise (Chang, 2010). While it was going on, workers prevented the sort of disorderly and irrational behaviour that often characterises spontaneous strikes. This reflected their awareness of the need to show internal solidarity, act strategically and communicate with the public. The Nanhai Honda strike became an example for other enterprises to copy. Despite the fact that the strike wave involved many enterprises and several regions, both labour and capital over a wide area were able to act rationally and resolve their disputes through consultation and negotiation.

The 2010 strike wave demonstrated, for the first time in China, the potential of action by organised labour in the labour market. Evidence of its power was a 20 to 30 per cent wage rise across the striking enterprises; such a large increase was unprecedented. In addition, some enterprises that did not experience strikes themselves none-the-less voluntarily increased their wages in order to prevent them. The strike wave also influenced the more general rise in wages across the country. In 2011, 24 provinces adjusted their minimum wage standards, leading to an average increase of 22 per cent. It was the highest percentage increase since minimum wages were introduced nearly twenty years earlier (Xinhua News Agency, 2011). The collective bargaining power of the workers was thus demonstrated through the most fundamental indicator of the price of labour, the minimum wage.

The main focus of any labour movement is its members' economic interests, reflected in its ability to improve their wages and working conditions. One of the most prominent features of the 2010 strikes was that the workers' demands shifted from rights towards interests. A rights dispute is concerned with whether or not legal or contractual rights have been breached. An interests dispute is concerned with whether the contractual terms of employment should be altered. Rights disputes can be individual or collective, but interests disputes usually apply collectively. Before 2010, collective labour disputes were usually related to the violation of rights of groups of workers. In this strike wave the bulk of the disputes hinged on interests, with workers demanding wage rises, improvement of working conditions and fairer treatment. It is generally the case that the improvement of conditions affecting their interests can only be achieved directly by the workers mobilising collective strength and then engaging in collective negotiation. The growth of interests disputes from about 2010 indicates that Chinese workers were beginning to organise themselves. The strike wave emphasised the important role of a labour movement in a market economy in advancing workers' interests.

The shift from rights disputes to interests disputes is directly linked to growing labour consciousness as a result of exposure to markets. This refers to the awareness that a collective group of workers has of their own positions as hired labour in a market-determined labour process. The labour consciousness of Chinese workers is being gradually formed through the process of marketisation. The prerequisite for the generation of labour consciousness is the worker's self-identification as hired labour. Workers start to identify their role in the market economy as 'I am a hired worker, hired by the boss'. The author interviewed dozens of workers in the striking enterprises. On the issue of their work-related personal identity, all the workers in non-state-owned enterprises perceive themselves as labour. Only one or two workers in the state-owned enterprises believed that they still enjoyed the status of the 'master' of the enterprise.

The introduction of the Labour Contract Law in 2008 gave legal recognition to the changed identity of urban workers as a transition from the state-owned regime to hired labour. It also confirmed the change of rural workers from rural labour (*nongmingong*) to hired labour (*guyong laodongzhe*). It was highly significant that the Labour Contract Law did not differentiate between state-owned enterprise workers and rural migrant workers, but simply described them as 'workers'. It indicated that there was no longer any difference in the legal status between the urban workers and rural workers.

There are, in effect, a number of layers of labour consciousness; they include legal awareness, rights awareness, solidarity awareness and action awareness. These may be deepened and enhanced as labour consciousness increases. Collective consciousness is the fundamental aspect of labour consciousness in a market economy. Its awakening releases the innate power that initiates a labour movement. Workers' collective consciousness has been substantially enhanced by the recent development of labour relations, by the experience of workers' struggles across China and by the implementation of the Labour Contract Law and other regulations. The self-perception as 'masters' in the state-planned economy has been replaced by self-perception as 'workers' in the market economy. As a result they see the benefits of following the example of workers in market economies in building collective solidarity in order to take action to defend and fight for their rights and interests.

Workers' collective action has been the driving force behind the transition towards collective labour relations in China. The 2010 strike wave was a direct result of the development of China's labour relations and of its labour movement. It has demonstrated not only the bottom-up organising potential of Chinese labour, but also that this can play a unique role in balancing labour relations and in regulating the labour market.

Top-Down: The Trade Union and the Construction of Collective Labour Relations

A labour movement is built up of workers' collective actions. They provide the impetus for the transition to collective labour relations. But the institutional structuring of the transition depends upon how far it is recognised and assisted by the state. At the same time as workers may be spontaneously pushing for collective labour relations, the construction of a parallel structure led by the government is also taking place. Unlike the bottom-up movement organised by workers, this is a top-down administrative process.

The Chinese government is well aware, from its own and international experience, of the need to shape and regulate collective labour relations. It is also aware of the politically sensitive and unavoidably associated issue of collective action by workers. Since the economic reforms started in the late 1970s, the government's labour policy has mainly relied on a top-down approach, using administrative power to build collective labour relations. At the same time, it has tried to prevent strikes, and to fragment and weaken spontaneous action. The official mind-set has been one of mobilising the full resources of public authority to control labour relations. Its main intention has been to ensure that labour relations fit in with the government's overall goals of political security, economic development and social stability (Li and Duan, 2014). The main official executor of this policy is the trade union. It is the instrument given the task by government of achieving the transition towards collective labour relations.

The nature of Chinese trade unions is much debated. One view is that the official trade unions are no more than agents of administrative power; in this sense they cannot be described as 'trade unions' (Taylor and Li, 2007). The present author has argued a contrary view, that the Chinese official union movement has both legal basis and social foundation. It is also the official representative of China in the International Labour Organisation. This 'trade union with Chinese characteristics' is unique to China's post state-planned economy (Chang, 2013). The ACFTU operates in accordance with government thinking but in a quite distinctive way.

The ACFTU is distinctive, first, in its belief that labour relations in China are fundamentally different from those in Western countries. For example, the ACFTU maintained in 2015 that 'no change has been made to the status of the working class, and all workers are masters of the country and society; and no change has been made to the socialist nature of labour relations'. Conflicts between labour and capital in the current stage of economic development are seen as 'conflicts of deriving from differences in substantive interests based on the broad alignment of fundamental interest'. These kinds of conflicts of substantive interests are 'internal conflicts amongst the people' (*Workers' Daily*, 2015). On this basis, the enterprise unionism designed by the ACFTU is defined by the working principle of 'promoting enterprise development and safeguarding workers' rights and interests'. This prioritises the enterprise's interest before that of the workers, despite the fact that the Trade Union Law stipulates that 'safeguarding workers' legitimate rights and interests' is the fundamental duty of the union. Another indication of this broader prioritisation of the ACFTU was the theme of the report of its 16th Representative Congress in 2013: 'unite and mobilise millions of workers to fulfil the Chinese dream' (Li, 2013).

In 2005 the ACFTU set out the *Socialist union development road with Chinese characteristics*, pointing the direction of travel for the Chinese trade union movement. This statement set out its guiding ideology, political role, tasks, functions, organisational structure, foreign relations, and so on. It specified eight commitments or 'adherences' (*jianchi*): to the leadership of the Party; to the socialist nature of the trade unions; to the development of the working class; to harmonious labour relations; to safeguarding the legitimate rights and interests of workers; to improving the socialist legal system of work; to promoting the formation of a new order in the international labour movement; and to the spirit of reform and innovation to strengthen the trade unions' own structure (*Workers' Daily*, 2013).

These eight principles were essentially a political statement that expressed the ACFTU's loyalty to the Party. The question of the identity and duty of the union under the market economy had deliberately been left vague. This excessive politicisation of the unions, even to the extent of treating them as a political organisation, not only lacks any legal basis, but also deviates from the nature of trade unions' duties as prescribed by the law. By increasing the distance between the unions and the mass of workers it has a perverse effect on the ability of unions to perform their legal functions. This also reflects a continuing debate. The author participated in discussions during the drafting of the 1992 Trade Union Law. In the initial draft concerning the nature of the Chinese trade unions, there was the statement: 'the union is an important social and political organisation'. This provoked much controversy. After repeated deliberation, the Party Central Committee decided to delete it.

The building of harmonious labour relations has been only one component of the objective of a union with Chinese characteristics. The involvement of the Chinese trade unions in labour relations is limited to carrying out specific tasks under the principle of 'government led control'. These tasks include: establishing a workplace venue for supporting workers' communal activities (*zhigongzhijia*); promoting democratic management of the enterprise; developing transparency in factory affairs; delivering welfare and care; participating in the drafting of labour legislation; providing legal support; promoting the tripartite consultation mechanism; safeguarding legal rights; establishing grassroots unions;

and promoting collective consultation. Undoubtedly these union activities have a positive role in regulating labour relations. They also succeed to a greater or lesser extent in representing and safeguarding workers' rights and interests. The ACFTU itself considers that the construction of collective labour relations has been its most important work since 2010, with the promotion of 'two universals' (*lianggepubian*) as its key objective, that is, to establish unions universally in all enterprises and to develop collective consultation universally.

The official targets required that at least 90 per cent of the registered enterprises in the country should set up a union within three years and that at least 80 per cent of those enterprises that have set up a union should establish a collective wage negotiation system (Wang, 2010). Through the efforts of local trade unions, as of the end of June 2013, there were 280 million trade union members, 2.75 million grassroots union organisations, covering 6.38 million enterprise units, and a union membership density of 81.1 per cent in these unionised units (Xinhua Net, 2013). 'By the end of 2013, a total of 2.42 million collective contracts were signed in the whole country, covering 6.33 million enterprises and 287 million workers. The three-year planned goals were thus smoothly accomplished' (*People's Daily*, 2014). The rates of unionisation and of collective contract signing are seen as important indicators of collective labour relations. Thus, on the face of it, the ACFTU has had a substantial impact in building a collective labour relations framework, expanding the social impact of the unions, enhancing the awareness of labour relations amongst workers and enterprises, and defending the rights and interests of the workers.

There are, however, serious problems associated with this pursuit of quantitative targets by government administrative methods. The main problem is that the task of achieving unionisation is handed over to the enterprise management. The consequence is that many new trade unions are just nominal or 'shell unions' with no substance. What is more serious is that many of the new unions are controlled by the employer and became 'bosses's unions' (*laoban gonghui*). The local government is heavily involved when collective contracts are signed and the rate of such signing is part of its performance evaluation. This has encouraged a rapid increase in the number of collective contracts signed, and the breadth of their coverage. But the quality of the contracts suffers from this emphasis on formality, quantity and political performance, so that there has been little attention to their content, quality and real achievement (Wu, 2012).

The big problem with these administrative methods of furthering collective labour relations is that it becomes a mere formality, and a numbers game. The danger is that superficial union activities owe nothing to workers' requests and result in little involvement with the workers. Although the three-year targets may have been achieved, the new unions have not in reality organised the workers. Nor have the collective contracts played any significant role in regulating labour relations. More important, this employer control (*laobanhua*) and pure formality (*xingshihua*) of the enterprise unions not only fails to involve the workers effectively in labour relations; it also damages the chance for workers to develop genuine solidarity, thereby exacerbating the imbalance of power in labour relations. As a result, far from eliminating workers' self-organised collective action, and providing a substitute for it, these new enterprise unions have actually widened the gap between the union and the workers, provoking yet more unofficial worker activity.

Conflict and Cooperation: The Interaction of the Two Sources of Labour Power

The 2010 strike wave was not only a landmark of the start of the transition towards collectivised labour relations, it also marked the emergence of two new forces and directions in the Chinese labour movement. The problem of the relationship between the official unions and workers' unofficial grass-roots activity arose at a deeper level. The two sources of labour power (*laogongliliang*) are, first, the union organisation within the official system that is represented by the ACFTU and, second, the labour movement that has been developed spontaneously by the workers outside the official system. The former carries out union activities in a top-down and administrative mode. The latter is a bottom-up force, which is mainly apparent in the form of spontaneous strikes to defend and advance workers' rights and interests.

The emergence of these two separated forms of labour power with distinct paths within the labour movement is mainly caused by the distancing of labour as an effective institutional actor. In the legal sense, labour as an institutional actor is composed of both the union and the workers. That is, workers are the ideological subject (*yizhizhuti*) of the labour side, and the union is the formal subject (*xingshizhuti*) (Chang and Zhang, 1993). However, in reality, because of the administrative absorption of the trade union at the local government level (*difang gonghui xingzhenghua*) and the tendency for a 'boss's union' at the enterprise level (*qiyegonghui laobanhua*), the separation between union and workers is becoming more and more serious. If trade unions are unable effectively to represent and safeguard the interests of workers within the official system, then workers will naturally choose the path of self-help.

The resulting divergence in the sources of labour power within labour organisations has become a distinctive Chinese phenomenon.

There is an important dynamic that arises from the interaction of these two forms of power and their associated organisations. The official trade union movement led by the government has a clear legal basis and its own practical needs. It owes its existence to the need to redress the imbalance of power between capital and labour. Its purpose is to safeguard workers' rights and interests. Although the bureaucratic nature of the official union can seriously affect how it pursues this role, the existence of the union is in itself a counter-balance to the pressure of capital. Moreover, because of the high political status of the ACFTU, it has played a very active role both in drawing up labour legislation and in policy making on labour matters. Its authority and influence are currently indispensable and irreplaceable in China.

The potential of the grass-roots power of labour is inherent in any industrial society. Strikes are a manifestation of workers' power. Since this aspect of their power lacks the stability that would be derived from power based on legal support and organisational continuity, it is neither sustainable nor enduring. Currently, it dissipates as soon as the strike or other defensive action is over. Nevertheless, as Engels said, the experience of strikes will become 'the military academy for workers, in which they will be trained and be ready to be involved in this inevitable great struggle' (Engels, 1845). The significance of the many strikes of recent years rests not only in the direct defence of workers' rights and interests, but also in training worker leaders and activists. As in the early stages of the Chinese market economy, the development of the labour movement involves workers developing themselves. A good example was the Li De workers' communication team (*lidegongren xuanjiantuan*) which, after the 2015 Li De Shoe Factory dispute, was organised by the striking workers to disseminate strike ideology and experience to workers in other enterprises. At the time that the author interviewed them, in June 2015, this team had spoken at five different sites in Guangzhou and Shenzhen, with audiences of between 20 and 50 workers.

The mutual dependence between the official union and the unofficial worker organisation is of critical importance in a competitive market. Both face employers trying to maximise profits, and they share the common goal of fighting for and defending the workers' rights and welfare. When the union has won recognition from an employer for collective consultation, it is able to engage in wage negotiations. Should there be a strike, the union is legally required to get involved in resolving the strike as the workers' representative. This is in itself a tacit support for the striking workers. Such strikes provide the impetus that requires the union to carry out its work, while demonstrating the need for the union for their resolution. In the current system, successful cases of strike resolution show that, if the two sources of union power are handled properly, they can support each other effectively. The successful work stoppages in Guangzhou and Dalian in 2010 provide examples. Many union officials believed that it was those strikes that raised the status of the trade union and increased its impact. The workers confirmed to the author that the active involvement of both the union and the workers' representatives was important for the successful outcome.

In the 2010 strike wave, some local unions, such as the Dalian Development Zone Federation of Trade Unions and the Guangzhou Municipal Federation of Trade Unions, were able to stand on the side of the workers to resolve the disputes and win the workers' support. But they were the exceptions. The vast majority of enterprise unions involved in the strike wave were rejected by the workers. Some even helped the employer to suppress the workers and became the object of workers' contempt. For example, at the Nanhai Honda strike in May 2010, a hundred people with yellow hats and trade union identity cards surrounded the workers. Three workers were injured in the ensuing violence, which strengthened the striking workers' resolve. Next day the union publicly apologised (Business Sohu, 2010). This experience had an enormous impact on the official unions. The ACFTU came in for substantial criticism, because it is supposed to 'organise and lead the mass of workers'. The pressure felt by the official unions was a powerful incentive for them to improve. In July 2010, the ACFTU responded by proposing the focus of union work on the 'two universals'. It was a direct response to pressures from the 2010 strike wave.

An essential pre-condition for the mutual cooperation of these two aspects of union power is that each recognises the legitimacy of the other. The legitimacy of the official unions is unquestionable, however much disillusioned workers might question it. There are, however, sharp differences of opinion as to legitimacy of unofficial grass-roots worker activism. The workers believe that the inability of the official unions to protect their interests is sufficient justification for them to take action themselves. The author's research team has conducted dozens of interviews with striking workers. A typical statement from one was that 'The union does not represent us now because their responsibility is to their leadership. They are in the same camp as the company. We workers have no choice but to use our own power to protect our interests.'

There is an argument that collective action, including work stoppages, does not violate the law. This is based on the narrow view that everything which is not prohibited by the law is allowed. Strikes are not illegal as such; therefore, workers can legitimately use strikes to defend their rights. To a certain extent, local governments have tacitly acknowledged the legitimacy of spontaneous strikes, because this is the premise when they become involved in strike resolution (Chang, 2010).

Contrary to this, however, the ACFTU has publicly stated that it 'does not approve' of strike action. Li Binsheng, one of the Secretaries of the Secretariat of the ACFTU, said: 'We are not in favour of the saying that a strike is the last resort of labour dispute resolution. The use of aggressive means to resolve conflicts in labour relations is not suitable to China's national conditions. Nor is it in line with the nature of labour relations at the present stage, or with the fundamental interests of the mass of workers' (*People's Daily* online, 2011). The ACFTU has thus adopted a more critical attitude towards the unofficial grass-roots labour movement. The ACFTU vice-chairman and Party Secretary Li Yubin controversially declared in 2011 that:

Labour relations conflicts have entered a period of high confrontation and frequent occurrence. Collective work stoppages and mass events occur regularly. The penetration of foreign hostile forces has increased. They attempt to use labour relations as a breakthrough point. By supporting illegal organisations 'defending rights', their personnel are competing with the union for the workers, and undermine the solidarity of the working class and the unity of trade union organizations.

Within hours of this statement there were several thousand overwhelmingly critical responses on-line. This public ACFTU statement indicates the substantial differences between the official trade union leadership and the unofficial labour movement.

This disagreement reflects differences in political ideology as well as institutional self-interest. Politically, the ACFTU and its affiliates is the only legal union organisation. Founded and led by the Party, acceptance of the Party's leadership is its basic principle. As the official agency responsible for work, the ACFTU's core duty is to organise, unite and control the mass of workers, and to prevent them from forming any breakaway organisations. Any self-organising and spontaneous actions by workers are seen as a threat to the union. Thus, preventing the emergence of 'independent unions' or a 'breakaway union' is crucial for the ACFTU, and its favoured strategy is one of deliberately politicising any spontaneous labour action. Because the official union is currently defined as the sole representative of labour, it is in its interest to protect the *status quo*. The emergence of any independent labour organisation would threaten the monopoly of the ACFTU in the handling of labour relations because it would create different voices and generate competition within the labour movement. It is understandable that not all those involved in labour issues are happy with this situation.

Under the current political and legal framework, the co-existence of the two bases of labour power is unavoidable. The official union movement could be crudely characterised as having organisation but no mass basis. By contrast, the labour movement outside the official system has the masses but no organisation. At present, the goals and demands of the two are basically the same: to protect and improve workers' status and their terms and conditions through legal means. What differs between them are the methods to be used. But these could be accommodated. If mutual support and complementarity can be achieved, this would encourage the unification of collective labour power and the effective conduct of labour relations. The key to achieving this is that the ACFTU must fulfil its duties according to the law. It must overcome its tendency to resort to administrative solutions and to take the employers' side. It must absorb the external, unofficial worker organisations into its system.

This can be done. Some local union leaders have adopted an understanding and cooperative attitude towards collective actions and towards labour-oriented non-governmental organisations (NGOs). For example, in Guangzhou, where workers' unofficial organisations and labour NGOs are the most vigorous, the Municipal Federation of Trade Unions Chairman, Chen Weiguang, observed: 'the labour NGOs are undertaking activities to protect the interests of the rural migrant workers. They can work as a supplement to the union system and help union organisations to better connect with the masses' (Chen, 2012).

Judging from the present situation, however, the official and unofficial aspects of labour organisation not only diverge in their understanding and values, but they also have conflicting interests. The present realities of the union system and the political situation directly impact upon the relationship between the two. How this relationship should be dealt with is still a matter for negotiation and experiment.

Developments since 2010

The two distinct aspects of collective labour power have developed further since 2010. The unofficial labour movement has increased in scale and become more orderly, while there have been significant changes within the official system.

The first development of the informal system is that the frequency of strikes continues to rise. Of the 2,831 strikes during the four years from January 2011 to January 2015 that were picked up by the China

Labour Bulletin database website, 185 incidents occurred in 2011, 382 in 2012, 656 in 2013 and 1378 in 2014. This represents an increase of 106 per cent, 72 per cent and 110 per cent in successive years (Lu, 2015). The number of major disputes was particularly frequent after early 2014. For example, in March 2014, over 40,000 workers in Yu Yuan Shoe Factory in Panyu, Guangdong province went on strike to fight for their social security entitlements. During May and August 2014, workers in Wal-Mart Changde Store protested against the corporation on the grounds of unfair dismissal of workers as a result of store closure. In addition, in May 2014, Ge Shi Bi Shoe Factory went on strike; in June, the Guangdong Foshan General Souvenir Factory went on strike; in August, sanitation workers in Guangzhou University City went on strike; in May 2015, over 10,000 workers from the China No.2 Heavy Machinery Group Corporation went on strike. All these strikes had an impact nationally.

Both workers' organising capacity and their strategic capability have improved substantially. The Li De Shoe Factory strike illustrates this well. Beginning in August 2014, more than 2700 workers went on strike to recover the social security and pension fund arrears that the company owed them and also to get compensation for company relocation. The workers held a meeting at which they elected representatives for collective bargaining purposes and at which fund raising and administrative arrangements were decided. A spokesperson was selected to liaise with the media, and a leader was elected for the picketing team. Although the strikers were confronted with a variety of obstructions and much hostile pressure, they remained united and did not back down. They had three successive strikes, totalling ten days, over the course of eight months, during which there were six rounds of collective bargaining. They guarded the plant for five nights during the strikes. Their battle was finally won with the employers paying the workers more than RMB 120 million in compensation (Xie, 2015).

The Li De case resulted in the largest amount of compensation being paid to workers in the history of Chinese labour disputes. More importantly, the use of worker representatives, strike funds, external liaison and picketing showed that they had mastered the basic elements of strike organisation in a market economy. During the bargaining process, Li De workers, through their representatives, proposed that 'it is agreed by both the labour and capital that no third party agency or personnel would be invited to participate in collective bargaining at the site the next morning', thus rejecting the involvement of the official union in the collective bargaining process. Indeed, the official union was completely marginalised in the Li De event. During the author's interview with the negotiating representatives they explained: 'the reason why we propose not to invite a third party is because we don't want the union to be involved in the negotiation, because we don't trust them. Their involvement will make the issue more complex. The employer agreed to the proposal, aware that the third party also includes our negotiation adviser. But even without the adviser being present, we still have the ability to negotiate' (Interview notes, 16th June 2015).

Clearly the workers' organising awareness had become more astute. It is significant that they called for the establishment of a workers' union, and opposed what they perceived as the 'boss's union'. In the Nanhai Honda strike five years earlier, workers had only requested the 'restructuring of the union'. More recently there have been numerous cases where workers have clearly rejected what they see as the 'yellow union' controlled by the boss, and requested that the higher levels of the ACFTU should support workers' efforts to set up their own union. In April 2014, the women workers of Guangzhou Sumida proposed to set up their own union in opposition to the 'boss's union'. This request failed as a result of opposition from the higher level union and the enterprise owner (Wang, 2014).

Another example of more sophisticated awareness in unofficial unions is provided by Wal-Mart. In 2006, after consultation between the ACFTU and the senior management of Wal-Mart, all 63 Chinese stores of Wal-Mart established a trade union. As a benchmark model for the ACFTU's campaign for grassroots union establishment, this case was claimed to be a great achievement. It put to an end Wal-Mart's worldwide opposition to union recognition of more than forty years. But even back then some workers claimed that it was in fact no more than setting up yellow unions across Wal-Mart's Chinese stores. In May 2015, these doubts came to a head when Wal-Mart workers complained to the Shenzhen Federation of Trade Unions. They pointed out that the Wal-Mart union's then president and the official collective consultation representatives were all members of senior management, and that the workers had neither elected them nor trusted them. According to the law, these executives were not qualified to represent workers in negotiations. The workers called for the 'yellow union' to be abolished and replaced by one with union officials who were directly elected.

The grass-roots labour movement is continuing to develop. Workers' organisational and strategic skills are becoming more mature. There are some signs that the government is less inclined to use criminal punishment against those who lead strikes. In May 2013, for example, Wu Guijun, the workers' negotiating representative at a strike at Shenzhen Diweixin, was detained for 'organising a mob to disrupt orderly traffic', but he was freed in June 2014, and awarded compensation of RMB 74,000. Despite such examples, because there is no clear legal protection of labour activists, workers' organisations tend to be transitory, existing only during strikes. The constant political pressure for the maintenance of stability makes the informal labour movement relatively weak and it struggles to survive. In general, strike organisers still face damage to their career prospects.

A policy statement was published in 2015 which, if implemented, might improve the way strikes are dealt with. Currently strikes are treated as 'mass labour relations incidents' and are usually suppressed by the co-ordinated action of several government departments through the 'Emergency Response Mechanism'. On 21 March 2015 the Party Central Committee and the State Council announced their *Opinions on building harmonious labour relations*. For the first time, this clearly differentiated 'work stoppages' from 'mass labour relations events'. It called for 'collective work stoppages' to be dealt with by application of the 'tripartite mechanism of coordinated labour relations', but that 'mass labour relations events' should be dealt with through the 'Emergency Response Mechanism'. Workers' collective actions are to be regarded as 'labour disputes' and not as events requiring 'maintenance of stability'. This reclassification has a very significant meaning to those local governments that used to suppress strikes in the name of 'maintaining stability'.

Recent adjustments in ACFTU policy are primarily related to how enterprise unions can represent the workers, and how collective contracts might be standardised and made more effective. The ACFTU announced that 'it will promote the direct election of grassroots unions to gradually replace the traditional procedure of union members electing a grassroots committee and the committee then electing a chairperson'. To further this, the ACFTU drew up *Procedures for chairpersons of enterprise unions*. This document provides regulations on, among other things, the underlying ideology of direct election, basic electoral procedures and criteria for the candidates. Even before the issue of the *Procedures*, the Shenzhen Trade Union had already started to adopt direct elections in 165 enterprise unions.

It has been argued that worker activism is the driving force behind this union reform. To prevent the emergence of a radical workers' movement, the union must reform itself in order to respond to this pressure (Clarke and Pringle, 2009). The reason that Shenzhen was pioneering direct union elections was because it was experiencing increasing levels of worker activism and additional pressure was coming from the flourishing growth of labour NGOs (Wen, 2014). Trade unions were seeking to win the workers' trust through direct elections. At the same time the ACFTU was shifting its attention from the crude quantity of union coverage to its quality. Local trade unions were called on to organise training courses aimed at raising the quality of union personnel. As yet there has not been whole-hearted promotion of direct union elections, presumably because of institutional constraints and hostile parochial interests. But, even if there were, while it may be possible to improve the quality of officials in newly established unions, they alone cannot alter the attitudes of the employers who are in effect controlling them.

Aware of the difficulties being faced in implementing collective contracts, in March 2014, the ACFTU published *Opinions regarding the enhancement of the quality of collective consultation and the effect of collective contracts*. In this document, it was admitted that:

There are still major and pressing problems to be solved in collective consultation. For example, workers' participation levels are low in some collective consultations, the consultation process is a mere formality, and some collective contracts lack substantive content and have limited effect. In order to address these issues effectively, and to raise the quality of collective consultation, and increase the effect of collective contracts, the following opinions are put forward.

The document then set out the guiding ideology, goals and tasks, working principles and measures for raising the quality of collective consultation and for increasing the effectiveness of collective contracts. For the overall goals, the document requires:

From 2014 onwards, within a five-year period, on the basis of maintaining an 80 per cent level of establishment of collective consultation, 90 per cent of the workers covered by collective contracts should have developed an awareness of collective consultation, and there should be a steady increase in the workers' overall satisfaction rate regarding the [union's] work on collective consultation and collective contract signing.

It will not be difficult to achieve the five-year goal of making 90 per cent of the workers aware that there is a collective agreement.

The ACFTU acknowledges the problems associated with the establishment of formal grass-roots union organisation and collective contracts and it has taken action to tackle them. This is undeniably a positive step. However, it still adheres to the old administrative and often superficial style of operating, and it fails to touch upon the real issues. To what extent the ACFTU can improve on this is perhaps still an open question. The deep-rooted problem of the ACFTU, that it is detached from the mass of workers, is not only a long-term complaint of the wider society, but it is also attracting a high level of attention from central government.

In July 2014, the Deepening Reform Leadership Group of central government requested that the ACFTU and other mass organisations carry out reforms. It clearly stated that the key to reform is to prevent and overcome: excessive bureaucracy, detachment from the people, the emergence of a self-promoting worker aristocracy and being entertainment-oriented (*xingzhenghua, jiguanhua, guizuhua, yulehua*). It was the first time that a Central Government document had pointed out so sharply what was seen to be a problem of the union and other mass organisations. The Central Government requested that the Shanghai Trade Union Reform Experiment group produce a plan within two months, indicating the urgency of union reform in the view of the Central Government. If the Shanghai Union can produce a reform plan focussed on the union's 'organisational design, management style, working methods, and staff management', then perhaps there may be effective changes. It should be said, however, that because many of the problems afflicting the union involve much broader issues of the system within which it operates, one cannot be optimistic about this reform experiment.

Conclusion

The co-existence of, in effect, two trade union movements in the transition towards collective labour relations is not unique to China. It has also been a response to the opening up of markets in other post-socialist countries, such as Russia and Vietnam, as discussed in Chapter 10 (and Pringle and Clarke, 2011). But this takes a more complex form in China because of the political system of single-party rule and a single legitimate trade union. The emergence of the market economy creates a need for regulation through collective labour relations. It has become necessary for workers to be able to mobilise collective power and to have legal labour organisations that truly represent their interests. This is a requirement for legitimate labour relations in a market economy. At present, China has yet to develop standardised labour organisations that are suitable for competitive markets. The emergence of the two forms of labour power and two labour movements is a direct consequence.

Current trends in economic development in China suggest that this problem cannot be solved in the near future. But it will become the most critical issue in the regulation of labour relations. As the workers' awareness of the potential of solidarity and action continues to grow, the scale of the problem will become more obvious. The solution requires wider reform of the Chinese political system. But even within the framework of the current political system, the Party as the leading agency and its official union may still have it in their capacity to reduce the tensions between the two aspects of organised labour. They could enable them to work more positively together. They would thereby strengthen the regulation of labour relations and workers' rights. This would, however, raise important political issues and challenge relationships between existing interests, so that it is unclear in what direction the two forms of the labour movement might evolve.

References

Business Sohu (2010), 'Nanhaiqu zonggonghui, shishanzhen zonggonghui zhi bentian yuangong de gongkaixin', [An Open Letter from the Trade Union Federation of Shishan Town, Nanhai District Trade Union Federation to the Workers and Staff of Honda], internet source: http://business.sohu.com/2010 0603/n272552380.shtml.

Chang, K. and Zhang D. Y. (1993), 'Gonghui fa tonglun', [*The General Theory of Trade Union Law*], Beijing: The Press of the Central Party School Press.

Chang K. (2010), 'Guanyu bagong hefaxing de falv fenxi – yi Nanhai bentian bagong wei anli de yanjiu', [A legal analysis of the legitimacy of strikes – a case study of Nanhai Honda strike], *Strategy and Management*, 8.

Chang, K. (2013) 'Laodong guanxi de jitihua zhuanxing yu zhengfu laogong zhengce de wanshan', [From individual to collective labour relations and towards better labour policies], *Social Sciences in China*, 6, 91–206.

Chen W. G. (2012), 'You yu si: sanshinian gonghui gongzuo ganwu', [*Worries and Thoughts – Reflections of Thirty Years of Trade Union Work*], China Social Sciences Press.

Clarke, S. and Pringle, T. (2009), 'Can party-led trade unions represent their members?' *Post-communist Economics*, 21, 1.

Engels, F. (1845), *The Condition of the Working Class in England, The Complete Works of Marx and Engels*, Volume II, Gottingen: Weigand.

Li, J. G. (2013), 'Gaoju qizhi, gaige chuangxin, tuanjie dongyuan yiwan zhigong zai shixian zhongguomeng lishi jincheng zhong zhongfen fahui zhulijun zuoyong', [Hold high the banner of reform and innovation, unite and mobilise millions of workers to play the leading role in the historical process of realising the Chinese dream], report in the 16th National Congress of Chinese Trade Unions Representatives (18th October 2013).

Li, Q. and Duan, Y. (2014), 'Jiti laodong guanxi de tiaozhan he celue: jiti laodong zhengyi de zhengce shijiao fenxi', [Challenges and strategies of harmonious collective labour relations – a policy-oriented analysis of collective labour disputes], Conference paper presented in the Sixth International Labour Relations Conference, Beijing.

Lu, J. (2015), 'Jiti xingdong zhong de laogong yishi jiqi suzao', [Labour consciousness in collective action and how it is shaped], PhD thesis, Renmin University, China.

People's Daily Online (2011), 'Qiangguo luntan: quanzogn shujichu shuji libinsheng tan cujin hexie laodong guanxi', [Strong China Forum, 'Li Binsheng, the Secretary of the Secretariat of the ACFTU, talking about promoting harmonious labour relations], 10th March, www.people.com.cn/GB/32306/143124/147550/14112975.html, accessed on 2nd August 2016.

People's Daily (2014), 'Quanguo qianding jiti hetong 242 wan fen, fugai zhigong 2.87 yi ren', [Collective contract signing in the whole country reached 2.42 million copies, covering 287 million workers], 14th October.

Pringle, T. and Clarke, S. (2011), *The Challenge of Transition: Trade Unions in Russia, China and Vietnam*, Basingstoke: Palgrave Macmillan.

Tang, J. G. (2004), 'Xing'ang xiechang gongren saoluan diaocha', [Stella shoe factory labor unrest investigation], *China Newsweek*, 39.

Taylor, B. and Li, Q. (2007), 'Is the ACFTU a union and does it matter?' *Journal of Industrial Relations*, 49(5), 701–715.

Wang J. S. (2014), 'Cong zizai dao ziwei: Guangdong panyu shengmeida gonghui xuanju anli yanjiu', [From being-in-itself to being-for-itself: A case study on Sumida Union Election in Panyu, Guangzhou], www.gdlaowei.com/a/opinion/jthot/201410/12973.html, accessed on 2nd August 2016.

Wang Z. G. (2010), 'Zai zhonghua quanguo zonggonghui shiwujie sici zhiwei huiyi shang de jianghua', [Speech in the 4th meeting in the 15th ACFTU Executive Committee Session], *Chinese Labour Movement*, 8.

Wen X. Y. (2014), 'Gonghui zhuxian: guangdong shijian de jingyan yu jiaoxun', [Union direct election: Practical experience and lessons from Guangdong], *Open Era*, 5.

Workers Daily (2013), 'Zhongguo tese shehui zhuyi gonghui fazhan daolu de jiben neihan', [The basic meaning of the path of developing socialist trade unions with Chinese characteristics], 6th October.

Workers Daily (2015), 'Tuijin zhongguo tese hexie laodong guanxi de lilun chuangxin', [Developing theoretical innovation in promoting harmonious labour relations with Chinese characteristics], 21st April.

Wu, Q. J. (2012), 'Jitixieshang yu "guojia zhudao" xia de laodong guanxi zhili', [Collective consultation and 'state-led' labour relations governance], *Sociology Studies*, 3.

Xie Y. H. (2015), 'Shichanghua jititanpan chenggong anli – panyu lide xiechang laozi jititanpan fenxi', [Successful cases of collective negotiations under marketisation – an analysis of the collective bargaining of Li De Shoe Factory in Panyu], *China Workers*, 2.

Xinhua News Agency (2011), '24 ge shengfen niannei tiaozheng zuidi gongzi biaozhun', [24 provinces adjust the minimum wage standard in this year], *Beijing News*, Section A05 Edition, 30th December.

Xinhua Net (2013), 'Zhongguo gonghui huiyuan renshu dadao 2.8 yi', [Chinese trade union membership reached 280 million in total], *Xinhua Net*, 11 October 2013, http://news.xinhuanet.com/fortune//c_, accessed on 2nd August 2016.

4   The Response of Trade Unions to Market Pressures

Chang Cheng

Chinese trade unions are constituted with dual loyalties; they are legally required to represent the interests of both the state and the workers. As a result, their officials often find themselves in the middle, not only between the employers and employees, but also between the government and their members. It is a dilemma that has become more acute with the increased exposure of the Chinese economy to market forces. This chapter will trace how the role of unions has developed under China's economic reforms and explore how they have coped with this ambiguity and the consequent tensions. It starts with the official function of Chinese trade unions. It then describes their structure and organisation. This leads on to their recent growth. There is a discussion of the nature of union influence at the workplace. The chapter concludes with the unions' response to increased pressure from their members.

The Trade Unions' Dual Function

Socialist countries have generally required their trade unions to have two functions. Lenin argued that trade unions should protect both the workers and the workers' state (Lenin, 1920). They are expected to represent labour and if necessary to confront enterprise management when workers have grievances. But they are also expected to mobilise labour in order to facilitate production. Disputes are typically seen by those in authority to be individual rather than collective in nature (Pravda and Ruble, 1986).

The unique history of trade unions in China has placed particular emphasis on their role in promoting production. This happened long before 1949 brought the command economy dominated by unitarist assumptions for labour relations. The Communist Party of China (CPC) founded the All-China Federation of Trade Unions (ACFTU) in 1925. At the start, the ACFTU, led by the Party, organised industrial workers to engage in political strikes and other protests in cities. After the

The author wishes to thank Cao Xuebing and Fang Lee Cooke for their helpful comments.

alliance between the CPC and the Nationalist Party broke up in 1927, however, the CPC-led labour movement was suppressed by the Nationalist Party in urban areas, and the ACFTU had little opportunity to build its capacity to organise. In rural areas where it had influence, workplace union branches were in charge of mobilising the workers to co-operate with the factory management in order to raise production and support for military needs. This production function developed further in the initial period after 1949 when the PRC was established. During the early years of the state-planned economy, when the country closely followed the Soviet model, trade unions developed their emphasis on political mobilisation and on activities such as increasing production, distributing welfare and promoting members' well-being. Their role of protecting the economic well-being of the workers was displaced by the state's comprehensive control of society. Later, from the mid-1960s to the mid-1970s, union organisation was disrupted during the Cultural Revolution (Wilson, 1986).

The unions' dual function was severely challenged after the country started its economic reforms in the late 1970s. Among the issues debated was the so-called 'three-in-one' function that proposed that the union should take production as its central function, while at the same time being responsible for the workers' livelihood and their education (Chang and Zhang, 1993; Ng and Warner, 1998). In 1988, the ACFTU's National Congress proposed four functions through which unions should protect workers' interests as well as the interests of the state. These were summarised as: 'protection', concerned with safeguarding members' interests; 'participation' in management; 'construction', or mobilizing productive activity; and the 'education' of workers in political thinking. This primacy of the dualist function of the union was specified in the 1992 Trade Union Law, which stated that 'the trade union protects the overall interest of all people of the nation; while it represents and protects the legal rights and interests of workers'. The 2001 revision of the Law upheld this, emphasizing the union's unique authority for protecting workers (Howell, 2003). The legal framework provided unions with the right to intervene in issues such as labour disputes, and to be involved with tripartite institutions as well as participating in policy making processes. It provided the union with some leverage to protect its members (Chen, 2003). All these functions were to be located within a political framework in which Chinese unions remain the 'bridge and bond between the Party and the workers, social pillars of state power, and the representatives of their members' (Trade Union Constitution, 2013).

In the late twentieth century, private and foreign-owned enterprises had been first permitted and then encouraged to develop, greatly expanding the sectors of employment where union organisation was absent. The result was that the trade union had to rebuild its organisational base in a new economic and social environment. This development has continued to be within the framework of dual commitment. In 1988 the ACFTU announced policies to help adaptation to the market economy. Most were not implemented because of the temporary cessation of political reforms in 1989. These policies were revived by the then president of the ACFTU, Wei Jianxing, a member of the Politburo Standing Committee of the Party who was a strong advocate of trade union activity. In 1994, the ACFTU published its statement on *General thinking on trade union work* to promote the work of trade unions (ACFTU, 1994). Supported by the introduction in 1995 of the Labour Law, it highlighted the trade union's function of protecting members' interests and proposed that the introduction of collective agreements should become the highest priority. Trade unions should safeguard labour rights and the interests of employees through negotiation of collective contracts. Augmented by the 2001 Trade Union Law, this general approach was intended to allow the union to become more active in labour relations and to play a pivotal role in protecting workers' rights and interests (Wu, 2004).

A change to a more political union strategy came in 2002 when a new leadership headed by Wang Zhaoguo took over. The policy document *The road of socialist trade unionism with Chinese characteristics* set out the primary aim of union work to be 'firmly and conscientiously accepting the leadership of the Party, adhering to the socialist nature of Chinese trade unions and persistently safeguarding the workers' legitimate rights and interests' (Wang, 2009). The trade union was given multiple duties including carrying forward the spirit of model workers, accelerating the pace of unionisation and improving institution building (ACFTU, 2005). The basic principle for the workplace trade union was promoting enterprise development and protecting workers' rights and interests (ACFTU, 2006). The union function of worker protection that had been highlighted earlier was now outweighed by attention to the interests of the enterprise. Underpinning this was a dominant official message of non-adversarial employment relations. Contrary to the earlier emphasis on trade unions adapting to the needs of a market economy, this introduced a more conservative tone which emphasised their political responsibility for the overall interests of the Party (Chen, 2009). It was an approach that echoed the messages from the Party's social governance framework (Zhang, 2007). Trade unions have to work in a co-operative framework that is 'led by the Party, supported by and co-operating with the government and other actors'. It is a framework by which the union is fully integrated into the government in terms of ideology, political affiliation, underlying policies, functions, organisational arrangements and communications with trade unions from other countries. This political direction has provided the fundamental rules for union activity in the face of increasing market exposure.

Trade Union Structure and Organisation

The national trade union, the ACFTU, is by law the only union. It is composed of an overlapping structure of affiliated regional (or local) unions (*defang gonghui*), sectoral (or industrial) unions and enterprise unions. It is a single centralised hierarchical organisation based on its regional structure. This authority structure descends from province or city, to county or district, then to township or street federation unions. Within it are currently ten sectoral trade unions (*quanguo chanye gonghui*) at the national level. Not all regions have all the industrial unions and, at provincial level and below, they come under the authority of the corresponding regional unions (Baek, 2000). The structure is set out in Figure 4.1.

Full-time officials working for the ACFTU and its branches have the status of civil servants (Chen, 2009). They are recruited through the civil servant admission examinations and they have the same scales of pay and welfare provisions as civil servants working in the government system. This special status has tended to distance them socially from ordinary workers. The appointment of officials at the local branch level is jointly determined by the higher level union and local Party committee at the same level (Cooke, 2011). In practice, it is the Party committee that controls personnel matters such as the selection and appointment of trade union officials.

An important feature of the union is the use of concurrent appointments to key positions in both the ACFTU and the Party. In 2009, for example, among the 9972 union chairs and deputy chairs above county level, 11 per cent were members of the Party Standing Committees, 18 per cent were members of the People's Congress, 10 per cent were members of the Political Consultative Standing Committee and 9 per cent were vice chairmen of the People's Congress (Xu and Wu, 2011). Some officials in the federation trade unions have previously worked in key positions in government departments (Cooke, 2011). The use of concurrent appointments between the union and the government has enhanced the unions' political status and influence, but it has not helped the perception of their role as representing the members.

Unions at the workplace are financially tied to the employer. Their financial resources do not come from membership dues in other than

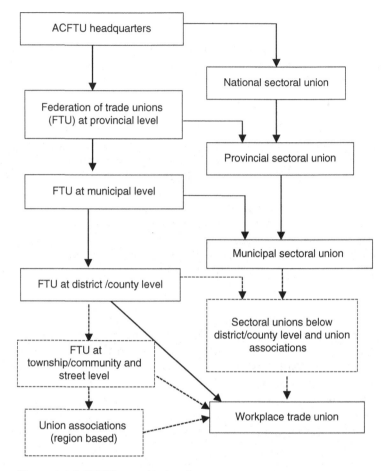

Figure 4.1 ACFTU organisational structure
Note: Dotted lines and boxes refer to forms of union organisation developed after the 2001 Trade Union Law. The sectoral unions, synonymous with industrial unions, are established and controlled by the regional unions for the purpose of developing sectoral bargaining within particular geographical boundaries that are normally below the municipal level.

a nominal sense. The main source is a 2 per cent levy of each enterprise's overall payroll. To this is added a payment per union member by their employer of 0.5 per cent of wage costs. Part-time union officials at the enterprise level are normally managers paid by the enterprise; the union president is often the enterprise head of human resources. There are also financial contributions arising from the trade unions' own commercial activities and from a government subsidy (Article 42, revised Trade Union Law). The unions' administrative structure is financed by a 40 per cent levy from the enterprises' contribution (Cooke, 2011). Some have argued that this transfer of money from enterprises may compromise union independence (Feng, 2006; Qian, 2008).

Although most union membership in the 1990s was in the state-owned enterprises, the ACFTU was aware that the private sector presented the major challenge if it were to expand its membership base. But achieving trade union recognition faced serious opposition in the private sector, not only from enterprises but also from those local governments which were wary of the potential disruption to economic expansion that might accompany private sector trade unionism (Taylor *et al.*, 2003: 125). In 2000 the ACFTU replaced its efforts at direct mobilisation of grass-roots workers by initiating a top-down campaign aimed at establishing more robust enterprise-based union organisation. This required the higher levels of the trade unions to give local union officials performance targets for both unionisation and collective contracts.

The focus of the unionisation campaign was shifted to union branches just above the enterprise. These were at the bottom of the union administrative structure. They were set up because the higher level authorities realised that there was a need for union institutions to assist union activity at the workplace. In contrast with the union federations, these union organisations were not initially granted government funds and their officers were normally not government officials although this was later relaxed to provide them with more resources. They served as the interface between trade unions at the higher levels and the enterprise trade unions. They typically took the form of township union federations, or street union federations, and 'union associations'. Union associations are formed by the association of unions in small- and medium-sized enterprises. Sometimes they have been formed under the leadership of a regional union organisation, around an industrial zone, or even a market square. Sometimes they arise under the leadership of a sectoral union organisation, for example in connection with an industrial programme, sectoral collective consultation or an agricultural supply chain. Because they can come in such a variety of forms, the unions have often preferred the use of union associations over other types of union structure.

These lower level organisations were regarded as 'the essential organisational guarantee to accelerate unionisation and the functioning of workplace trade unions in township and village enterprises' (Chen, 1996: 240). They played the crucial role in enlarging the grassroots base of trade unions, by setting up workplace unions and assisting them to sign collective contracts, recruit members and establish smaller union associations. The law stated that the local federation of trade unions should guide the enterprise union in signing collective contracts, or directly sign them itself where the enterprise trade union was absent, or it should sign sectoral collective contracts with the local employer associations. The number of the union associations grew rapidly in the early 2000s, especially after the revised Trade Union Law of 2001 granted them formal status (China Labor Bulletin, 2008). After a set-back in 2003, their number has subsequently increased every year, with a surge following the launch of the ACFTU's campaign for collective contracts in 2010.

Lower level trade unions normally work with town government bodies under one roof, and their presidents are government officials who concurrently hold the post in the union (China Labor Bulletin, 2008; Chen, 2009). In a hierarchical system, it is unavoidable that the low level trade union officials do not have the political status of their colleagues at higher levels, but their closeness to government provides the advantage of access to administrative resources to enhance the union's leverage. By so doing, the union can promote the establishment of union institutions at workplaces without having to mobilise grassroots action (Wu, 2012). An example of how this works is provided by the setting up of a collective agreement. The relevant government departments would be obliged to provide the framework of the collective contract, set out the legal terms of the signed contract, and co-ordinate the two sides. The local trade unions, which would mostly be union associations and township unions, working with the employer associations, would then be obliged to provide their subordinates in enterprises with guidance and supportive information.

Dependency on local government has tended to increase. The rapid growth in the number of enterprises has brought difficulties in raising the union levy; such difficulties have been met by local government being increasingly involved in enforcement (Wen, 2012). There is evidence from several cities that government control of tax administration increases the ability of local trade unions to collect the union levy from enterprises, substantially increasing the funds raised (Dong *et al.*, 2015). This may strain the workers' identification with the union. The effective denial of discretionary income for grassroots trade unions prevents their having significant organisational capacity to protect workers' interests. The denial of both resources and authority, combined with the fact that unions have to act as representatives of both the state and the workers, effectively eliminates the possibility of their deploying effective bargaining sanctions. Trade union officials are, to varying extents, heavily dependent upon both enterprise management and the government (Pravda and Ruble, 1986; Clarke *et al.*, 2004).

Expanding the Union Base

Building union membership became a high priority. This was not a problem for the state sector. Unionisation there was much higher than in the private sector, supported by government authority and easily embedded in the unions' traditional practices (Kong, 2000). By contrast, unionisation had been far less successful in the private sector. Back in 1998 the union density had been only an estimated 11.5 per cent in the private sector (Qiao, 2006). It became a serious challenge in terms of membership expansion as the state-owned and collective sectors declined in size after the 1990s. To tackle this problem, at the end of the 1990s, the ACFTU started to accelerate the pace of unionisation in the private sector with the slogan 'where there are workers, there should be a trade union' (Wei, 1999). There were top-down campaigns throughout the country, with local union officials given targets for workplace unionisation, aiming to establish more robust enterprise-based union organisations. Under the pressure of these targets, local union officials often persuaded employers to set up workplace trade unions without consulting workers (Liu, 2010; Taylor *et al.*, 2003). To encourage management's co-operation, the local trade unions tended not to enquire too closely how far the new workplace trade unions were controlled by employers (Wu, 2012). As a consequence, workers could be unaware of the existence of the trade union in workplaces which were officially unionised (Cooke, 2011; Liu, 2010). Regulations intended to prevent undue management influence over union organizing were not strictly enforced. Since the mid-2000s, the union had also expanded its membership coverage by actively recruiting migrant workers (Cooke, 2011).

The 2010 strike wave put further pressure on the ACFTU to increase its coverage. In July 2010, the ACFTU launched a nationwide campaign to increase both union membership and the coverage of collective contracts. It called for a unionisation rate of 90 per cent of all types of enterprises and 80 per cent coverage of collective contracts. This became the prime objective of the ACFTU in an effort to meet the rising concerns of workers (Wu, 2012). The result, as Figure 4.2 shows, has been that trade union membership has increased steadily. Before 2003, at a time when the highly unionised state sector was shrinking and the private sector was expanding, aggregate membership had fluctuated around

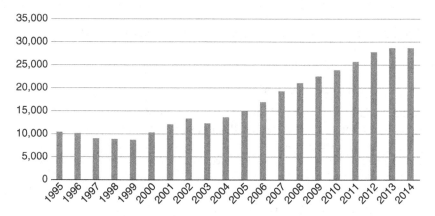

Figure 4.2 The number of trade union members in the ACFTU,
1995–2014
Note: numbers of union membership in ten thousands
Source: National Bureau of Statistics of China

100 million members. But from 123 million members in 2003, it rose
without interruption to 288 million members in 2014.

Closely associated with the extension of trade union membership have
been efforts to spread the coverage of collective contracts. This is discussed in Chapter 7 on collective consultation. Developing the system of
collective consultation and collective contracts was envisaged, as was
mentioned earlier, to be the primary role of the union by the ACFTU at
the time of its *General Thinking* statement in 1994 (ACFTU, 1994).
Trade unions are officially authorised to represent workers for consultation with employers and for signing agreements on, for example, specific
pay issues, working time, rest and vacations, occupational safety and
health, professional training and insurance and welfare (Cooke, 2011).
As part of its campaign to provide comprehensive coverage of collective
contracts, in 2009 the ACFTU adopted a 'Rainbow Plan'. The rainbow
metaphor was as a bridge to connect workers and capital in the development of the market economy. By 2013, the ACFTU estimated that
630,000 enterprises covering 84 million workers had followed the
Rainbow Plan (*Workers Daily*, 2013).

The ACFTU assigned targets for collective contracts for its union
federations at provincial, city and county levels. The appropriate levels
of government were also monitored to secure compliance (Wu, 2012).
Three methods are used to implement collective contracts. The first is
a combined strategy by which territorial, regional and sectoral trade

unions act together to make a claim for contracts to multiple enterprises. The second is a Party and government-led approach, using the authority of local government to encourage management to sign contracts and to monitor them. The third approach is to have supplementary regional collective consultation in order to include workers in smaller enterprises within the relevant geographical boundaries. But, as with union recruitment, the target-driven approach is problematic. Focussed on meeting quotas on the number of collective contracts, it does not develop into a process of effective negotiation between union and management. It is largely based on a dialogue between the employer and the employer-controlled trade union. The results are generally formalistic, duplicating existing legal provisions. It should be added that, more recently, senior officials of the ACFTU have declared that the quality of collective agreements is more important than their number and have suggested raising the standards by which this quality is judged (Workercn, 2014).

However superficial the process, it did raise worker expectations. There have been many reports of confrontation during the unionisation and consultation process as a result of workers seeking active participation in their unions. The ACFTU response to workers' efforts to reduce employers' control of workplace unions has been judged to be ambivalent (Chen, 2009; Liu, 2010). An example was at the Danish company of Olewolff in Shangong, where a union was established with support from the ACFTU in 2006. The newly established union assisted the workers in labour disputes but, within a year, several of the union committee members resigned in the face of management opposition. Another example was of workers in the Japanese company of Sumida, in Guangdong province, who tried to form a workplace union organisation in 2013. There was an impasse between workers and management that had to be mediated by higher union officials. The workers then accepted the proposal that the company should be in charge of the union election process, but most of the original worker activists were excluded from the reconstituted union committee.

The ACFTU launched a unionisation campaign among foreign and privately owned enterprises in 2006. One of the major multinational corporations targeted was the American retail chain Wal-Mart, which had a long-standing anti-union policy. Local union federations had failed to make headway against the aggressive approach of Wal-Mart management. In response, the ACFTU set about mobilising Wal-Mart workers through an education programme. Within two months, it had successfully established the first workplace trade union organisation in Wal-Mart China. In five carefully selected stores, grass-roots union activists, guided by the ACFTU, organised union elections. In the face of a highly publicised campaign, Wal-Mart eventually dropped its opposition to unionisation, and began ostensibly to welcome the union in its workplace. Within a few months this campaign had spread throughout China's Wal-Mart stores (Chan, 2006).

Although initially regarded as 'a breakthrough in unionisation work' (*Workers Daily*, 2006), it became apparent that the unions' independence was severely limited. Wal-Mart managements in many stores gradually regained control (*China Youth Daily*, 2008; Estlund and Gurgel, 2012). This provoked a dispute in May 2015 when a group of Wal-Mart workers signed an open letter of complaint to the Shenzhen Federation of Trade Unions, the Guangdong Provincial Federation of Trade Unions and the ACFTU headquarters (Lin, 2016). It reported that the management had manipulated the union election, that union representation was controlled by management, and that there had been little progress on the improvement of pay and working conditions. They appealed to the higher level trade union to help them regain influence in the shop union.

Union Influence at the Workplace

State-Owned Enterprises

Workplace trade unions take the form of union committees and their functions and performance differ in different types of enterprise. In state-owned enterprises, trade unions maintain their subordinate position as, in effect, a department of management (Taylor *et al.*, 2003: 118). They are affiliated organs of the Party branch within the enterprise. Because union presidents typically take concurrent positions in the enterprise administration as well as in the Party branch, the trade union is usually active and well developed, and is given substantial authority within the enterprise (Lüthje, 2012). Its main functions are distributing welfare for those in financial difficulty, and organising sports and entertainment activities. It also assists workers to engage in various forms of democratic management, such as providing 'reasonable suggestions' (*helihua jianyi*) which includes suggestions on the enterprise's production plans.

An example is provided by an enterprise in Changchun employing about 2300 workers that was visited by the present author in 2011. The union president was the secretary of the main Party committee, and both the union vice-president and the union secretary were full-time union officials. There was an active workers' congress and union branch. A collective wage contract was signed annually. The trade union to some extent co-managed wage issues. The size of the wage fund was fixed by the parent company, but monthly meetings were held in the factory to determine each worker's incentive payment. The enterprise also made a point of showing a sense of social responsibility, for example by employing a dozen disabled workers. Despite average pay being lower than the average in Changchun, an ethos of socialist redistribution was cherished. When interviewed, the factory director said that, 'by comparison with the private sector, profit or loss do not affect us much. Whatever the loss or the gain, our workers are protected by the iron rice bowl. As the factory director, I support this system, for it makes management and production easier – otherwise who would work for the factory?'

Since 2004, the number of state-owned and co-operatively owned enterprises has continued to decline. Those remaining are mainly in core industries in relatively monopolistic positions, such as petroleum and telecoms. But the privileges and protection of these industries have only been available for the shrinking number of regular employees. The ever-growing number of irregular workers – particularly dispatched (or agency) workers – have been excluded, despite the fact that in some state-owned firms dispatched labour accounted for as much as two-thirds of the workforce (Wang, 2012). This heavy reliance on insecure workers is, however, under legislative pressure. The addition of the Provisional Regulations on Dispatch Labour of 2014 to the Labour Contract Law of 2008, both of which the ACFTU was active in promoting, has placed clear limits on the use of dispatched labour – to no more than 10 per cent of the workforce – as well as on the occupations for which it can be employed.

The Private Sector

In joint venture enterprises, it is normal for the Chinese partners to be in charge of labour management. The status of trade unions and workers is thus dependent on the ideology and outlook of the Chinese management, and on the power relationship between the Chinese and foreign management. In joint ventures with strong government involvement, the trade unions, under the leadership of the Party, often acquire a secure and effective position in labour management. In some, the union has taken a strongly protective stance towards the workers. In these, the trade unions play an important role as a channel between the worker and the management. Their secure status enables them to exert a positive influence for workers in labour relations and dispute resolution (Lüthje, 2012).

Union density in domestic private enterprises and foreign-owned enterprises remains relatively low. This is mainly because of resistance from the entrepreneurs and local government. According to the ACFTU statistics yearbooks, only 0.45 per cent of 440,000 registered private enterprises had unions in 1996. This number had increased to 26.3 per cent of 4.68 million private enterprises in 2010. As a result of the unionisation drive, which targeted the non-state sector against the backdrop of the restructuring of state-owned enterprises, the non-state sector accounted for 76.9 per cent of the total union membership by 2010; state-owned enterprise employees accounted for only 23.1 per cent (ACFTU statistical yearbook, various years).

Despite the growth in union membership, the protective function of the workplace trade unions in domestic and foreign-owned private enterprises is generally relatively weak, partly because the Party's influence there is weak. In the absence of their traditional role as a branch of the enterprise management, the workplace union organisations in these essentially capitalist companies have very limited sources of influence (Clarke, 2005). This is reflected in the fact that to win any authority, the trade union will have to assist management in relatively trivial matters such as organising entertainment activities. As one union president, interviewed by the author in 2011, said, 'if you don't do it, you will have no authority. The more you do, the more authority you will have.' This took a considerable amount of the union's time and energy.

In these circumstances, where there is no chance of mobilising grass-roots action, two things can make a substantial difference to the trade union's influence. The first is the personal qualities of the union president. The second is the support provided by higher levels of the union. The importance of personal qualities was illustrated by the union president in an auto component company in Guangzhou visited by the author in 2011. He was a mid-level manager but passionate about union work. While in office, he had established functioning union institutions, including an effective union cell system and a strengthened union committee. When dealing with one recent labour dispute, he told the company that, in his view, the union had made valid criticisms and that if management refused to make concessions, the case would be submitted to the union committee and then to all the workers. The company backed down and concessions were mediated by the union.

The political and administrative status of the local trade union is of great importance in supporting workplace unions. In the regular wage negotiations that have been carried out in the Dalian Development Zone since the mid-1990s, for example, administrative assistance from above has been the main resource and source of authority for the workplace unions' involvement in bargaining. From 1997 onwards, the local Dalian government put pressure on foreign partner firms to pay acceptable wages by setting them pay guidelines. These provided the firms with high, middle and low levels as three reference points for the minimum rate of wage increase. The annual wage increase had been around 2–3 per cent before 2008. After 2008, as a result of the local government's increasing pressure behind its guideline policy, the wage increase for many enterprises reached 10 per cent for the first time. One of the union presidents commented to the author that collective bargaining 'should be a top-down process. The higher level union's role is important. Without "the word" from the higher level union, how could we bargain?' In particularly difficult cases, and especially in strikes, where the political risks are high, shelter provided by the higher level is essential to protect the lower level officers. In 2010, in a case studied by the author, the company union worked with the district union to deal with a dispute. The company union president had followed guidance from the district union closely because, as he said: 'on some key issues, especially if they contain political factors or risks, we cannot make a decision, but the district union can'.

The benefit of support from higher union levels and the government has its limits. First, enterprise unions are largely controlled by their enterprise managements, and the union presidencies are held by managers. This reduces the willingness of the enterprise union to fight for workers' rights and to call for the higher union level to intervene. Secondly, the lower levels of a union have less leverage and, as it is often the union associations or lowest union level which have direct contact with workers at the grass-roots, they are not capable of providing adequate resources and support. Thirdly, the union is constrained by the objective of maintaining social stability, which may run counter to the use of autonomous collective action by workers. It might well be rational for the union to support management, on the grounds that they should represent the 'overall interests' in a conflict between the workers and the state, or between the workers and the management. Union officials at local levels often lack the motivation to engage with difficult worker activists to prevent industrial action.

The position of workplace trade unions has been weakened by the widespread but somewhat tokenistic campaigns to establish a union presence. A by-product of the numbers games resulting from these campaigns for unionisation driven from the top were large numbers of management-controlled enterprise unions. Usually the local trade union and the enterprise management would together set up a union organising committee in order to deflect pressure from higher management and local government. Once established, these enterprise unions typically ceased to bother about effective scrutiny of management behaviour (Baek, 2000;

You, 2010; Wu, 2012). The perceived latent risk of mobilisation of grass-roots worker power often induced the higher level unions to turn a blind eye when management exercised autocratic control over workplace unions. After all, they might say in self-justification, the formal task of unionisation from above had been fulfilled.

A trade union in a foreign-owned enterprise that was studied by the author in Guangzhou city in 2011 provides an example. The union had been established a year after the factory started production, and the process of unionisation was organised by the company's legal consultant because, as the company's vice-president put it, 'the company's institutions need to be formalised for when it comes onto the stock market'. A mid-level manager was elected as the first union president and, even though many of the workers might not have been aware of it, they all became union members. Such practices were widespread in the union-isation campaign of the mid-2000s and, as noted in previous chapters, it resulted in many 'shell unions' or 'boss's unions' appearing at workplace level (Chen, 2009; *Yangcheng Evening News*, 2010; Chang, 2014).

The Union Role in Workplace Dispute Resolution

The union has been playing an increasingly flexible role in dispute resolu-tion. Informal worker protests and work stoppages have been increasing and have tended to shift from rights disputes to hybrid disputes combin-ing both rights and interests (Elfstrom and Kuruvilla, 2012). These pressures from below pose severe challenges to the ACFTU and highlight its constitutional weaknesses. As discussed in Chapter 9, union officials are neither allowed to organise a strike, nor are strike activities released from tort liabilities. The trade union's prescribed function in a strike is to articulate the workers' grievances and, more importantly, to assist the government and management to defuse it (Chen, 2003; Pringle, 2011). The union is the legitimate body in resolving conflicts at a workplace. During a strike it should 'understand the situation, listen to workers' opinions and voices, and transmit the workers' opinions and demands to the party and higher trade union' (Article 27, Trade Union Law). In practice, the union has been exercising this role with some creativity.

The degree of independence shown by the union in recent strike resolution episodes varies across the country. One approach is that the trade union does not act independently of the government and the man-agement. Disputes get settled because both sides compromise and reach agreement through union mediation. But the position of the trade union with regard to workers, management and government is ambiguous, and the workers may perceive the union officials as part of either government or management. A consequent lack of trust may make effective negotiation difficult because workers are fearful lest their representatives might suffer from subsequent retaliation. Examples where the pressure to end strike action triggered the authority's use of direct force, which in turn provoked more worker discontent, were at Honda Nanhai (Chan and Hui, 2012) and in the Dalian Development Zone in 2010 (Chen, 2010). The trade unions were highly integrated into government and relied on its power and the personal influence of the union president to win workers' compliance. This approach reflects a low level of institutionalisation of conflict resolution (Chen, 2010; Elfstrom and Kuruvilla, 2012).

In a contrasting approach, however, the union acts with more independence of government and consults directly with the management and the workers. The union's role is to help or represent workers in bargaining with management. By articulating the workers' demands it can exert some degree of influence over them. Mutual trust and support between the workers and the union can help deploy grass-roots pressures for the union which improve its negotiating position. Examples are provided by the cases of Denso Nanhai in 2010 (Chang, 2014) and Wal-Mart Changde in 2013 (*Financial Times*, 2014). At different organisational levels, the union played a positive role in articulating workers' interests. In Denso, once the district union had decided on a bottom-up strategy, it allowed the workplace union to implement it while protecting it from government intervention. In the Wal-Mart Changde dispute, the workers' campaign led by the workplace trade union improved the outcome for the workers. In this approach, while still responding flexibly and pragmatically, the union's representation of worker interests is more explicit.

Responding to Pressures from below

The environment in which the Chinese trade unions operate in the mid-2010s has altered substantially since the early 2000s. Increasing labour shortages have enhanced the bargaining power of workers, and particularly of skilled workers. It also led to the emergence of employer associations, discussed in Chapter 5, which have adopted a more strategic approach in dealing with tighter markets, as well as in lobbying government on new legislation. At the same time, the direction of government policy has shifted to the rebalancing of the Chinese economy, with trade unions required to play a key part in raising domestic consumption and in developing institutions to harmonise social relations.

The ACFTU and its constituent unions have responded to these challenges in various ways. One is by shaping the legislative and institutional framework. As has been mentioned, it has been actively involved in the major advances that have been taking place in labour law and institution building. The ACFTU and local union federations mobilised support and lobbied on successive drafts of the 2008 Labour Contract Law. From 2009 sectoral bargaining was formally encouraged in its policy directive *Guidance on the active promotion and implementation of sectoral wage bargaining.* The union was also effective in pressing for the restrictions on the use of dispatched or agency workers in 2014. Legislation has been an important arena for unions, particularly at the higher levels, allowing them to use their political authority to strengthen worker protections, increasingly in the face of employer resistance and lobbying.

The ACFTU's role in the development of sectoral bargaining is particularly notable. A consequence of labour shortages in some regions in the early 2000s had been that labour relations were sometimes characterised by chaotic competition between employers for skilled workers and the widespread infringement of workers' rights. The response was the development of sectoral, multi-employer bargaining. This was largely the result of locally initiated action, with ACFTU institutions playing a leading part. It led to a major structural change, permitted by the introduction of union associations mentioned earlier. The growth of sectoral negotiation at these lower levels has provided an important basis for working with employer organisations and thereby gaining substantial rights of union recognition which are the stronger for not being solely the result of government pressure. Local autonomy in labour matters has increased. The resulting collective agreements have included substantive clauses on matters particular to local circumstances, rather than the formulaic replication of legal requirements. It is also of interest that worker representation in this process, rather than being dictated by management, has involved some hybrid and partial use of elections by workers (Wen, 2011; Xie and Guo, 2011; Wen, 2014; Lee *et al.*, 2016).

Another response to changed circumstances has been that the ACFTU has been building connections and cooperation with labour non-governmental and other social organisations, with the purpose of mobilising a wider range of institutions to help achieve their objectives. For example, local unions have been purchasing legal services from law firms in Guangdong, Shanghai and Zhejiang (Chen, 2012). In an effort to expand collective consultation, the ACFTU and its regional branches are to provide negotiation training and expert assistance for workplace union officers (*Workers Daily*, 2015).

Progress on democratic reform has been sporadic and partial. Elections have been used at workplaces in foreign-owned enterprises in, for example, Guangdong and Zhejiang, but the wider development of these initiatives has been held back (Howell, 2008; Pringle, 2011). A number of pilot projects in coastal areas such as Guangdong, Zhejiang, Fujian and Shandong suggested benefits of direct elections for workplace labour relations (Wen, 2014). According to an investigation by the ACFTU, of more than 6000 union members in 193 enterprises which had direct elections for trade union presidents in Yuhang, Zhejiang province, 95 per cent judged their elected presidents to be well qualified for the role (Xinhua Net, 2013). Although this was encouraging for wider use of elections, the experiment has not yet spread to other parts of the country.

The delaying and frustration of democratic projects have tended to increase the separation of trade unions from the workers. The Party's response has been to urge union reforms. As discussed in Chapter 3, in July 2015 the central government called for substantial improvements in the conduct of senior officials. It was the first time a central government document had been so critical of the union and it posed a legitimacy crisis for the ACFTU (Chang, 2015). The criticisms reflected the findings of the Institute of Labour Studies survey of government officials of 2013 (described in Chapter 6), which had shown that, when asked to assess the union's function in protecting workers' interests, only 19 per cent of the regional labour officials were satisfied, while 31 per cent reported themselves dissatisfied (Institute of Labour Studies survey, 2013).

Pressure from the Party has led to moves for reform at different levels of the ACFTU. For example, Shanghai and Chongqing were chosen for one-year pilot projects concerned with the union's organisational structure and with the management of union officials. Reforms at workplace level have been carried out to improve the relationship between the rank-and-file officers and members. Rather than introducing radical changes, the reforms have focussed on formalising and improving existing locally developed arrangements which provide workers with greater involvement in trade union affairs. These include the strengthening of the workers' representatives' rights for consultation and participation, and the election of union presidents. A number of workplace institutions such as union committees, expenditure supervisors and female workers' committees have been required by some local laws. The recruitment of union presidents in, for example, Guangzhou, Yinchuan and Ningbo has been broadened to include people from outside management who are considered to have more relevant experience; their independence and external influence are enhanced because their wages are paid by the union (Wen, 2012).

In some cases the lower levels of unions have undergone organisational changes to make them more embedded in government. This illustrates not only the greater emphasis placed on union work by government, but also the policy of using joint meetings between the union and the government at relatively low levels. Unions have experienced a re-structuring of their organisation by simplifying and delayering it, so that more resources can flow down to the lower levels. For example, in Shanghai it was reported in 2015 that the number of City Federation of Trade Union agencies was reduced to allow more resources to flow to lower levels of the union (Xinhua Net, 2015). As a consequence, more work and resources should flow, for instance, to the union associations and street unions. Meanwhile, in the workplace, it is intended that the opinions of ordinary members will be brought to the attention of work-place union officials more than in the past. If achieved, these develop-ments will put more pressure on the union officers, increasing the challenge they face in balancing the sometimes contradictory interests of labour and capital.

These recent reforms suggest that the unions will rely more than in the past on the government to implement worker protections. In effect, legal support of trade union recognition has been strengthened. This includes legal support of the two basic requirements of unionisation and collective negotiation. Reflecting the same top-down approach, government agen-cies will be given the necessary responsibility for scheduling the proce-dures, mobilising action and checking the outcomes. As a result, the lower levels of the unions are being further embedded into government admin-istration, which has the effect of augmenting the dual functions under which unions operate.

Conclusion

The conflict of interests between labour and capital is a fundamental feature of any market economy. What makes things more complicated for the Chinese trade union is that the ACFTU's responsibilities are constitutionally divided between labour and the state. This has the advan-tage that organised labour can at times draw strength from the state in negotiating with employers. It reflects a degree of state support for trade union recognition by employers that is far greater than most Western trade unions have ever enjoyed. But it has the major disadvantage that the interests of labour may be subordinated when they are seen by the state to conflict with other objectives such as economic growth. We have described how pressures from below and the pursuit of social harmony have encouraged a degree of pragmatic flexibility in the way in which the ACFTU has responded to worker needs. It remains to be seen whether this might develop into sufficient independence for trade unions for them to be able to commit themselves more fully to the needs of the workers.

References

ACFTU Reports, Speeches and Regulations

gonghui gaige de jiben shexiang [*Basic thoughts on trade union reform*], October 1988

gonghui gongzuo zongti silu [*General thinking on trade union work*], December 1994

guanyu xinshengdai nongmingong wenti de yanjiu baogao, [*Research report on issues of the new generation of workers*], June 2010, www.youngmigrants.org/ew/uploadfile/20100718143155316.pdf, accessed on 2 August 2016.

qiye gonghui gongzuo tiaoli [*Regulation on the work of enterprise trade unions*], December 2006.

Wang, Zhaoguo (2009), *A Speech at the Seminar on Trade Union Theory and Practice in China*, Beijing, http://news.xinhuanet.com/politics/2009-06/02/content_11473867.htm.

Wei, Jianxing (1999), *A Speech at the National Conference on Union Organising in New Enterprises*, Ningbo, http://www.people.com.cn/GB/channel1/10/2000111 13/310516.html.

zhongguo tese shehui zhuyi gonghui fazhan daolu [*The Road of Socialist Trade Unionism with Chinese Characteristics*], July 2005.

zhongguo gonghuifa [*Trade Union Law of PRC*], April 1992.

zhongguo gonghuifa xiuzheng'an [*Revised Trade Union Law of PRC*], October 2001.

zhongguo gonghui zhangcheng [*Trade Union Constitution of PRC*], October 2013.

zhongguo gonghui nianjian [*Statistical Yearbooks 2004–2013*], Beijing: China Statistics Press.

zhonghua quanguo zonggonghui guanyu tisheng jiti xieshang zhiliang zengqiang jiti hetong shixiao de yijian [*ACFTU's Views on Improving the Quality of Collective Consultation and on Enhancing the Effectiveness of the Collective Contract*], March 2014.

References

Baek, S. W. (2000), 'The changing trade unions in China', *Journal of Contemporary Asia*, 30(1), 44–66.

Chan, A. (2006), 'Organizing Wal-Mart: The Chinese trade union at a crossroads', *Japan Focus*, 8 September, http://japanfocus.org/products/details/2217, accessed on 2 August 2016.

Chan, C. K. C. and Hui, E. S. L. (2012), 'The dynamics and dilemma of workplace trade union reform in China: Case of the Honda workers' strike', *Journal of Industrial Relations*, 54(5), 653–668.

Chang, C. (2014), 'The Emerging Role of Trade Unions in China and their Function in Strikes' PhD thesis, University of Cambridge.

Chang, K. (2015), 'Two forms of labour movements in the transition towards collective labour relations in China – characteristics of current development and prospects', Paper for the International Labour and Employment Relations

Association (ILERA) 17th World Congress, 7–12 September 2015, Cape Town, South Africa.

Chang, K. and Zhang, D. R. (1993), 'Gonghuifa tonglun', [*The General Theory of Trade Union Law*], Beijing: zhongyang dangxiao chubanshe.

Chen, B. Q. (1996), 'Zhongguo gonghui de gaige yu jianshe, (1984–1993)' [*Reform and Building of Chinese Trade Unions (1984–1993)*], Beijing: zhongguo gongren chubanshe.

Chen, F. (2003), 'Industrial restructuring and workers' resistance in China', *Modern China*, 29(2), 237–262.

Chen, F. (2009), 'Union power in China: Source, operation, and constraints', *Modern China*, 35(6), 662–689.

Chen, F. (2010), 'Trade unions and the quadripartite interactions in strike settlement in China', *The China Quarterly*, March, 201, 104–124.

Chen, W. G. (2012), 'You yu si: sanshinian gonghui gongzuo ganwu', [*Worries and Thoughts – Reflections of Thirty Years of Trade Union Work*], Beijing: zhongguo shehui kexue chubanshe.

China Labor Bulletin (2008), 'Shuilai weiquan, weishui weiquan: lun quanzong weiquan de zhengzhihua ji zhongguo gonghui yundong de chulu', [Who Protects? For whom do they protect? – The politisation of the ACFTU's protection function and the future of China's trade union movements], www.clb.org.hk/schi/files/No.14%20ACFTU(PS).pdf, accessed on 2nd August 2016.

China Youth Daily (2008), 'Wal-Mart: yige jiceng gonghui yu juwuba de jiaoliang', [In Wal-Mart – the battle between the workplace trade union president and the Maximal shop], 7 January, http://mnc.people.com.cn/GB/6788912.html, accessed on 2 August 2016.

Clarke, S. (2005), 'Post-socialist trade unions: China and Russia', *Industrial Relations Journal*, 36(1), 2–18.

Clarke, S., Lee, C.-H. and Qi, L. (2004), 'Collective consultation and industrial relations in China', *British Journal of Industrial Relations*, 42, 235–254.

Cooke, F. L. (2011), 'Unions in China in a period of marketisation', in Gall, G., Wilkinson, A. and Hurd, R. (eds.), *International Handbook on Labour Unions: Responses to Neo-Liberalism*, Cheltenham: Edward Elgar, pp. 105–124.

Dong, X. H., Ma, J. Y. and Wang, R. (2015), 'Guanyu wanshan dangqian gonghui jingfei daizheng jizhi de sikao he jianyi', [Thoughts and suggestions for the improvement of the taxation mechanism of trade union levies], *zhongguo gonghui caihui*, 2015(9), 16–17.

Elfstrom, M. and Kuruvilla, S. (2012), 'The changing nature of labor unrest in China', paper for the International Labor and Employment Relations Conference, Philadelphia, 2–5 July 2012.

Estlund, C. and Gurgel, S. (2012), *A New Deal for China's Workers? Labor Law Reform in the Wake of Rising Labor Unrest*, New York University Public Law and Legal Theory Working Papers, 3:1.

Feng, G. (2006), 'Qiye gonghui de zhiduxing ruoshi jiqi xingcheng beijing', [Institutional weaknesses of the trade union and the background of their formation], *zhongguo shehuixue zazhi*, 2006(3), 81–89.

Financial Times (2014), 'Official China union raises stakes in Walmart closure programme', 23 March, www.ft.com/cms/s/0/2038fd78-b262-11e3-b891-001 44feabdc0.html#axzz4ILTr0RyZ, accessed on 2 August 2016.

Howell, J. (2003), 'Trade unionism in China: Sinking or swimming?' *Journal of Communist Studies and Transition Politics*, 19(1), 102–122.

Howell, J. (2008), 'All-China federation of trade unions beyond reform? The slow march of direct elections', *The China Quarterly*, 196, December, 845–863.

Institute of Labour Studies survey (2013) 'Constructing Harmonious Labour Relations and the Government Regulation', unpublished, Renmin University of China.

Kong, X. H. (2000), 'Heilian, honglian? Zhongguo gonghui de gaige', [*Black Face, Red Face: The Reform of Chinese Trade Unions*], Guangzhou: huacheng chubanshe.

Lee, C.-H., Brown, W. and Wen, X. Y. (2016), 'What sort of collective bargaining is emerging in China?' *British Journal of Industrial Relations*, 54 (1), March, 214–236.

Lenin, V. I. (1920), 'The Trade Unions, the Present Situation – Speech to the Eighth Congress of Soviets, Communist Members of the All-Russia Central Council of Trade Unions and Communist Members of the Moscow City Council of Trade Union (30th December 1920)', online, www.marxists.org/a rchive/lenin/works/1920/dec/30.htm, accessed on 2 August 2016.

Lin, K. (2016), 'Workers Walk Out over Unfair Scheduling', *Labournotes*, July 2016, www.labornotes.org/2016/07/china-walmart-retail-workers-walk-out-over-unfair-scheduling, accessed on 2 August 2016.

Liu, M. W. (2010), 'Union organizing in China: Still a monolithic labour movement?' *Industrial and Labor Relations Review*, 64 (1), 30–52.

Lüthje, B. (2012), 'Diverging trajectories: Economic rebalancing and labour policies in China', *East-West Center Working Papers: Politics, Governance and Security Series*, 23, April, 2–36.

Ng, S. H. and Warner, M. (1998), *China's Trade Unions and Management*, London: Macmillan.

Pravda, A. and Ruble, B. A. (eds.) (1986), *Trade Unions in Communist States*, London: Allen & Unwin Press.

Pringle, T. (2011), *Trade Unions in China: The Challenge of Labour Unrest*, London: Routledge.

Qian Y. F. (2008), 'Shehuifa shiye zhongde gonghuifa', [The trade union law of China from the view of social legislation], *yunnan daxue xuebao (faxueban)* March 2008, 21(2), 26–32.

Qiao J. (2006), 'Zhongguo gongren: laodongzhe zuzhiquan de falv baozhang yu shijian', [Chinese Workers: Legal Protection and Practice in Workers' Rights to Organise], in Ru, X., Lu, X. and Li, P.L. (eds.), 2006 nian: zhongguo shehui xingshi fenxi yu yuce [*Analysis and Prediction in Chinese Society in 2006*], Beijing: shehui kexue chubanshe.

Taylor, B., Chang, K. and Li, Q. (2003), *Industrial Relations in China*, Cheltenham: Edward Elgar.

Wang, S. (2012), 'Lun guoyou qiye laowu paiqian yongong fanlan chengyin', [A discussion of the causes of the misuse of labour dispatch in the state-owned enterprises], *jilinsheng jiaoyuxueyuan xuebao*, 28(5), 128–130.

Wen, X. Y. (2011), 'Jiti tanpan de neibu guojia jizhi: yi wenling yangmaoshan hangye gongjia jiti tanpan weili', [The internal state mechanism in collective bargaining: evidence from the collective bargaining by the Wenling sweater industry], *shehui*, 2011(1), 112–130.

Wen, X. Y. (2012), 'Wu laogong canyu de tonghe zhuyi: zhuanxingqi zhongguo gonghui yunxing jizhi yanjiu', [Corporatism without Workers Participation – Analysis of Trade Union Operation in Transition], PhD Thesis, Renmin University.

Wen, X. Y. (2014), 'Gonghui zhixuan, nionizat shijian de jingyan yu jiaoxun', [Direct election in trade unions: experience and lessons of practices in Guangdong], *Opening Time*, 2014(5).

Wilson, J. L. (1986), 'The People's Republic of China', in Pravda, A. and Ruble, B. A. (eds.), *Trade Unions in Communist States*, London: Allen & Unwin Press.

Workers' Daily (2006), 'Wal-mart zujian gonghui de jiji yiyi', [The positive meaning of the unionisation in Wal-mart], 2 August, http://news.people.com.cn/GB/37454/37459/4659847.html, accessed on 2nd August 2016.

Workers' Daily (2013), 'Gongtong yueding xingdong, 'zhongguo tese' de gonghui dandang', [The co-operation agreement campaign – the trade union's responsibility with Chinese characteristics], 11 October, http://news.xinhuanet.com/politics/2013–10/11/c_125516095_3.htm, accessed on 2 August 2016.

Workers' Daily (2015), 'Zhuanzhi jiti xieshang zhidaoyuan duiwu jiang da wanren yishang', [Professional collective consultation supervisors increasing to more than ten thousand], 16 April, http://acftu.people.com.cn/n/2015/0416/c67560-26854282.html, accessed on 2 August 2016.

Workercn (2014), 'Jianding buyi tuijin jiti xieshang', [Steadfastly pushing forward collective consultation], 7 January, http://zgtv.workercn.cn/28411/201401/07/140107082741098.shtml, accessed on 2 August 2016.

Wu, Q. J. (2012), 'Establishing trade unions within foreign companies in China', *Employee Relations Journal*, 32(4), 121–141.

Wu, Y. P. (2004), 'Zongti silu de youlai, queding he fazhan', [The origin, establishment and development of general thinking on trade union work], in *Gonghui lilun yu shijian*, 18(5), October 2004.

Xie, Y. H. and Guo, Y. X. (2011), 'Zhongguoshi gongzi jiti xieshang moshi tansuo: wuhanshi canyin hangye gongzi jiti xieshang diaocha', [Exploring collective bargaining in the Chinese model – a survey of the collective consultation on wages in the catering industry in Wuhan], *Zhongguo laodong guanxi xueyuan xuebao*, 2011(6), 54–58.

Xinhua Net (2013), 'Zhongguo gonghui huiyuan renshu dadao 2.8 yi', [Chinese trade union membership reached 280 million in total], October 11, http://news.xinhuanet.com/fortune//c_, accessed on 2 August 2016.

Xinhua Net (2015), 'Shanghai shizong gonghui gaige shishi fangan', [Methods of implementing the reform of mass organisation in Shanghai

City], December 2015, www.sh.xinhuanet.com/2015–12/18/c_134929132 .htm, accessed on 2 August 2016.

Xu, X. J. and Wu, Q. J. (2011), 'Dui zhongguo gonghui xingzhi tezheng yu hexin zhineng de xueshu bianxi: jiyu guojia tizhi kuangjianei gonghui shehui xingwei de shijiao', [An academic differentiation and analysis of the Chinese trade union's nature, characteristics and core function – a perspective based on the trade union's social activities in the state institutional framework], *Renwen zazhi*, 2011(5), pp. 165–172.

Yangcheng Evening News (2010), 'Dengweilong: qiye gonghui zhuxi duobushi minzhu xuanju', [Most of the workplace trade union presidents are not directly elected by workers], 3 July.

You, Z. L. (2010), '60 nianlai zhongguo gonghui de sanci dagaige', [Three major reforms of Chinese trade unions from 1960s], *shehuixue yanjiu*, 2010(4), 76–105.

Zhang, C. W. (2007), 'Jianchi dangzheng zhudao, gonghui yunzuo de weiquan geju', [Insisting on the 'government leading and trade union operating' approach to protect workers' rights], *zhongguo gongyun*, 2007(1).

5   Employer Strategies in Collective
Labour Relations

Wen Xiaoyi   ●

How are employers adapting to China's changing labour relations? Employers' strategies are the broad policies and plans of action that they develop and implement. In Western countries in the twentieth century the question mainly referred to strategies adopted by employers to deal with trade unions, whether positively through collective bargaining or negatively through union avoidance. They were concerned with both the external strategies that employers may adopt with regard to other employers and government, and also their internal strategies with regard to control within the enterprise and responses to changing product and labour market conditions (Kochan *et al.*, 1984; Kochan *et al.*, 1986). When Kochan and his colleagues described the 'transformation' of American labour relations in the 1980s it was, in part, a shift from operating on a collective to an individual basis. Labour relations in China are currently undergoing at least as great a transformation, but it is in the other direction, from the individual to the collective (Chang, 2013).

With the flow of migrant workers from the countryside drying up, the Chinese economy is arguably reaching Arthur Lewis's 'turning point' at which enterprises are facing difficulty in hiring workers. The consequent labour shortages are encouraging both rising wages and increasing collective consciousness and willingness to strike by workers. In addition, the Chinese government has issued a succession of laws which constrain and regulate employers' employment practices. These challenges are forcing Chinese employers to develop new strategies. The chapter starts by reviewing these changing circumstances. It then looks at the diversity of employer approaches to labour relations. It discusses the rapid emergence of employer organisation in response to the growth of markets and legal constraints. It ends with the emerging strategies of individual employers.

The New Challenges Facing Employers

Labour Shortages

The greatest challenge facing Chinese employers has been a swing in the labour market from excess supply to excess demand. First signs of labour shortage appeared as a seasonal problem in manufacturing industry in the Pearl River Delta and the Yangtze River Delta regions in 2004, reflected in a shortage of women workers at the time of festival holidays (Chen and Zhao, 2010). Since the international financial crisis in 2008 this phenomenon has extended nationwide, even to those provinces of previously massive labour supply like Henan and Anhui (Li, 2014). Figure 5.1 presents the ratio of job vacancies to job seekers from 2001. It shows a steadily rising trend, with a slight dip at the time of the financial crisis in 2008 and 2009. In 2010, the ratio passed 1 for the first time, indicating that the supply had become less than the demand. By 2014, the ratio had risen to 1.12, the highest point in its history.

Apart from these recruitment difficulties, employers have also been experiencing increasing difficulty retaining workers. Employee turnover in Chinese enterprises is rising. Figure 5.2 shows this from 2012 to 2014. As a consequence, the dominant priority for personnel management at enterprise level has shifted to the recruitment and retention of workers. Other human resource functions, such as the management of pay, performance, manpower planning and training, have been relegated to lower priority. Recruitment posts account for 40 per cent of human resources

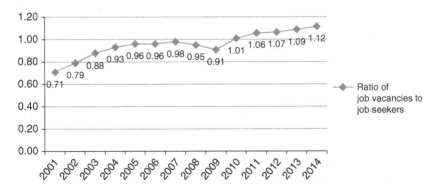

Figure 5.1 The ratio of job vacancies to job seekers, 2001–2014
Source: China Human Resources Market Information Monitoring Center, 'Report on the Nationwide Demand for and Supply of Jobs', 2001–2014

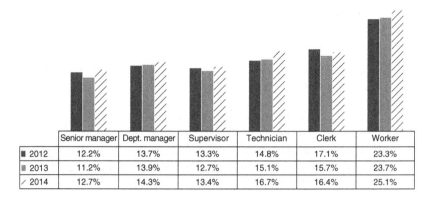

	Senior manager	Dept. manager	Supervisor	Technician	Clerk	Worker
■ 2012	12.2%	13.7%	13.3%	14.8%	17.1%	23.3%
■ 2013	11.2%	13.9%	12.7%	15.1%	15.7%	23.7%
⁄ 2014	12.7%	14.3%	13.4%	16.7%	16.4%	25.1%

Figure 5.2 Employee turnover rates, 2012–2014
Source: JOBS, White Paper on Human Resources in 2014, http://resea
rch.51job.com/free-355.html

posts appearing on the internet. Labour turnover is particularly high among migrant factory workers. Personnel departments in the Pearl River Delta now record turnover monthly rather than annually because so many workers resign in their first month. The annual peak in the labour turnover rate is the Spring Festival. According to a survey carried out by the *China Youth Daily* in 2013, 52 per cent of the surveyed workers said they were unwilling to come back to work after the Spring Festival. Of the employers surveyed, 35 per cent of them said that they had a significant number of employees who did not intend to return after the Spring Festival; only 16 per cent of employers said this was not a problem.

The Changing Attitudes of the New Generation of Workers

The increasing dominance of migrant workers who were born in the 1980s and 1990s changes the workforce to one which has largely grown up in more prosperous times, is better educated, is more aware of its legal rights and expects to be treated as individuals. This is increasing the daily challenges to management. Chinese enterprises have generally relied on an authoritarian style of leadership. This is partly because of a cultural tradition of patriarchy, and partly because of the discipline demanded of labour by large-scale manufacturing industry. Leadership tends to be highly centralised, emphasising obedience to orders, and stressing top-down absolute authority (Wen, 2013). Over the past twenty years, authoritarian leadership has become the mainstream management style for Chinese enterprises. Its key feature can be summed up in the phrase

'Do as I say', implying that employees are not expected to have their own opinions. The worst effect of this style of decision-making, emphasising absolute obedience, is one of denting the enthusiasm of employees and smothering the potential liveliness of organisations. Employees come to feel unappreciated, suffer from low morale and are reluctant to speak out even when they have valid opinions. This may result in their gradually losing their sense of personal responsibility. It is unavoidable that this kind of authoritarian leadership provokes conflict with those of the new generation of employees who have their own ideas and expect to have space for their own identities.

There is a very revealing difference in perception between management and the new generation of workers. A survey of employees who were born in the 1980s and 1990s identified the distinctive characteristics that they considered themselves to possess. These were having a strong sense of responsibility, being good at learning new skills, being realistic and thinking independently. In sharp contrast, the characteristics they were seen to have by human resource managers was that they were personally unstable, over-independent in their attitudes, have poor self-discipline and are over-confident. The distinctive characteristics of themselves that were most prized by these younger workers were precisely those considered to be the worst by human resource managers. Clearly, the perceived needs of enterprise managers are dissonant with those of their employees born in the 1980s and 1990s.

One might conclude that both sides of the employment relationship tend to be more self-centred and lacking in the most basic understanding of each other. But the essence of good management is to make those who are managed understand and meet the expectations and standards of the managers. This huge disparity causes managers to feel that they are trapped in a painful dilemma. Managers often appear hostile and unapproachable towards younger employees, reflecting their very different expectations. For the migrant workers, the tolerance and obedience that they displayed in the past in the face of harsh management methods has now changed into far more vocal protests and collective action.

A mix of circumstances is making migrant workers more willing to press for their interests. Prominent among them are their sense of relative deprivation compared to established workers, their greater awareness of their legal rights, the greater size of their social networks and their experience of living in enterprise dormitories (Cai, Li, and Feng, 2009). While the level of individual labour disputes continues to be high and rising, there has also been a surge in collective labour disputes. Disputes featuring strikes are now frequent, and have spread from the more developed coastal areas to much of the rest of the country. With ample job opportunities, workers are less afraid of losing their jobs. New social media make it much easier for workers to organise collective action. Strikes have become the preferred instrument for the new generation as a method of leverage with the greatest impact and rewards but at minimum cost to themselves.

The use of strikes is shifting from being grievances about rights to claims concerned with interests. Workers are seeking to improve on legal minimum provisions by raising their wage rates, improving their working conditions, shortening working time and getting paid for overtime. The trigger is typically an awareness of their enterprise's increasing profits. Instead of being satisfied with the statutory minimum wages, workers seek to have a share of rising profits in their wages. Their awareness of growing profits at a time of wage stagnation creates a strong sense of unfairness, which provokes workers to press for wage increases by taking collective action.

Incremental Government Regulation

The rise in labour conflict has been accompanied by increased legislation. The number and frequency of new labour laws has been increasing since 2008. These have included legislation on labour contracts, on mediation and arbitration and on social insurance, accompanied by many administrative regulations and judicial interpretations. These laws have raised the legal requirements for enterprise hiring and employment. For most employers, the Labour Contract Law of 2008 has increased labour costs. For example, the amendments to it in 2013 and 2014 were designed to reduce the increasing use of labour dispatch, also known as agency employment. In 2014, the Ministry of Human Resources and Social Security introduced provisions stipulating that no employment unit must have more than ten per cent of its workers on dispatch. This had a substantial impact on state-owned enterprises where use of dispatched workers in some cases had risen to high levels. In the case of China Mobile Communications Corporation, for example, it had reached as high as 60 per cent of its workforce (Chen, 2014).

It is government policy to encourage technologically advanced industrial development. This has had substantial effects on enterprises with labour-intensive methods of production. The Pearl River Delta region has taken the lead in actively discouraging labour-intensive enterprises from settling there. There are two reasons for this. The first is that the tax contribution from labour-intensive activity is less than that from more capital-intensive technologies. The second is that it is believed that labour unrest is more likely where large concentrations of relatively unskilled workers are employed, and that there are serious implications for social stability.

In 2008, Guangdong Province government proposed a policy on industrial structure known as *Emptying the cages for birds of other kinds*, which required governments at all levels in the Pearl River Delta region to develop policies to eliminate low technology enterprises. According to the policy of *Ten priorities for accelerating industrial transition for 2011–2015*, that was issued by Shenzhen government in November 2011, 'in the next five years, Shenzhen will clean up low-end enterprises which are uncertified or unlicensed and have serious safety risks, high pollution and high energy consumption. It will make room for 5 million square metres of industrial development by the end of 2013, and make room for 7.5 million square metres of industrial development by 2015.'

The resulting industrial transition and upgrading have brought mergers, reorganisation, relocation, transition and even closure and bankruptcy for enterprises. This aroused a new round of turbulence between capital and labour. The upheaval has provoked employees to make collective demands for employers to pay for their social insurance and housing fund, to pay economic compensation, to increase wages and to improve welfare. These demands increased the likelihood of major labour disputes. Such disputes mostly resulted from the workers' having had low wages for a long time, leading to a build-up of grudges. These accumulated grudges would sometimes explode when sparked by enterprise restructuring.

Official policy on dealing with individual disputes has moved away from one of heavy interference by local government. In the past, the fact that the government always intervened directly meant that what started as a conflict between labour and capital quickly became a political conflict with labour. Local governments are now gradually changing their responses. On the one hand, concerned about the costs to their perceived legitimacy of direct intervention, they are tending to deal more neutrally with labour conflict. They do this by playing the role of a mediator. They also provide a better platform for independent talks between workers and employers and they arrange tripartite consultations. On the other hand, they have changed their strategies in dealing with workers' collective action from one of oppression by direct administrative force to actively encouraging workers to elect their representatives. In this way, labour and capital are directed to solve disputes by themselves through negotiation. As long as the governmental attitude is neutral, employers must bear greater costs to settle disputes than in the past.

Differences in the Character of Labour Relations

The development of the market economy in China has had a profound effect on employers. At the same time as the number and size of enterprises has been increasing, the influence of employers on labour relations has been growing day by day. Most significant is the development and maturation of employer organisations, to which we shall return. First we shall consider the individual employer, who plays a leading role in labour relations. The philosophy and behaviour of employers have a direct influence on the character of labour relations and on how they are developing.

China's current laws have no definition of the concept of 'employer'. In Clause 2 of the Labour Law, the concept of the 'employment unit' is used to define the party to the employment relationship other than labour. There is a legal distinction between publicly owned economic organisations and non-public economic organisations for employers. The development of the legal concept of 'employer' is closely linked to the development of the economic and social system. In the early days after the People's Republic of China was founded, owners and operators of capital were essentially the same. But after the policy of reforming capitalist industry and commerce commenced, there was no real concept of 'employer' in China under the planned economic system. After the *Reform and opening-up* policy was implemented, with the development of a market-based economic system, the practical category of employers began developing gradually and matured bit by bit. With the advance of the marketisation of labour relations, people became accustomed to regular use of the term 'employer'.

The number of China's employers continues to grow. They play a crucial role in Chinese labour relations in terms of influence and voice. By the end of December 2014, 18.2 million enterprises were registered in China, having increased by 19.1 per cent since the previous year. Of these, 15.5 million were private enterprises, which had increased by 23.3 per cent over the previous year. More than 250 million employees are now employed by the private sector. The number of employees of private enterprises had increased by 14.3 per cent since the previous year (State Administration for Industry and Commerce, 2015). The rapid development of enterprises benefitted from the priority given to economic growth by both national and local governments.

Employers are generally classified in China according to three different types of enterprise ownership, and each is associated with a very different character of labour relations. Employers of Type 1 are state-owned enterprises. Although it is still controversial whether managers of state-owned enterprises should be called 'employers', it is undeniable that managers and employees of state-owned enterprises have different interests. With the continued spread of marketisation around state-owned enterprises, the relationship between employers and employees has been shaped accordingly. The labour relations of state-owned enterprises now have composite characteristics of both public ownership and private ownership. For many of their employees, state-owned enterprises generally have generous systems of employee welfare, relatively high wages and solid channels for employee participation. But the requirement for profitability that flows from marketisation tends to contradict their traditional employment principle of 'no firing'. As a result, use of labour dispatch has become very common in these enterprises, and consequently 'unequal pay for equal work' has become a principal characteristic of the labour relations of state-owned enterprises.

Employers of Type 2 are private enterprises. Having grown with the rise of marketisation in China, they have developed a distinctive form of employment relations. This type is especially associated with being in supply chains for foreign traded goods, processing raw materials on clients' demands, assembling parts for clients and manufacturing according to clients' samples. There are many private enterprises engaged in this sort of labour-intensive industry, where labour relations are not stable, and employer behaviour commonly breaches the basic rights of employees. Typical offences are illegitimately deducting or owing wages, gratuitously punishing or firing employees, failing to pay social insurance contributions and disappearing without paying wages. Because private enterprises of this type are so very numerous and generally have little awareness of the law, it is difficult to have effective law-enforcement and inspection of their labour conditions.

Employers of Type 3 are foreign-funded enterprises. Strongly influenced by the legal systems of their home countries, foreign-funded enterprises can be classified into a number of sub-categories (Chan, 1998). In general, there are three sorts. The first is Hong Kong and Taiwanese-funded enterprises, which are mostly engaged in manufacturing fairly basic equipment. They generally have low wages and also have relatively unstable labour relations. The second is Japanese and Korean-funded enterprises, which are mainly engaged in advanced manufacturing production. They typically have a standardised management system and relatively stable labour relations. The third is American and European-funded enterprises, which are mostly industry leaders and technologically innovative. They attach importance to the creativity of employees, have high-quality human resource management systems and a relatively high level of employee satisfaction.

Despite these very diverse types of employer currently operating in China, the same laws apply to them all. The government regulates the hiring practice of all employers. Of recent labour laws, the Labour Contract Law of 2008 has had the greatest influence on employers. This law raised statutory labour standards, emphasising the protection of the rights and interests of workers, and increasing the penalties to employers for illegal practices. It is controversial in academic circles whether the law is good or not. But enterprises commonly have a negative view of it, and employers often criticise it.

China has two systems for protecting workers. The first system determines statutory labour standards and sets out workers' legitimate rights and interests. These include a specified labour contract, salary, holiday entitlements and social insurance. The second form of protection is workers' collective consultation and the collective contract system. The Trade Union Law stipulates that 'the workers of an enterprise can sign collective contracts with their enterprise with regard to labour remuneration, working hours, rest breaks and vacations, occupational safety and hygiene, insurance and welfare, and so on'.

These two systems constitute the basis of national labour law and policies. However, because there are problems with the trade unions, collective contracts have not played their intended role. It is very rare that genuine negotiation occurs over a collective contract. The deficiencies in the way that collective labour relations operate mean that the only protection mechanism that workers can rely on in reality is the state acting to raise statutory labour standards. This does have the effect of gradually improving the practical realities of labour standards. But the consequences are not straight-forward. The intention of the legal system was to achieve a high level of enforcement for comparatively basic standards, whereas in reality it tends to achieve low enforcement of relatively high standards. A systemic problem with the current Chinese labour relations system is the widespread failure of enterprises to abide by the law.

The Development of Employer Organisation

Employer organisations have become an important aspect of Chinese labour relations. Employer organisations are those legally established by groups of employers, aimed at both representing and defending their interests to government as well as managing relations with employees and with unions. Unlike union organisation, which was established early in modern China, on a coherent political foundation, the development of employer organisations in China has been a gradual and decentralised process, reflecting the diversity of different employer interests.

The development of employer organisations in China is also characterised by diversity. We can classify these organisations by their levels and their active jurisdictions. At the national level, representing all organisations is the China Enterprise Confederation/China Enterprise Directors Association (CEC/CEDA). Also at the national level, representing non-public organisations, is the All-China Federation of Industry & Commerce (ACFIC). This represents, among others, the China Association of Enterprises with Foreign Investment, the China Private-Owned Business Association and the China Non-Governmental Enterprise Directors Association.

Below national level, employer organisations can be subdivided into four levels of provincial, local, county and town. According to the *Circular on the development status of members and organisations in the first half of 2015* issued by the ACFIC, commercial organisations grouped around chambers of commerce may be sub-divided further according to town, street, park, a market, building or village. Quite apart from formal organisations, many employers have spontaneously formed non-governmental organisations in order to be able to act together in dealing with labour affairs. Most of these take the form of an informal sodality or club with no formal constitution or organisation, typically based on districts or counties, and dominated by foreign-owned enterprises (Chang, 2005).

The employer organisations whose prime concern is regulating domestic labour relations have as their representatives the two national organisations of CEC/CEDA and ACFIC. These are mainly responsible for handling affairs related to relations between labour and capital, including carrying out negotiations with unions. They also participate in the design of labour legislation, in formulating labour policy and in labour arbitration. Because the state-owned enterprises are its main members, CEC/CEDA has developed a more governmental style of working, in which policy development is driven from the top down. By contrast, because private enterprises are its main members, ACFIC has developed an operating style in which policy is most easily developed from bottom to top. In the time since they were established, there have been a number of changes in their functions and operational methods, reflecting the importance that employers attach to these associations in coping with the turbulence that has been brought to labour relations by the growing market economy.

The CEC was established as the nationwide employer organisation with a legal personality under the approval of the State Council. Its predecessors were the China Enterprise Management Association (founded in

1979) and the China Factory Directors (Managers) Research Society (founded in 1984). Because of its strong official background, CEC has since its birth been given the absolute right of representation of enterprises. In August, 2001, the CEC, together with the ACFTU and the former Ministry of Labour and Social Security, formally established the National Tripartite Meeting System for Labour Relations Coordination. This officially confirmed CEC's central role in coordinating labour relations. In June 2003, CEC was included into the International Organisation of Employers as a full member, and was confirmed as the only internationally representative organisation of employers in China, representing it at the International Labour Organisation. By 2008, CEC had already built up an organisational network covering the entire country with almost 4500 direct enterprise members and 545,000 associate enterprise members. Members of CEC were, however, mainly state-owned enterprises.

A growing number of private sector employer organisations sprang up spontaneously outside the CEC because of the rapid growth of the market economy. This was driven by the need for private enterprises to avoid destructive competition between themselves and to be united to fight for market share from the state-owned enterprises. As an organisation of employers, originally founded in 1953, the ACFIC works on behalf of private enterprises and in a somewhat competitive relationship with CEC. Another name for it is the Chinese Non-Governmental Chamber of Commerce. As a grass-roots-based organisation of individuals and chambers of commerce, its members mainly consist of non-public enterprises and business people. Its structure and development are indicated in Table 5.1. Its expenditure is mainly financed by its own resources.

Since the opening up of the economy to markets, there has been a rapid increase in economic diversity in the private sector. The ACFIC's response to this has been a series of reform measures intended to develop a structure of non-governmental chambers of commerce. It started by selecting Shenzhen, Guangzhou, Wuxi and Wenzhou as pilot areas. Here they managed the transition from top-down control and administration to bidirectional interaction and cooperation. As a result, both ACFIC and non-governmental chambers of commerce achieved sustained growth (Pu, 2003). In 2008, the ACFIC proposed to the government that a new form of relationship between labour and capital should be developed for private enterprises. It also asked to be included in the Tripartite System of Labour Relations Coordination, and it successfully challenged CEC's authority as sole coordinator of labour relations. In 2009 the ACFIC was authorised to participate in coordinating labour relations. In 2010, both the ACFIC and the CEC became the official employer

Table 5.1 *All-China Federation of Industry and Commerce (ACFIC) organisational structure, 2006–2014*

| Year | Number of members | Organisational structure | | |
		Above county level	Primary level organisations	Sectoral organisations
2006	2,052,307	3120	22,781	7854
2007	2,190,403	3130	23,409	8846
2008	2,337,423	3130	23,993	10,337
2009	2,574,494	3295	24,722	12,326
2010	2,710,715	3345	26,359	14,251
2011	2,838,005	3348	43,855	15,965
2012	3,147,154	3331	49,219	17,036
2013	3,628,461	3381	22,474	10,051
2014	3,969,674	3394	25,586	11,395

Source: Report of the Development of Membership and Organisational Construction, 2006–2014, ACFIC www.acfic.org.cn/web/c

representatives in the Tripartite Negotiation System at the levels of enterprise, industry and locality.

At around the same time, other types of employer organisation, such as industry-based associations, chambers of commerce, economic leagues and entrepreneurial associations, were emerging, representing the varied interests of their members at different administrative levels. A network of employer organisations which contains nationwide organisations, regional organisations and organisations of different industries has evolved. Operating at different levels and for different industries, these are developing great diversity.

The emergence of employer organisations in China has many consequences for labour relations. First and foremost, in formulating its labour relations legislation, the government is facing an increasingly strong opposition from employer organisations. Before the introduction of the Labour Contract Law in 2008, a variety of employer organisations came together and bargained with the ACFTU, successfully forcing it to compromise on some key terms. In 2010, the Hong Kong Businessmen's Association successfully prevented the introduction of *Regulations on Democratic Management of Enterprises* in Guangdong Province and the introduction of *Regulations on Collective Bargaining* in the Shenzhen Special Economic Zone. In 2014, with powerful influence from the six major chambers of commerce in Hong Kong, the *Regulations on Collective Agreement for Enterprises in Guangdong* went through many stages of revision in favour of the employers before they became law.

Second, the employer organisations have gradually become a platform for enterprise managers to share information, discuss labour polices and adjust their salary strategies. In many industrial parks in the Pearl River Delta, enterprise managers regularly hold meetings to develop policies of salary adjustment, so that they can do better in retaining their workers while minimising competition between employers in their labour markets. They also exchange information about worker activists seen to be 'trouble makers'. In industrial parks in the Yangtze River Delta, the employer organisations take the form of human resources clubs. Their responsibilities include collectively lobbying local government on issues like labour legislation and use of the law. They also manage collective negotiations among the club members on recruitment, admission, resignations and welfare (Gallagher, 2010).

Last but not least, employer organisations need to intervene in internal disputes and on other labour issues that might be raised by the need to protect the interests of employers as a whole. Small, weak and dispersed enterprises are at the bottom of the global industrial value chain. Many of them are in furious competition with each other. This often results in severe damage to local relations between workers and employers and costly churning of workers. This can lead to employers fighting over skilled workers and incessant labour disputes. In these circumstances, employer organisations are forced to intervene in the conduct of labour relations by individual enterprises. This was the background for the emergence of collective negotiations on pay in China.

In 2008, the then premier Wen Jiabao issued special instructions calling for the collective negotiation of pay in the woollen sweater industry of Wenling, Zhejiang Province (Wen, 2016). This was given nationwide publicity, in which the ACFTU played a part. Wenling is a famous area for the production of woollen sweaters, made in a large cluster of small and medium-sized enterprises. Every year, these firms suffered from labour shortages. To complete production orders, the enterprises started to compete for workers, bidding up salaries in order to recruit. A vicious spiral of labour cost competition developed. Many firms could not fulfil the high salaries that they had promised on recruitment and workers took strike action in response. This prompted the Wenling Woollen Sweater Association to take the lead and initiate the setting up of a labour union for the Woollen Sweater Industry, involving worker representatives who came straight from the production line. The Association and the labour union held collective negotiations on issues relating to labour costs. After some intense arguments and discussions this led to agreement on common wage scales across all associated firms and, in due course, to a small pay rise. The turbulence of labour relations fell sharply. Similar examples of the collective bargaining over wages at industry level occurred in other industries, such as the ceramic industry of Yixing, Zhejiang Province, the metal plate processing industry of Pizhou, Jiangsu Province, the shoe industry of Quanzhou, Fujian Province and the clothes industry of Yingkou, Liaoning Province. All these are clear cases in which employer organisations have taken a lead to intervene and to innovate in labour relations (Lee *et al.*, 2016).

Strategies of Employers at Enterprise Level

As pressures increase, employer strategies develop. One example is the reaction of state-owned enterprises to the tightening of legal constraints on the use of dispatched or agency labour within their workplaces. Their response is to make more use of outsourcing work through commercial contracts. Another example is the response of large private sector enterprises to rising labour costs, where they are having to choose between investment in more capital-intensive technologies or moving their production sites elsewhere.

Chinese capital is increasingly moving westwards within China and outside the country altogether into Southeast Asia. Rising unit labour costs are prompting an increasing number of low technology manufacturing enterprises in the Pearl River Delta, especially clothing factories and toy manufacturers, to move to low labour cost inland areas of China and beyond. Those enterprises which choose to move outside China have targeted Vietnam and Cambodia as their first choices; those which intend to move inland see Hunan and Guangxi as their preference. Industrial parks aiming to attract industries in transition are being built in inland areas to draw factories from the Pearl River Delta.

The alternative strategy for many enterprises is one of reducing their dependence on labour by increasing investments in more capital-intensive, automated equipment, optimising control over work flow and getting the most advanced manufacturing technology. The chairman of the massive electronics company Foxconn declared in 2011 that 1 million robots would be introduced to improve production within three years. By 2017, China has been predicted to overtake the EU and the US as the economy that uses most industrial robots.

New employer strategies go far beyond their investment decisions. There are also innovations in their handling of individual and collective labour relations and collective disputes. Their new strategies are closely related to the changes in the labour relations environment.

Handling Individual Labour Relations

The way enterprises recruit workers is changing drastically. In the past they were not worried about labour shortages. Peasant workers would line up for interview as soon as the recruitment ads were posted at the gate of the plant. But with more recent recruitment difficulties, strategies of enterprises have changed. They are increasingly dependent on recruitment agencies to hire workers, and at the same time, vocational schools have become the most important channel from which enterprises now hire workers. Both enterprises and recruitment agencies invest energy and resources in lobbying managers of vocational schools. As a consequence, many vocational school students find themselves spending most of their time working in factories as interns instead of studying in school. Both the schools and the factories are avoiding official supervision by taking advantage of loopholes in labour law.

The local government authorities of the big inland population centres have started to collude in helping recruitment. The best known example is of local governments helping Foxconn with their recruitment. The human resources departments of all levels in Chengdu and Sichuan Province, as well as all the big agencies, were assigned to help Foxconn to hire more workers in Chengdu. The tasks were distributed down from city level to the level of county, township and village. Local human resource agencies would be rewarded with over 1000 yuan for each worker they recruited. In Henan Province, the local government helped Foxconn to find 200,000 workers. Responsibility for recruitment was delegated, and those local officials who could not meet the targets would be reprimanded or even held financially liable. In one county of north Henan, responsibility for recruitment was delegated down to the village level, and in one village, both the village secretary and the village officer were warned by town officials that they would be dismissed if they missed the targets (Sun, 2012).

The interpersonal style of management is also changing. In the past, the emphasis was on strict labour discipline and the obedience to orders. The unquestioned authority of those at the top was seen as essential to maintain the stable operation of factories of many thousand employees. There were, for examples, strict restrictions on going to the washroom or for drinking water. The style adopted by foremen and first-line supervisors was often harsh with frequent use of physical and verbal abuse. But, in response to labour shortages and disputes, this is quietly changing. The churn rate of workers used to be treated as a warning indicator for the performance of human resources departments. Now it has become a warning indicator for the performance of line managers. This means that departmental managers are being given responsibility for lowering the churn rate of employees within their departments. A direct consequence is a decrease in the use of verbal and physical punishment of workers.

Department managers increasingly find it necessary to consider and respect the feelings and aspirations of workers. In many firms, employee relations have become the central focus of management. Lecturers on psychology and organisational behaviour are often brought in to improve department managers' skills in understanding employees and retaining them. Effort is also being put into team-building, improving the culture of the workplace and its welfare system. Many enterprises now regularly organise consultative meetings between managers and workers to identify sources of discontent and to discuss solutions.

Handling Collective Labour Relations

Attitudes towards labour unions are changing. Previously, employers typically had two attitudes towards unions. The first was that they were confrontational organisations which did nothing but ask for a pay raise. The second attitude saw the union as a shell with no content, built in response to official requirements, with the sole purpose of collecting union dues. Increasing intensity of labour relations and high labour turnover are making many enterprises change their attitude in the hope that the union might help placate worker discontents.

Employers are increasingly trying to influence the form of the union in their enterprise. Three different models are apparent. The first model is the welfare union. This calls for substantial investment in the workers' welfare system, and the union's main function is seen to be to provide cultural and entertainment services. In some Taiwanese enterprises the management of the staff dormitory is the responsibility of the union.

The second model is of a monitoring union which has authority to observe day-to-day management in order to prevent problems arising that might provoke labour discontent. An example is provided by Foxconn which, after a crisis of bad publicity over worker suicides in 2010, appointed the secretary of the chairman and founder of Foxconn as the chair of the labour union, backed by a large number of full-time union officials. Its involvement with management is such that it even has power to stop the production lines if necessary.

The third model is that of the representative union. In some Japanese-owned enterprises, workers are encouraged to elect their union representatives in order to build a platform for labour relations and win the workers' loyalty to the enterprise by, for example, making pay rises open to collective negotiation. The electronics company Ricoh in Guandong Province provides an example. Its union has been constituted democratically for the workers. They elect all the union representatives within the workplace. First, the workers elect worker representatives. Second, the trade union committee implement multi-candidate elections. Finally, the union chairman is elected from multiple candidates by the trade union committee. Since its establishment, the Ricoh labour union has achieved steady improvements in the workers' pay and welfare provisions through collective negotiation. The company, in return, no longer has its previous problems of high labour turnover and frequent labour disputes. Its labour turnover has fallen below 4 per cent in an industry where it is typically around 20 per cent.

Employers are generally hostile towards collective consultation. This is partly because they consider that the officially encouraged collective consultation system places too much emphasis on wage growth. For most employers, it means that wages can only rise not fall. They feel that government encouragement of collective consultation is unfair to them. At the same time, collective consultation mostly has to be carried out at the level of the enterprise. If the enterprise is not running well, it limits the potential for effective collective negotiation. The attitude of small- and medium-sized enterprises is even more hostile. They typically use labour-intensive production methods and their profit margins are too slight to allow any concession through collective consultation. This employer hostility was made clear in Guandong Province through a co-ordinated series of boycotts against the legislation.

The picture is very different for foreign-invested enterprises. Many US and EU-owned companies implement individualistic human resource management policies instead of more negotiation-based industrial relations. By contrast, many Japanese-owned companies, with large-scale production and high profit margins, hope to achieve a stable industrial order through collective bargaining. Their labour unions are typically composed of representatives elected by the workers. What would generally be considered to be collective bargaining over pay is carried out on a regular basis between the union and the enterprise management. Worker representatives have a substantial role in a genuine negotiation process, in which the two sides converge on an agreement through a series of rounds (Lee *et al.*, 2016). What is especially important is that the outcome of the negotiation is usually a pay rise that reflects the current level of profitability of the enterprise. By allowing a share of its profits to go to the workers, the enterprise is likely to improve stability of both its workforce and its production, and the labour union also wins worker support.

Managing Strikes

Strikes are always a major challenge for employers. They disrupt production and damage profitability. Most employers lack experience of dealing with strikes. In the past, many strikes were stopped by the use of the power of local government. This has brought increasingly serious consequences because police intervention sometimes provokes a larger riot. As far back as 2000, the Ministry of Public Security published *Regulations on police action for the restoration of peace in group disorder events*. These clearly specified that police force should not be used directly to end strikes within enterprises. Most employers felt abandoned with this withdrawal of access to governmental power. In the past, following a strike, management often acted as if they subconsciously relied upon police support, by shouting at the strikers or even firing them on the spot. Such action could have the perverse effect of intensifying the conflict, making workers more united, and sometimes even refocussing their attacks on the management, making the underlying problem much trickier to resolve. Punishing or firing strikers is not an effective way of restoring production and defusing conflict.

Because the number of strikes is increasing, employers are acquiring the experience to deal with them. They usually attempt to weaken the unity of the workers. They will generally get help from the local labour department and labour union. They will try to calm emotions down and encourage the striking workers to select representatives with whom they can discuss the problem and negotiate. They will then offer some concessions to satisfy the main demands of most of the workers so as to restore production as soon as possible. Typically, the employers will then try to identify the strike organisers and the activists. After some time has passed, they will find excuses and opportunities to fire them. By this time, most of the workers, having benefited from the strike, will not risk further action to reinstate them. In this way, the employer will have eliminated the organisational basis of the strike. In some places in the Pearl River Delta, employers have established blacklists to prevent these strike activists from ever being rehired in the region. In anticipation of major changes such as plant relocation which might lead to substantial collective resistance by the workers, the enterprise management may hire consultants who specialise in breaking worker solidarity. Employers are learning how to mobilise their own power.

Conclusion

The increase in collectivism of Chinese labour relations has had a massive impact on employers. The era of unlimited labour supply has passed. Workers have collectively gained the capacity to organise and to negotiate. This presents a comprehensive challenge to the time-honoured authority of Chinese management. Top-down control is no longer able to constrain the new generation of workers. Furthermore, the government is setting aside its limited engagement of the past and introducing laws that support worker rights and that place constraints on employers' freedom to hire. This presents huge challenges that employers have never faced before but now have to deal with on their own.

In response, employers are starting to change both their management style and the form of their organisations. In terms of individual labour relations, employers are using softer management policies by which they emphasise the importance of dialogue in building employee relations. In terms of collective labour relations, employers are gradually changing their attitudes towards unions in the hope that unions can play a role in stabilising enterprise labour relations. Many foreign-owned enterprises have even encouraged workers to form a representative labour union through elections. In coping with strikes, employers are showing more proficiency in undermining workers' unity. Employers are inherently hostile to collective labour relations, and especially to any form of institutionalised collective bargaining, but they are increasingly expressing this resistance by building their own organisations.

References

Cai H, Li, C. H. and Feng J. H. (2009), 'Liyi shousun nongmingong de liyi kangzheng xingwei yanjiu', [A behavioural study of the interests of peasant workers suffering losses], *Sociological Research*, 1, 139–161.

Chan, A. (1998), 'Labour relations in foreign-funded ventures, Chinese trade unions, and the prospects for collective bargaining', in O'Leary, G. (ed.), *Adjusting to Capitalism: Chinese Workers and the State*, Armonk, NY: Sharpe.

Chang, K. (2005), 'Laoquan lun', [*The Theory of Labour Rights*], Beijing: Zhongguo laodong shehui baozhang chubanshe.

Chang, K. (2013), 'Laodong guanxi de jitihua zhuanxing yu zhengfu laogong zhengce de wanshan', [The collective transformation of labour relations and the improvement of government labour policy], *Chinese Social Sciences*, 6, 91–206.

Chen, B and Zhao, Y. (2010), 'You mingonghuang yinfa dui liuyisi guaidian de sikao', [Some Thoughts about the Lewis Turning-Point caused by labour shortage], *Commercial* Times, 3, 4–5.

Chen, B. (2014), 'Zhongyidong tiaozheng laowugong', [China Mobile has adjusted the status of labour dispatch workers], *The 21st Century Business Herald*, November 18.

Gallagher, M. (2010), 'Quanqiuhua yu zhongguo laogong zhengzhi', [*Globalisation and Chinese Labour Politics*], Zhejiang: Zhejiang renmin chubanshe.

Kochan, T. A., McKersie R. B. and Cappelli, P. (1984), 'A strategic choice theory of industrial relations', *Industrial Relations*, 16–39.

Kochan, T. A., Katz, H. C. and McKersie, R. B. (1986), '*The Transformation of American Industrial Relations*', New York: ILR Press.

Lee, C-H., Brown, W. and Wen, X. (2016), 'What sort of collective bargaining is emerging in China?' *British Journal of Industrial Relations*, 54(1), 214–236.

Li X., (2014), 'Labour shortage spreads to Midwest', *China Business News*, May 5

Pu, W. (2003), *The Market Economy and Non-governmental Chambers of Commerce*, Beijing: Zhongyang bianye chubanshe.

Sun, X. (2012), 'Fushikang daguimo zhaogong renwu cheng he'nan jiceng zhengfu fudan', [Foxconn recruitment became a burden for local government in Henan Province], *Southern Metropolis Daily*, September 28.

Wen, X. (2013), 'Qiye renli ziyuan guanli de tiaozhan yu laodong guanxi guanli tixi jianshe', [Challenges for enterprises in human resources and the construction of a labour relations management system], *Chinese Human Resources and Development*, 11, 81–86.

Wen, X. (2016), 'Employer-initiated collective bargaining: a case study of the Chinese sweater industry', *Employee Relations*, 38(2), 267–285.

6 The Changing Role of Government Towards Labour

Tu Wei

No country has more deep-rooted a tradition of a centralised state than China. For thousands of years Chinese society has been most stable when the central government has been strong. When the People's Republic came to power in 1949, it renewed this tradition. This chapter is concerned with how it has regulated labour relations and, in particular, with how this has altered with the emergence of a market economy. The chapter starts with a general consideration of the role of government in labour relations, and with an overview of the position in China. The second part discusses central government regulation of individual labour relations, and the third part goes on to look at the regulation of collective labour relations by both central and local government. The fourth part considers the impact of the increased collectivism of labour on governmental intervention strategies. Finally, the changing nature of Chinese labour policy is considered from an historical institutionalist perspective.

The Role of Government in Labour Relations

The state is a theoretically abstract concept, unlike employers and workers, the other two actors in labour relations (Meardi, 2014: 617). Definitions of the state focus on it as a complex, centralised combination of institutions, acknowledged in the international community and concerned with, among other things, the organised use of violence, property rights and social regulation (Levi, 2002: 40). The nature of the state differs greatly from country to country. Historical and other environmental factors shape the state in ways which are unique to each country, even where countries have ostensibly similar legal systems and government

The author wishes to thank Wolfgang Streeck who inspired the original idea of this chapter. Thanks are also due to Sebastian Kohl, Katharina Sass, Irina España, Torsten Kathke, Chang Cheng, as well as Max-Planck-Institut für Gesellschaftsforschung (MPIfG) in Cologne, Germany where most of the chapter was written.

agencies. For example, the state in liberal market economy countries such as the United States and Britain is generally seen to be an independent actor, distinct from the wider society. By contrast, in countries with a corporatist tradition, such as many in Western Europe, the boundaries of the state are much less clear, and it plays a more active role in labour relations.

Rather than dwell on the state in an abstract sense, it is more productive to focus on the specific roles it plays and the institutional settings it occupies. Analysts have noted that generally the state influences labour relations in six distinct ways. It affects the labour market indirectly through macro-economic policies and directly through active policies, such as training of the unemployed, or creating jobs. It establishes a structure of procedural provisions which set out the status, rights and obligations of those involved and the procedural rules of labour relations. It also sets labour standards, which directly regulate the treatment and conditions of employment of workers. The state may act as a neutral third party to facilitate the resolution of labour disputes. Having responsibility for the public sector, the state itself is usually the largest employer, with a substantial demonstration effect on other employers (Hyman, 2008: 264; Meardi, 2014: 620).

The institutions of labour relations are an important source of competitive advantage affecting the economic performance of different countries (Hall and Soskice, 2001: 9–12). State power is of critical importance in shaping power in any labour relations system. The state establishes the basis of orderly operation of labour relations and labour protection and, in most countries, the labour relations system is directly or indirectly dominated by the state (Hyman, 2008: 260). The intervention of the state in labour relations is not itself problematic. The problems arise with the degree of intervention, the methods used and the specific objectives.

Interest in the way that institutions have evolved historically has grown in recent years with an awareness of the variety of forms that capitalist societies can take. This has shifted attention from the analysis of theoretical equilibria towards better understanding of the historical processes through which functional institutions evolve in different countries (Thelen, 1999; Frege and Kelly, 2013: 24–27). This historical institutionalist approach considers how different combinations of state institutions are produced and what mechanisms maintain them. The starting point is different from the traditional static analysis which assumes that economic equilibria are normal. On the contrary, its premise is that political and economic systems are constantly changing, often in subtle ways. From this historical institutionalist viewpoint, we should be concerned with incremental developments which may ultimately produce discontinuities (Pierson and Skocpol, 2002). It has been argued that generally there are five main types of gradual institutional change. These are the displacement of institutions, the layering of them, their drift, their conversion and their exhaustion. These are different from their internal mechanisms of change (Streeck and Thelen, 2005:18–30). These theories help us to understand the mechanisms by which the state shapes labour relations, and they provide some core concepts with which to understand how a country's labour relations system evolves.

The Chinese Government's Role in Labour Regulation

As a planned economy in the years following 1949, Chinese society was based on vertical lines of executive authority. This included the regulation of labour, described as 'administrative labour relations', which meant that labour relations were in effect a relationship between the state and the workers. The Chinese state was the only employer, and was responsible for the allocation of workers to jobs, their wage standards, social welfare standards and work rules. Enterprises were not independent actors but were the representatives of the state with responsibility for managing firms and for the implementation of labour policy.

With the deepening of economic reforms, fundamental changes have taken place in this dominant role of the government in labour relations. First of all, it has forced administrative labour relations to move towards market-oriented labour relations. The system in China is gradually showing some signs of convergence with those of countries such as Britain and the United States. This is especially evident in the widening divergence of interests between labour and capital when enterprises gain more freedom as employers. The direct dependence of both enterprises and workers on government is diminishing, and the previous importance of the state in labour relations has been weakening.

Since the 2008 financial crisis, however, the state has expanded its intervention in the market economy, and more generally has become an important driver of China's economic development. Labour relations are being shaped by the state in new ways (Liu, 2013: 335–340). The government is still the most powerful actor in the labour relationship. Indeed, it has been argued that China has state-led labour relations, whereby stability is achieved by direct control from top to bottom (Chang, 2005: 1). It has been suggested that the Chinese state plays four distinct roles in labour relations: regulation; monitoring; damage control; and mediation and arbitration (Taylor *et al.*, 2003: 29–35). But such analyses generally overlook the extent to which the form of intervention that is used by the state differs at different levels. For example, the state operates as the regulator through legislation at the central level, but through the role of labour arbitrator at the local government level. The role of the state varies with the purpose of its intervention.

Labour relations can be divided between two basic aspects: individual and collective. It has been argued that subordination is the dominant feature of individual labour relations (Huang, 2003:94–96). Employees have to subordinate their personal identity to the employer. They have to submit to work rules, instructions, supervision, monitoring and, if appropriate, punishment from the employer. They are also subordinate in economic terms. The employer owns the production facilities and tools, supplies the raw materials and confronts the employee with occupational risks. The state mitigates this subordination of employees in individual labour relations, providing workers with basic rights by setting labour standards, such as minimum wages, and by providing protections against dismissal and occupational health hazards.

The second aspect, which is often seen to be more significant, is collective labour relations. It consists of the relationships between trade unions, as the main representatives of employees, on the one hand, and employers or employers' organisations on the other. The trade union is the main interest group involved. Because trade unions share comparable procedural status with employers in the labour market, trade unions are better able to protect employees' rights and to overcome many disadvantages to which employees are vulnerable at the individual level. The intervention of the state in collective labour relations is totally different from its intervention in individual labour relations. It provides the institutional guarantee for negotiation procedures, and it can do this without any need for direct intervention in the actual conduct of negotiations.

The intervention of the Chinese state in labour relations can be considered under these same two headings. There is the regulation of individual labour relations, which is mainly done by setting labour standards and through the labour contract system. There is also the regulation of collective labour relations which is mainly carried out through the exercise of administrative power. The Chinese political system has been described as 'decentralised legal authoritarianism' which is defined as the 'twin strategy of decentralised accumulation and legalistic legitimation of authoritarian rules' (Lee, 2007:10–11). Interventions in individual labour relations in China are controlled mainly through the central government's use of legislation. In collective labour relations, on the other hand, because central legislation is lacking, a more active role is played by local government through the use of its administrative power. For example, the process of spreading collective consultation across China was achieved by the higher levels of government, which put pressure on local governments by giving them mandatory targets, setting out the number of collective agreements that had to be achieved (Wu, 2012). Similarly, it is in accordance with national emergency planning rules to 'maintain the stability of society' that local governments may be required to repress strikes.

Labour relations in China have changed in response to substantial changes in the economic environment which have obliged the state to make gradual adjustments. The focus of legislative changes has shifted with regard to employment law. Before 2008, the state's labour policy was mainly one of supporting measures for market-based economic development. After 2008, the government began to develop policies to protect workers. From the point of view of intervention in collective labour relations, it was changes in the external environment that forced changes in the intervention strategies of local governments.

The Regulation of Individual Labour Relations

The Historical Development of Individual Labour Relations Policy

Unlike in most developed countries, China's market-oriented labour relations have not evolved gradually in the process of economic development, but are adapted from a centrally planned economic system. This is an important aspect of economic reforms since the 1980s. When legal rights of ownership and management were changed, it was unavoidable that employment institutions would have to make corresponding changes. The reforms confirmed the principles of 'property rights' and of 'independent operation' in the state-owned corporations. This was linked with the reform of labour institutions which stripped workers of any of the property relations they possessed under communism in the planned economy and forced them to compete in a labour market. The objective of this was to establish free labour markets, and to build market-oriented labour relations. The then Ministry of Labour in 1993 issued an *Overall plan of labour reform for the period while the socialist market economic system is being established*. This proposed that:

we should establish a new regulation system for labour relations, adapted to the requirements of the socialist market economy, through the use of legislation and labour standards by the government, through independent coordination by employees and employers, through coordination by trade unions and business representatives under the guidance of the government, through administrative supervision and through the use of judicial arbitration to protect the interests of both sides in labour relations.

This marks the point when China's market-oriented labour relations start to develop, the market economy begins and the planned economic system begins to draw to a close.

The reforms progressed through successive stages. The first stage, from the mid-1980s to the early 1990s, saw the implementation of labour contracts mainly in the state-owned enterprises. The second stage, from the early 1990s to the early 2000s, was marked by the establishment of a modern enterprise system, fully implemented in both private and state-owned enterprises. Employees of most state-owned enterprises became wage labourers under the new market economy. Millions of farmers abandoned agricultural work and were hired as migrant workers by the modern industries, becoming market-oriented wage earners. An important landmark of this stage was the introduction of the 1995 Labour Law. The third stage, from the beginning of the twenty-first century to the present, saw further improvements. The introduction of the Labour Contract Law in 2008 marked the completion of the main structure of government regulation of individual labour relations. At present, the main task is to consolidate the reforms, and to develop and refine the institutions of labour relations.

The focus has been on reforming labour market institutions through mandatory administrative action from top to bottom. The intention was to improve labour allocation and utilisation by market competition in ways that were not available under a planned economy. The reforms were intended to reshape the identity of both labour and capital. The reform of individual labour relations was the starting point for wider reforms.

The Effectiveness of Regulations

The regulation of individual labour relations has been primarily achieved by fixing labour standards such as minimum wages and maximum working hours at the macro level, and by building on the labour contract system at the micro level. Although 'labour standard' is not an accepted legal term, it covers usefully many different benchmarks for employment conditions, including minimum wages, working hours, protections for particular types of worker and safety protections. For example, Article 36 of the Labour Law specifies the institution of the eight hour day. Article 48 is concerned with a minimum wage system, but authorises local government to set the standards of minimum wages within provinces. Chapter 6(article 52–57) provides regulations for occupation safety and health protection. Chapter 7(article 58–65) provides a system of labour protection for female and for youth workers.

The government regulates the balance of rights and obligations between employee and employer through the labour contract system. The introduction of the Labour Law in 1995 was based on a labour contract either with or without a fixed period (Article 20). The termination of a labour contract could take three forms: legal dismissal; dismissal by negotiation; and termination by the expiry of the contract. After more than ten years' experience, the labour contract became the main method of adjusting employment relationships. But problems arose from its poor implementation. The number of contracts signed was low, and much use was made of short-term contracts (Chang, 2008; Zheng, 2008). The Labour Contract Law of 2008 was built on the 1995 Law and was designed to eliminate these problems. It increased the penalties for not signing contracts. It also increased the statutory conditions for non-fixed-term contracts, removing some conditions that allowed contract termination on contract expiry, and tightening the statutory conditions for the termination of contracts by employers. Overall, the Labour Contract Law strengthened the central position of the labour contract and it encouraged employers and employees to establish long-term employment relationships. Of particular importance was that it protected the rights of migrant workers (Li and Freeman, 2015).

There was a fierce academic debate on the changes incorporated in the Labour Contract Law and about potential social and economic consequences. The argument focussed on whether the state had authority to intervene in the labour market and labour relations. Chang Kai of the Beijing School argued that the law should be used for improving on workers' weak position in labour relations. The contrary view, expressed by Dong Baohua of the Shanghai School was that the law already favoured workers' protection too much, and that the consequences might be damaging. This so-called 'North-South debate' in academia lasted until after the Law was passed. In addition to this argument among lawyers, economists also expressed critical views on the consequences of the Law. Wang Yijiang (2006) stressed that the elements of labour participation and of government intervention implied in the Law would cause market inefficiencies that would lead to higher unemployment rates in the long run, with adverse consequences for labour. Similar arguments were made by academic advocates of neo-classical economics who were critical of, for example, the minimum wage system. It was argued that statutory minimum wages are a price control, which hindered efficient contracts and had adverse consequences.

What are the views of the local government officials who have operational responsibility for labour relations? Light was shed on their attitudes towards the Labour Contract Law by a study jointly

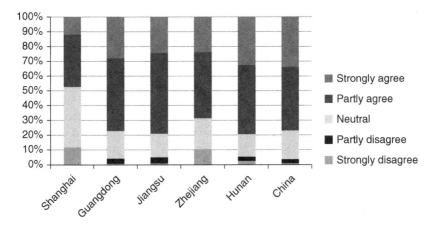

Figure 6.1 Local government officials' response to the proposition that the Labour Contract Law was having a positive effect in stabilising labour relations in 2013
Source: 2013 Institute of Labour Studies survey, Renmin University of China (2013)

carried out in 2013 by the Labour Relations Institute at Renmin University of China and the Ministry of Human Resources and Social Security. They surveyed the officials in charge of labour relations for the local governments in 29 of China's 31 mainland provinces (excepting Tibet and Shandong), both at the city level and county level, to assess their views about government's role in promoting harmonious labour relations. The number of questionnaires returned was 2169, of which 1874 were from county level. Figure 6.1 provides some of the results. The survey found that the great majority of provincial government officials (85.6 per cent) believed that the Labour Contract Law was having a positive effect in stabilising labour relations. It was considered by 89.9 per cent of the county government officials that the Law strengthened the legal foundation of their work. From only one of the provinces was it reported that the introduction of the Law did not have positive benefits for the development of the local economy. There were, however, substantial discrepancies between provinces in their assessment of the influence of the Law on economic development. At one extreme, Shanghai held more negative views, with 11.8 per cent of the officials expressing adverse criticism. By contrast, Jiangsu was more positive, with 78.7 per cent of the officials considering the effects on economic development to be beneficial.

Redirecting Individual Labour Relations Policy

Early on in the market reforms, the main objective of the government was to establish a market for labour that had not existed under the planned economy. But it became clear that this process of market reform could damage the interests of workers. For example, reform of state-owned enterprises resulted in large numbers of workers being laid off. Deep division between the urban and rural labour markets created severe problems with the many migrant workers whose long-term interests were neglected (Li, 1998; Sun, 2002; Yu, 2010). The emphasis on labour flexibility in the reforms encouraged massive use of short-term employment contracts. The consequent deepening of the division of interests between enterprises and workers increased labour conflict. The number of individual labour disputes rose from about 19,000 in 1994 to 666,000 in 2013. Collective labour disputes increased in number from 1,482 in 1994, to 6,783 in 2013.[1]

It has been argued that the most important issue for government during this early period of reforms was to reduce the social shock in order to achieve a smooth transition of labour relations in state-owned enterprises. The policies were essentially restorative measures. They were intended to provide substitutes for the previous political and social functions of state-owned enterprises, but also to compensate workers for the loss of their economic and political status in order to maintain stability (Li, 2003; Zheng, 2009).

With the introduction of a series of laws from 2008, including the Labour Contract Law and the Social Insurance Law, government intervention in individual labour relations addressed new targets. The protection of labour rights gradually became an independent policy goal. In contrast with the 1995 Labour Law, the prime legislative purpose of the Labour Contract Law changed to one of 'building and developing harmonious and stable labour relations' (Article 1). The protection of workers' rights was now a quite distinct policy objective (Chang, 2008; Cooke, 2011: 186).

The government's single-minded focus on the flexibility of the labour market had evolved to focus on the stability and flexibility of labour relations. The Labour Contract Law changed the law in order to reduce the flexibility of employment contracts. It did this by imposing strict limits on fixed-term contracts, while broadening the scope of contracts without a fixed period. The Law changed the overall structure of employment, reversing the trend towards short-term contracts (Wang, 2008). It was

[1] China Statistical Yearbooks (1995–2014).

appreciated that labour is a special commodity and that its excessive commercialisation would create social problems. Despite the fact that the government had given considerable autonomy to employers, it was felt that some kind of restriction must be put on their rights (Yang, 2011).

To summarise, the government has intervened in individual labour relations by setting labour standards and regulating employment contracts. The enactment of the Labour Contract Law completed this process, providing the basis for balancing the legitimate rights and interests of both enterprises and workers. A practical consequence, however, has been to awaken workers' awareness of their rights and of their potential solidarity. This laid the foundation for the development of collective labour relations.

The Regulation of Collective Labour Relations

In sharp contrast with the individual picture, the institutions of collective labour relations are still deficient after thirty years of market reforms. In many ways the system of the planned economy continues with little change of the out-dated legislation. The government dominates collective consultation and conflict resolution in a system that has been described as 'being led by the Party and government and managed by the exercise of power' (Li, 2013). There are three key features of this arrangement. The trade unions are controlled by the Party and government and use of collective consultation is determined by administrative power. Appeals and arbitration procedures exist to deal with collective labour disputes. Strikes, described as mass worker incidents, are dealt with by emergency provisions.

The Regulation of Collective Consultation

Apart from the Labour Law, the Trade Union Law and the Labour Contract Law, the regulation of collective consultation and collective contracts is mainly covered by the Collective Contract Provisions of 2001. These provisions specify the legal requirements of collective consultation: the principles, content, agents, procedures and the supervisory responsibility of the government. Trade unions would normally be the representatives of the employees' side, but if there is no trade union, representatives could also be elected by the workers directly. There are prohibitions of 'yellow dog clauses' that make non-membership of a union a condition of employment, and also of dual representation. Article 33 states that 'collective contracts should be signed by the enterprise and trade union representatives of the workers. If the enterprise does not establish trade unions, companies should sign the contract with representatives elected directly by workers'. Article 24 adds that 'employer representatives shall not serve concurrently as employee representatives'.

The legislation sets out the basic content of the collective agreement. Article 51 of Labour Contract Law provides that, through consultation between the employees and employers, both sides may sign a collective agreement on pay, working hours, rest breaks, vacations, health and safety, occupational insurance, benefits and other matters. Article 52 permits special collective contracts on health and safety, protection of female employees and pay fixing arrangements. The legislation sets out the necessary procedure to sign a collective agreement. This is that a proposal should be discussed and adopted by the employees, and then submitted to the enterprise's labour administration department. There are also specified procedures for the collective consultative process.

Regulations for Collective Labour Conflict

China's social structure has been described as a 'broken society' because many people are excluded and there is a lack of mechanisms for regulating conflict between stakeholders (Sun, 2013). Faced with growing social conflict and the need to limit risks, the Chinese government has made social control its first priority. It has been described as 'rigid stability' because the political and social fabric of society lacks the necessary toughness and ductility. There is no buffer, with the result that those in control are always in a state of high tension, willing to use any resource to sustain control (Tang, 2012; Yu, 2012). As a consequence, all activities that may lead to social disorder, including marches, demonstrations and other protests, are strictly controlled by the government. Labour strikes come into this category because they involve many participants and may have wider social impact. If the conflict cannot be resolved quickly, it can lead to petitions, and even to violent action such as workers committing suicide by jumping off buildings (Chang, 2005).

The number of collective labour disputes has increased rapidly in recent years, raising government concerns about potential side effects. This gives labour conflict two completely different faces from the point of view of the government's conflict resolution strategy. The main form of labour conflict is legally defined as a 'collective labour dispute' when the number of participants 'consists of ten workers or more, and they have a common request'. This is defined as such in Article 7 of the Mediation and Arbitration of Labour Disputes Law, and Article 13 of the Rules on the Arbitration of Labour Disputes.

There is, however, a second face to collective labour conflict, which is that events are perceived as mass incidents by workers, and as threats to social stability. 'Mass incident' is not a formal legal term. But it features prominently in government political reports. In 2000 the Ministry of Public Security defined mass security incidents as 'the joint implementation of the violation of national laws, regulations or rules; disturbing social order; endangering public safety; violations of the safety of citizens or of public or private property'. Mass incidents have been classified into five types: action in defence of rights; public expression of anger; social unrest; social disputes; and organised crime. Worker action in pursuit of their legal rights is one of the most important types of protest (Yu, 2009). According to one analysis of data collected between 1990 and 2009, 35.0 per cent of protests are related to work issues and, of these, wage issues (12.6 per cent) and lay-offs (10.8 per cent) were the most common causes (Wedeman, 2009). Workers' participation in mass incidents accounts for 36.5 per cent of all incidents, and they are the main type of mass incident (Li, 2013).

Two completely different approaches are used by local governments to deal with collective labour conflict. The first is with the Mediation and Arbitration of Labour Disputes Law which permits an approach to dispute resolution through normal legal channels, including the use of mediation, arbitration and litigation. The second is to use emergency planning powers whereby a mass incident is considered a threat to social stability. Available to local government at all levels, this permits direct intervention and suppression.

Use of Arbitration Procedure   The main feature of the collective dispute resolution provisions is that the collective dispute is considered to be a special form of an individual labour dispute, and to be solved by application of the normal individual procedures. There had been no innovation in collective dispute resolution for nearly twenty years, after the 1993 Regulations on the Treatment of Enterprise Labour Disputes and the 1994 Labour Law and Collective Contract Provisions. Since 2012, however, there have been four laws relating to collective disputes, including the Labour Law, the Labour Contract Law, the Trade Union Law and the Mediation and Arbitration of Labour Disputes Law. In addition there have been a number of special administrative regulations, relating to collective contract provisions and the regulation of arbitration. But these newer regulations still broadly follow the principles set out in 1993.

The procedures for collective disputes follow from the Mediation and Arbitration Law. Article 7 states that where 'the number of workers in a labour dispute is more than ten and they have a common request, they may elect a representative to participate in mediation, arbitration or litigation'. That is to say, the law has no special procedure to deal with collective disputes, other than allowing workers to elect representatives to participate. Collective disputes are essentially considered to be the sum of individual disputes. If the dispute involves pay or industrial injury compensation, workers can also appeal directly to the relevant government departments. In addition, collective disputes on some issues can also be submitted to labour inspectors. The departments can investigate whether there has been illegal behaviour that might merit criminal prosecution.

Use of Emergency Plans   Generally local governments deal with mass incidents under the remit of an 'emergency plan'. All provinces have an emergency plan for public incidents, in which mass worker incidents are classified as an incident category. In Jiangsu province, for example, there are four levels of event, from 'very urgent' down to simply 'urgent'. The very urgent level is defined as occurring when 'the number of participants is more than 5000, and will seriously affect social stability'.[2] The procedure is jointly coordinated by the provincial Party committee and the provincial government.

By their unpredictable nature, mass worker incidents pose a potential threat to social stability. Local governments follow the guidelines that are 'for and only for the maintenance of stability' (Li, 2013). This has a double significance. First, in dealing with mass worker incidents, a local government clearly has no intention of helping either the workers or the employers; their purpose is to maintain social stability. Secondly, the involvement of local government is strictly limited to preventing immediate unrest, and they have no intention to construct an ongoing resolution process. Although 27 of the 31 mainland provinces have their own collective consultation regulations, for most of them (16 of the 31 provinces) their content exactly follows the national provisions. The regulations of two of the others do not consider the resolution of collective labour disputes as such. Only the regulations of Shanghai and Hunan provinces expanded the definition of 'collective labour disputes', but in their resolution procedures they still comply with the principle of 'coordination by government' that is mentioned in the Special Regulations on Collective Contract Provisions (Tu, 2013).

The instructions for local government cover, among other things, interpretation and implementation of the law, provision of compensation, persuasion and the discouragement and repression of strikers (Li, 2013).

---

[2] www.gov.cn/yjgl/2006–03/22/content_233536.htm.

The main tactic for local government officials is to divide the workers and to decentralise the protest. Police are to be used as a threat to control the scale of the event, and in some cases to punish worker activists. It has been suggested that local officials have developed three main tactical responses for the control of unrest. These are, bargaining with the protestors, smothering them in legalistic bureaucracy and using patronage to win them over. The objective is to de-politicise the workers' collective action in order to maintain social stability in a context of market exchange (Lee and Zhang, 2013).

There are two sorts of intervention. If the number of participants is small and they only concentrate inside the factory, local government officials tend to take a wait-and-see approach and rarely intervene directly. However, if workers gather on a large scale with more than 1,000 participants and the action is illegal, or if the number of participants is smaller but involves a wide social range, local officials tend to intervene strongly. This may include sending police to control the site, and arresting the main organisers and activists. In recent years, some local governments have shown signs of acting in a more conciliatory way, as the mediators of a bargaining process, but so far the number of such cases is relatively small. An example was the strike of Guangzhou Sheng Lian Plastic Hardware Mold Co. Ltd in 2013, where local officials mainly played a mediation role (Li, 2015).[3]

The Effectiveness of Regulations

Formalisation of Collective Consultation   The construction of collective labour relations from the top down, led by the Party and government, has progressed in step with labour market reforms. It included the reform of trade unions as the main actor in the labour market and the promotion of their role in collective consultation. The Trade Union Law specifies that the basic duty of the trade union is to protect the legal rights and interests of workers. Trade unions safeguard the overall interests of the whole people, but they also represent and safeguard the legal rights and interests of workers, which is generalised as the 'dual protection' principle. Under this principle, as labour becomes exposed to markets, trade unions should establish a form of workers' club. Its responsibilities should be to promote democratic participation in the enterprise; to spread information about factory issues; to help disadvantaged workers; to participate in applying legislation; to promote tripartite consultation; and to help workers to claim their legal rights.

---

[3] See https://clbchinese.org/1267.html.

The Labour Contract Law placed particular emphasis on widely promoting the establishment of trade unions and the development of collective wage consultation at enterprise level. These became the focus of All-China Federation of Trade Unions (ACFTU) activity after 2010. There were 2,767,232 trade union units in 2013, and the total membership reached 288 million in 2013 (including 110 million migrant workers);[4] 2.42 million collective contracts had been signed, covering 6.33 million enterprises, and 287 million employees.[5] The ACFTU have been active in spreading collective consultation, broadening the social impact of trade unions, and safeguarding the rights and interests of workers.

A serious problem for the trade unions is the superficial nature of much of their presence. In general, as discussed in earlier chapters, both trade unions and collective consultation are controlled and spread as an administrative exercise by the Party and government. This has the effect that the setting up of trade unions within enterprises is mainly controlled by the employers. As a result many new enterprise unions are no more than a token. They are meaningless from the point of view of the workers because they typically take the side of the employers when there is conflict with labour. It is true that the number and coverage of collective contracts has been increasing in response to targets set by the Party and government. But this often means that the collective contract is no more than an empty administrative act. The collective contract system, far from the original intention of protecting the rights and interests of workers and improving working conditions, has become a hollow performance index for local government.

Unionisation rates and union density only become useful indicators of effective collective labour relations if the associated collective agreements are the result of a real negotiation, and if their content is both substantial and is implemented in practice. If the trade union in an enterprise is not representative, it is not possible to have what would generally be considered to be proper collective bargaining. Collective agreements that are no more than formulaic and without substantial content will have no effect in regulating working conditions. What is currently normal at enterprise level, and especially in the private sector, is that the employer is faced with fragmented and unorganised workers instead of effective trade unions.

Failure in Strike Prevention   The use of labour arbitration and emergency measures may have had some limited effect, but they have not

[4] http://gb.cri.cn/42071/2014/07/03/6071s4600890.htm.
[5] http://acftu.people.com.cn/n/2014/1015/c67502-25840765.html.

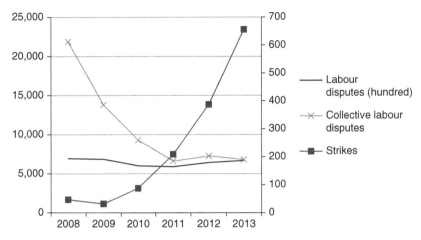

Figure 6.2 Labour conflict in China, 2008–2013
Sources: The data of individual labour disputes (100) (left hand side) and collective labour disputes (left hand side) are from China's Labour Yearbook (2009–2014). The data on strikes (right hand side) are from the website: China Labour Bulletin & China Strike.[6]

provided an effective long-term means of preventing a rising trend of strikes. The number of collective labour disputes that are officially registered with the arbitration system did decline after 2008 and, at time of writing, appears to be relatively stable. By contrast, however, the number of work stoppages is continuing to increase. This reflects a major change in the form of collective labour conflict. Arbitration within the legal system is being gradually abandoned as more and more workers choose instead to defend their rights by taking strike action. It has been argued that the dispute mediation and arbitration system has reduced the number of workers involved in officially registered collective labour disputes, but it has not significantly decreased their frequency (Zhuang, 2013; Zhuang and Yue, 2014).

Arbitration procedures have failed to reduce the number of conflicts between labour and capital. Instead, because of its low efficiency and perceived corruption, workers may well become disillusioned with the law (Zhuang, 2013). They may gradually lose the desire to fight for their rights through legal channels, and instead choose to defend their interests by strike action. This implies that the increase in the incidence of worker

[6] China Labour Bulletin only provide data from 2008 to 2010, so China Strike used as the data source for 2011–2013.

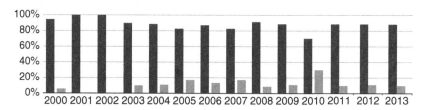

Figure 6.3 The percentage share of rights disputes and of interest disputes in China, 2000–2013
Sources: Data from 2000 to 2010 are from *A decade of change: the workers' movement in China 2000–2010*,[7] p. 14; data from 2011 to 2013 are from 2013 Institute of Labour Studies survey.

mass incidents may be caused by loss of confidence in legal channels. This possible displacement effect is supported by the evidence in Figure 6.2, showing the incidence of different types of labour dispute from 2008 to 2013. The number of individual labour disputes registered remained fairly unchanged. The number of registered collective labour disputes declined from 2008 before levelling out in 2011. But, with the caution that it was necessary to link two different data sources, the number of strikes appears to have grown rapidly over the period from 2009.

Changes in the Nature of Collective Disputes   After 2008 the nature of workers' unrest began to change. Collective grievances gradually altered from being about the defence of legal rights to more assertive calls for better working conditions and higher wages (Butollo and Brink, 2012; CLB, 2012; Elfstrom and Kuruvilla, 2014). Since these demands are beyond what the law permits, the official arbitration procedures cannot resolve them. Workers are clearly aware that their ambitions cannot be achieved through the arbitration agency, so they may try other legal channels, but they also continue to consider strikes and other non-legal means.

Survey data support this view that the nature of collective labour conflict has changed. Before 2003, disputes of interest (relating to improvements of pay and working conditions) were comparatively rare but, as Figure 6.3 shows, they rose afterwards to amount to typically around ten per cent of all disputes, with a 'spike' of around 30 per cent in 2010. It should be noted that a different data source was required for the years 2011–2013.

---

[7] www.clb.org.hk/en/sites/default/files/File/research_reports.

If we consider rights disputes on their own, the main cause of grievance has changed. In the past, the majority of cases involved the employer failing to meet agreed working conditions, such as not paying arrears of wages. Because of the Labour Contract Law and the consequences of industrial restructuring in some provinces, disputes are now more often about financial compensation for factory closure, merger and relocation. For example, in Shenzhen in 2011, there were 282 collective petitions, 415 collective labour disputes and 692 strikes, most of which arose from the enterprise restructuring.[8] In Zhejiang Province in 2008, disputes over wage arrears accounted for 80 per cent of all the labour dispute cases, and in some areas within it they reached 90 per cent. But after 2008 this dropped to about 60 per cent, with other types of labour dispute increasing.[9] In Anji, a county within Zhejiang Province, 44 conflicts provoked by enterprise restructuring took place in the one year 2014, involving 3512 employees.[10] It has also been shown that a quarter of strikes between 2011 and 2013 in China were associated with the relocation or closure of enterprises, of which 90 per cent occurred in the manufacturing sector (Dai and Li, 2014).

Lacking autonomy in their industrial policies, local governments had to intervene directly in collective labour relations to meet their prime objectives of political security, economic development and social stability (Li, 2015). Because the top priority is placed on maintaining stability, local governments strive to control collective labour relations in order to avoid the short-term escalation of conflict that might increase social tension. In the longer run, however, this use of direct controls does not reach the fundamental causes of collective labour conflict.

Local Government Response to Collectivism in Labour Relations

The arrangements described were sufficient to maintain the basic stability of Chinese society through the main period of economic reforms, without major strike waves or uncontrolled social unrest. But things have changed since 2008. Changes in the nature of labour conflict are presenting a major challenge of collective labour problems to the unilateral leadership style of the government. This section looks at the

---

[8] http://finance.people.com.cn/n/2013/0225/c70846-20590604.html.

[9] www.lawyer800.com.cn/ZXDT/20121227/126187.html.

[10] http://acftu.people.com.cn/n/2014/1016/c67502-25843411.html.

attitudes, resources, and behaviour of government – and mainly of local government – in the face of the collective transformation of labour relations.

Attitudes

Local governments generally still have a positive view of the degree of harmony in China's labour relations. Evidence on this comes from the 2013 survey of local government officials conducted by the Institute of Labour Relations at Renmin University. When asked about this, 61.0 per cent of them judged local labour relations to be 'harmonious', and 9.5 per cent said 'very harmonious'. This suggests that, although reports of labour conflict are increasing, they were not considered to be affecting China's overall social stability. Collective labour disputes were reported by local government to be under overall control. But some provinces are more cautious in their reporting of harmony in their local labour relations than others. The provinces that appear to be less harmonious are Sichuan, Inner Mongolia, Shanxi, Hubei and Shaanxi. These are characterised by their relatively fast economic development at the time of the survey, which could have resulted in wider divergences of interest between labour and capital.

Despite this apparent local government belief that labour conflict is generally controllable, officials still believe that it has a negative impact on the local economy and society. For example, 35.1 per cent of the local government respondents considered that strikes are not 'normal' as a means of conflict resolution. Consequently, they believe that they should intervene in the bargaining process between employees and employers to maintain control. This might stem from a mistrust of the rationality of the behaviour of both employers and employees in labour disputes. Nearly 20 per cent of them said that they thought that workers who engaged in collective action are not behaving rationally. The local government officials also did not display much trust in the employers' strategy for resolving collective conflicts. Although 60.4 per cent of them said they believed that the employers' strategy is 'generally reasonable', 14.5 per cent considered it 'not reasonable'. This apparent mistrust of both sides is likely to have an influence in local officials' intervention in dispute resolution.

Resources

After the opening up of labour markets in China, the government has put a lot of resources, both financial and organisational, into labour market

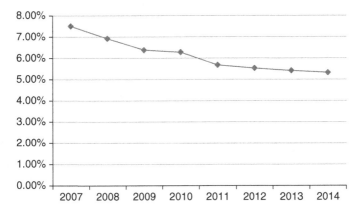

Figure 6.4 The proportion of spending on public security in general
public budget expenditure, 2007–2014
Source: China Statistical Yearbook (2008–2015)

reforms. This has played a positive role in stabilising labour relationships
and dealing with unavoidable conflicts between labour and capital.
It could be argued, however, that the increase in administrative resources
has not kept pace with the rise in collective labour disputes. Investment in
administrative resources appears to have reached a limit, and in some
respects human resource inputs may have begun to decline.

On the financial side, total expenditure on human resources and public
security at the national level has ceased to grow as a proportion of total
national expenditure since 2011; by 2013 it had declined by 8 per cent of
budget. Spending on public security as a proportion of the general budget
of public expenditure has, as Figure 6.4 shows, been declining since at least
2007. After rapid growth in the late 1990s, the number of people employed
in the labour inspectorates has declined by 7 per cent since 1997.[11]

The percentage of cases resolved by arbitration, and the change in the
back-log of arbitration cases left over from the previous year, are shown in
Figure 6.5. It appears that the percentage successfully resolved dipped
down to 50 per cent in the years before 2007, but then recovered and has
been between 60 and 70 per cent since 2009, which is a level of success
fairly typical of public mediation and arbitration services in other countries. The same figure shows that the backlog of cases unresolved from
the previous year spiked in 2009, then diminished, but was increasing by
2014.

[11] www.mohrss.gov.cn/SYrlzyhshbzb/zwgk/szrs/.

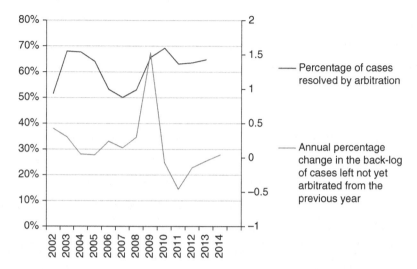

Figure 6.5 Labour disputes resolved by arbitration, 2002–2014
Sources: Labour Yearbook (2003–2015) – the percentage of
cases resolved by arbitration (left-hand axis), and the annual
percentage change of cases left for arbitration from the previous
year (right-hand axis)

There are, however, other signs that the local capacity to deal with
disputes may be suffering from constraints. Figure 6.6 shows that inactive
labour inspection, defined as the number of cases inspected only after
the workers make a claim and not proactively initiated, expressed as
a percentage of all the cases inspected by local government, has been
increasing. In 2002 the percentage was 51 per cent but by 2013 it had
increased to 91 per cent. The reach of the labour inspectorates may also
be diminishing. Figure 6.6 also shows that the proportion of all employees
who are covered by labour inspection, which has never been higher than
32 per cent in 2007–2008, had in 2013 fallen to 24 per cent.

Finally, there is independent survey evidence that local staffing is
inadequate. Local Ministry of Human Resources and Social Security
offices, in an effort to deal with collective disputes, introduced a policy
of co-ordinating labour relations with an E-platform at the grass-roots
level which is designed to help the staff to share current information
concerning collective conflict. In practice, however, according to the
2013 Institute of Labour Studies survey (by the present author), only
about one-fifth of local government offices actually fully implemented

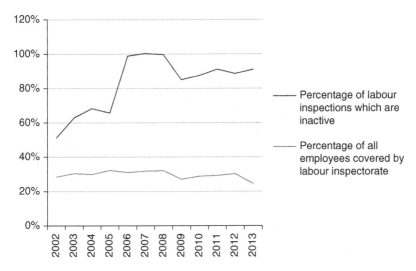

Figure 6.6   Inactive cases and coverage of labour inspection, 2002–2013
Sources: As in Figure 6.5

this. Although more than half of local governments do have labour relations coordinators, responses to open-ended questions suggested that there may be insufficient staff. Most of the coordinators were reported to be part-time employees, who were not in a position to play a serious role in the rapid resolution of collective disputes.

Changing Strategies

Local governments are changing their approach to labour conflict. This may be partly as a result of their limited resources. It may partly arise from their persistent mistrust of the competence of employers and workers to sort out their problems on their own. Evidence from the 2013 Institute of Labour Studies survey in Figure 6.7 suggests that a growing proportion of them are encouraging negotiation (under close supervision) between employers and employees to resolve conflicts, and fewer are resorting to suppression by force. The proportion of local government officials reporting that they attempted to coordinate the resolution of collective disputes rose from 46 per cent in 2008 to 58 per cent in 2013. Over the period from 2008 to 2103 there has been a decline of 7 per cent in the proportion of disputes resolved by voluntary collective bargaining without government interference. At the same time there has been a slight fall of 4 per cent in

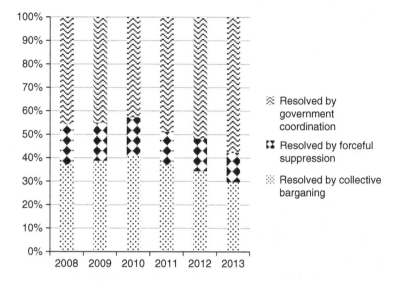

Figure 6.7 Collective labour conflict resolution strategies of local government, 2008–2013
Source: 2013 Institute of Labour Studies survey

the disputes settled by forceful government intervention. This does not mean that government intervention in labour disputes has decreased, just that the form it takes has changed.

The priority given to the maintenance of stability has not fundamentally changed. The combined percentage of local government coordination and suppression has not decreased but has increased in recent years. That is, local governments still play a leading role in collective labour dispute resolution, and the independence of the employers and workers in dispute resolution has decreased rather than increased. This is consistent with the view that local government intervention strategy has been shifting from simply repressing strikes towards trying to eliminate their causes (Elfstrom, 2014).

There is every sign that local government continues to see that it has an important role in controlling labour conflict. But officials are concerned about the risks associated with strikes because they consider that the disputants' behaviour is often irrational. The spread of labour conflict is placing increasing strain on the capability of government to control the problem by direct administrative coercion. Their response is increasingly one of actively facilitating negotiations between the disputing parties.

Conclusion: The Evolution of Government Labour Policy

The two linked goals for the Chinese government's labour policy during the process of economic reform have been establishing a working labour market and protecting labour rights (Wu, 2012). This contrasts with most advanced industrial countries where the two were developed quite separately (Hyman, 2008:273). The Chinese government both fixes statutory individual labour standards and provides a legal basis for employment contracts with which to regulate individual labour relations. By comparison with other countries, this has been a very substantial labour market intervention. But, in the past decade or so, the nature of it has been changing. The objectives of employment legislation have moved substantially since 2008 from an early concern to achieve labour market flexibility to a greater concern now with the stability of labour relations. The protection of workers' rights has become an independent objective.

In marked contrast, the regulation of collective labour relations is still deficient. As the freedom of employers and workers is constrained, local government plays an active role in resolving labour conflict. It intervenes directly to protect political security, economic development and social stability. But the current arrangements for collective labour relations face two major problems. The first is the artificial nature of collective agreements, both in terms of their content and of their extent. The other is the ineffectiveness of local government methods of strike resolution. This places the government under great pressure to improve collective labour law, and especially the law concerning collective bargaining and industrial action.

The Possible Evolution of Labour Policy in the Future

Labour policy in China is facing historical challenges which raise the possibility of further change. This raises the theoretical questions discussed at the start. Theories of rational choice and path dependence emphasise the role in institutional change that is played by exogenous shocks, such as political upheaval or war, while historical institutionalism concentrates on endogenous mechanisms of change. The different approaches draw our attention to different influences underlying institutional change and stability. Historical institutionalist theory suggests that the possibility of change lies in the internal characteristics of the system (Thelen, 1999; Streeck and Thelen, 2005:16–18; Hacker *et al.*, 2015).

Although institutions are designed to regulate social behaviour, they also need to reproduce themselves and to adapt in changing circumstances. Achieving this is far from automatic, and it always faces unique challenges of timing, which force the key actors to be creative and realistic. They are not mechanically driven by the institutional rules, but have the ability to reinterpret and even by-pass them.

There is currently considerable debate about the possibility of change in Chinese labour relations and about the path which it might follow (Chang, 2013; Li, 2013; You, 2014). Fundamental change in collective labour relations may not seem possible because the government will still play an important role in its regulation (Chang, 2009). But might there not still be gradual, incremental change in China? The analysis of this chapter suggests that, whether in individual or collective labour relations, there are challenges from the wider environment that are causing the government to adjust its policies. This suggests that labour relations policies in China are most likely to change gradually, in response to what has been described as 'the changing impact of existing rules' in response to external changes (Mahoney and Thelen, 2010:15–16). This sort of transition arises when, because of changes in the environment, strategic actors ignore some aspects of the rules, giving rise to change in the way institutions function but, despite these alterations in detailed implementation, the main body of the institution does not undergo a fundamental reform (Streeck and Thelen, 2005:31; Hacker *et al.* 2015: 184–6).

Although China's labour policies have faced huge challenges, they have not been fundamentally transformed. On the contrary, the government has changed its policies partially and incrementally. The growing shortage of labour and the workers' increasing awareness of their rights have led to changes in the nature of labour conflict, with disputes concerning legal rights increasingly being replaced by disputes of interest, such as demands for higher wages and better working conditions. The limitations of protections for individual labour relations, and the inadequacy of regulation of collective labour relations, have generated sufficient pressure on government for labour policy reform. Constraints on the resources of local governments are forcing them to intervene more selectively in order to improve the way that labour relations are conducted. This implies that labour policies are evolving. It is also possible that the government may introduce additional market-related institutions, such as it has with sectoral collective bargaining, as an alternative of direct regulation (Li, 2015; Lee *et al.*, 2016). China's labour relations will continue to be heavily influenced by government, and the most likely approach is one in which the government leads more by coordination than coercion.

References

Butollo, F. and Brink T. (2012), 'Challenging the atomization of discontent: Patterns of migrant-worker protest in China during the series of strikes in 2010', *Critical Asian Studies*, 44(3), September, 419–440.

Chang, K. (2005), *Laodong guanxi xue* [Labour Relations], Beijing: Zhongguo laodong shehui baozhang chubanshe [China Labor Social Security Publishing House].

Chang, K. (2008), 'Lun laodong hetongfa de lifa yiju he falv dingwei', [On the legislative foundation and legal position of the labor contract law], *Faxue luntan* [Law Forum], Vol.3: (23).

Chang, K. (2013), 'Laodong guanxi de jitihua zhuanxing yu laogong zhengce de wanshan', [The collective transformation of labour relations and the improvement of government labour policy], Zhongguo shehui kexue [Chinese Social Sciences], 6.

China Labour Bulletin (2012), 'A Decade of Change: the Workers' Movement in China, 2000–2010', Hong Kong, www.clb.org.hk/en/sites/default/files/File/re search_reports/Decade of the Workers Movement final.pdf.

Cooke, F. L. (2011), 'The enactment of three new labour laws in China: Unintended consequences and the emergence of new actors in employment relations', in Lee, S. and McCann, D. (eds.), *Regulating for Decent Work*, Basingstoke: Palgrave Macmillan.

Dai, C. and Li, Q. (2014), 'Xingdongxing jiti laodong zhengyi de yingxiang ji yingdui', [Influence and Countermeasures of strikes], *Gaige neican* [The reform reference], 19, 20–28.

Elfstrom, M. (2014), 'Labour disputes and changing governance in China', Conference Paper in Capital University of Economics and Business.

Elfstrom, M. and Kuruvilla, S. (2014), 'The changing nature of labour unrest in China', *Industrial & Labor Relations Review*, 67(2), 453–479.

Frege, C. and Kelly, J. (2013), 'Theoretical perspective on comparative employment relations', in Frege, C. and Kelly, J. (eds.), *Comparative Employment Relations in the Global Economy*, Abingdon: Routledge.

Hacker, J. S., Pierson P. and Thelen K. (2015), 'Drift and conversion: Hidden faces of institutional change', in Mahoney, J. and Thelen, K. (eds.), *Advances in Comparative-Historical Analysis*, Cambridge: Cambridge University Press.

Hall, P. A. and Soskice, D. (2001), *Varieties of Capitalism*, Oxford: Oxford University Press.

Huang, Y. (2003), *Laodongfa xinlun* [Labour law], Beijing: Zhongguo zhengfa daxue chubanshe [China University of Political Science and Law Press].

Hyman, R. (2008), 'The state in industrial relations', in Blyton, P. (ed.), *The Sage Handbook of Industrial Relations*, Los Angeles; London: SAGE.

Lee, C. K. (2007), *Against the Law: Labor Protests in China's Rustbelt and Sunbelt*. Berkeley: University of California Press.

Lee, C. H., Brown, W. and Wen, X. (2016), 'What sort of collective bargaining is emerging in China?' *British Journal of Industrial Relations*, 54(1), 214–236.

Lee, C. K. and Zhang, Y. (2013), 'The power of instability: Unravelling the microfoundations of bargained authoritarianism in China', *American Journal of Sociology*, 118(6), 1475–1508.

Levi, M. (2002), 'The state of the study of the state', in Katznelson, I. and Milner H. V. (eds.), *Political Science: the State of the Discipline*, New York/ London: W. W. Norton & Company.

Li, P. (1998), Zhongguo shehui jiegou zhuanxing de zhongjinqi qushi yu yinhuan [The recent trend and hidden dangers of the transformation of Chinese social structure], *Zhanlue yu guanli* [Strategy and Management], 5, 1–17.

Li, Q. (2003), *Gaige yu xiufu: dangdai zhongguo guoyou qiye de laodong guanxi yanjiu,* [Reform and repair: Research on the labour relations of state owned enterprises in contemporary China], Beijing: Zhongguo laodong shehui baozhang chubanshe [China Labour Social Security Publishing House].

Li, Q. (2013), 'Gongren jiti xingdong yu zhengfu yingji yu'an', [Collective worker protests and governments emergency plans], Huiyi lunwen [discussion paper].

Li, X. and Freeman R. B. (2015), 'How does China's new Labour Contract Law affect floating workers?' *British Journal of Industrial Relations*, 53(4).

Liu, M. (2013), 'China', in Frege C. and Kelly J. (eds.), *Comparative Employment Relations in the Global Economy*, Abingdon: Routledge.

Mahoney, J. and Thelen, K. (2010), 'A theory of gradual institutional change', in Mahoney, J. and Thelen, K. (eds.), *Explaining Institutional Change: Ambiguity, Agency, and Power*, Cambridge: Cambridge University Press.

Meardi, G. (2014), 'The state and employment relations', in Wilkinson, A., Wood, G. and Deeg, R. (eds.), *Oxford Handbook of Employment Relations: Comparative Employment Systems*. Oxford: Oxford University Press.

Pierson, P. and Skocpol, T. (2002), 'Historical institutionalism in contemporary political science', in Katznelson, I. and Milner, H. V. (eds.), *Political Science: The State of the Discipline*, New York/ London: W. W. Norton & Company.

Statistical Yearbooks, zhongguo gonghui nianjian, Beijing.

Streeck, W. and Thelen, K. (2005), *Beyond Continuity: Institutional Change in Advanced Political Economies*, Oxford: Oxford University Press.

Sun, L. (2002), 'Women zai kaishi miandui yige xinde shehui?' [We are facing a cracked society?], *Zhanlue yu guanli* [Strategy and Management], 2.

Sun, L. (2013), *Duanlie-20 shiji 90 niandai yilai de zhongguo shehui,* [Fracture: Chinese society since 1990s], Beijing: Shehui kexue wenxian chubanshe [Social Science Literature Press].

Tang, H. (2012), 'Zhongguoshi weiwen: kunjing yu chaoyue', [Chinese stabilisation: Dilemma and transcendence], *Wuhan daxue xuebao (zhexue shehui kexue ban* [Journal of Wuhan University (Philosophy and Social Science)], 5(65), 17–25.

Taylor, B., Chang, K. and Li, Q. (2003), *Industrial Relations in China*, Cheltenham: E. Elgar.

Thelen, K. (1999). 'Historical institutionalism in comparative politics', *Annual Review of Political Science*, 2, 369–404.

Tu, W. (2013), 'Zhongguo jiti laodong zhengyi chuli de falv guizhi jiqi cunzai wenti', [The current legislation of collective dispute resolution and its problems], *Zhongguo renli ziyuan kaifa* [Human Resources Development of China], 12, 104–112.

Wang, Q. (2008), 'Laodonghetongfa shishi hou de laodong guanxi zouxiang', [The future orientation of labour relations after the implementation of the Labour Contract Law], *Shenzhen daxue xuebao (renwen shehui kexue ban)* [Journal of Shenzhen University (Humanities & Social Sciences)], 5(25), 67–72.

Wang, Y. (2006), 'Shichang jizhi ke youxiao baohu laodongzhe quanyi', [Marketing mechanisms can protect the labour's rights], *Caijing* [Finance and Economy], 5, 24–25.

Wedeman, A. (2009). 'Enemies of the state: Mass incidents and subversion in China', APSA 2009 Toronto Meeting Paper.

Wu, Q. (2012), 'Jiti xieshang yu guojia zhudao xia de laodong guanxi zhili', [Collective consultation and the governance of labour relations under state dominance], *Shehuixue yanjiu* [Review of Sociology], 3, 66–89.

Yang T. (2011), *Gebie laogongfa* [Employment Law], Taipei: Wunan tushu chuban gufengyouxiangongsi.

You, Z. (2014), 'Dui zhongguo laodong guanxi de lingyizhong jiedu – yu chang kai jiaoshou shangque', [Another explanation of the collective transformation of labour relations in China: discussion with Chang Kai], *Zhongguo shehui kexue* [China Social Science], 6, 165–168.

Yu, J. (2009), 'Dangqian woguo quntixing shijian de zhuyao leixing jiqi jiben tezheng', [The main types and basic features of mass incidents in China at present], *Zhongguo zhengfa daxue xuebao* [Journal of China University of Political Science and Law], 6, 114–120.

Yu, J. (2010), *Kangzhengxing zhengzhi: zhongguo zhengzhi shehuixue jiben wenti* [Contentious politics: the basic issue of political sociology in China], Beijing: Renmin chubanshe [Beijing: Renmin Publishing House]

Yu, J. (2012), 'Dangqian yali weiwen de kunjing yu chulu – zailun zhongguo shehui de gangxing wending', [The current predicament and pressure on social stability: a discussion of rigid stability in China], *Zhengming yu tansuo* [Exploration and Discussion], 9, 3–6.

Zheng, S. (2008), 'Laodonghetongfa de gongneng yu zhidu jiazhi fenx', [An analysis of the functions and institutional values of the Labour Contract Law], *Shenzhen daxue xuebao* [Journal of Shenzhen university], 5, 73–77.

Zheng, Y. (2009), 'It's not what is on paper, but what is in practice: China's new Labour Contract Law and the enforcement problem', *Washington University Global Studies Law Review*, 8(3), 595–617.

Zhuang, W. (2013), 'Tiaojie youxian neng huanjie jitixing laodong zhengyi ma – jiyu 1999–2011 nian shengji mianban shuju de shizheng jianyan',

[Mediating to harmony: A panel data analysis on arbitral mediation and collective labour disputes, 1999–2011], *Shehuixue yanjiu* [Sociology Study], 5, 145–171.

Zhuang, W. and Yue J. (2014), 'Cong falv zouxiang jietou', [From the court to the street], *Zhongshan daxue xuebao* [Journal of Sun Yat-Sen University], 1, 145–157.

7   The Development of Collective Consultation

Lei Xiaotian

Introduction

Collective consultation has become important in the restructuring of labour relations in China. The past thirty years have seen the country's transformation from a planned to a market economy. But in marked contrast to the collective bargaining systems that developed in Western market economies, the collective consultation that has been established in China has unique features. It differs in terms of who are the key actors, the trade unions' role, the content and outcomes of the collective procedures, and in the implementation of collective employment contracts. The biggest difference lies in the role and responsibility of the state. The introduction of the Chinese collective consultation system has been so dominated by the state that its development has been completely different from Western countries (Warner and Ng, 1999; Clarke *et al.*, 2004; Brown, 2006; Wu, 2012). It has not been the result of a bottom-up contest of interests between labour and capital. It did not arise from labour disputes and the institutionalisation of a labour movement. Its development has been propelled by the government and has relied on top-down direction through the use of administrative power. Its development has been rightly described as a kind of 'compulsory institutional change' (Li, 2003). For these reasons, despite the fact that commentators often refer to 'collective bargaining' in China, this chapter will use the term 'collective consultation'.

Collective consultation has been promoted by a government campaign driven by administrative power which has, on the face of it, been hugely successful. There has been a steady rise in the number of the collective contracts and in the number of workers and enterprises covered. According to trade union data, by the end of 2013, 2.42 million collective contracts had been concluded, covering 6.32 million enterprises and 287 million workers. Despite this apparent success, however, substantial reservations have been expressed. Commentators have questioned whether management and unions should be subject to such direct government guidance, with wages and employment conditions tied to official guidelines. Workers, it has been argued, have little participation in the collective consultation process (Warner and Ng, 1999; Cheng, 2004; Clarke *et al.*, 2004; Xie, 2012). Such criticism has gained force since 2010, with the growing transformation from individual to collective labour relations (Chang and Brown, 2013). This has brought many challenges to Chinese collective consultation. For a new generation of industrial workers there has been an awakening of consciousness, with increasing tendency for disputes to be about matters of interest (as opposed to rights) and a growing propensity to strike, especially in China's coastal areas. One consequence has been the emergence of fresh forms of collective consultation.

This chapter will discuss the challenges to collective consultation and how it is changing. The first part will review its historical development in China. The second will analyse the characteristics of state-dominated collective consultation. The third will reflect on the challenges brought by the transformation to collective labour relations. The chapter concludes with a discussion of contemporary adjustments in collective consultation, particularly with regard to sectoral agreements.

The Development of Collective Consultation since the Opening-up of the Economy

Collective consultation can be traced back to the 1950s in China. At that time it was introduced in textiles, railways and electricity and other key industries. In the 1960s, however, political constraints caused it to stagnate. Later, as the policy for comprehensive market economic reform developed, collective consultation attracted more and more attention. In 1979, the All-China Federation of Trade Unions (ACFTU) proposed to restore collective contracts in state-owned enterprises. At that point, however, the provisions for collective consultation were still couched in general principles, and not in terms of specific operational norms. This contributed to unusually slow progress.

Private ownership developed rapidly in the 1990s, followed by increasingly difficult industrial disputes. Pressure grew for new labour legislation, not least for the development of collective consultation. The 1992 Trade Union Law and the 1994 Labour Law were important landmarks in the construction of Chinese collective labour law. After that the ACFTU took collective consultation as the focal point for labour laws concerned with workers' rights. It was seen as an important means both of employee participation and of labour relations regulation. But in the absence of direct government involvement, the promotion of collective contracts was proving very slow. Employers mostly turned a deaf ear to union requests to negotiate and were reluctant to sign collective contracts. This forced the unions to take action with the support of the local Party and drawing on government executive power. On 17 May 1996 a joint notice was issued by the Ministry of Labour, the ACFTU, the State Economic and Trade Commission and the Chinese Enterprise Association which ordered their branch organisations at all levels to work closely together to promote collective consultation. From this point onwards the implementation of collective consultation became not only the main task of the union, but also a national policy priority. This general mobilisation behind the collective consultation system became the distinctive feature of the first stage of its development.

The focus of the market-oriented reforms of the 1990s was on reducing administrative control at enterprise level and on cultivating freer markets as quickly as possible. These reforms did not safeguard labour rights. This was reflected in the two problems which became the main subject of labour conflicts at the beginning of the twenty-first century. One problem was labour lay-offs; demonstrations by laid-off workers posed a threat to social stability. In 2003, the number of employed or laid-off workers participating in such mass incidents reached 1.4 million, accounting for 46.9 per cent of all types of mass incidents (Qiao, 2010). The second problem was unpaid wage arrears which became particularly serious in construction and catering. This led to an explosion of labour disputes involving migrant workers.

The government responded by introducing policies aimed at 'building a harmonious socialist society, building a harmonious labour relationship'. This was accompanied by adjustments to the labour legislation. At the end of 2001, revisions to the Trade Union Law refocussed the basic responsibilities of trade unions in China towards workers. At the same time, the extension of collective consultation made great progress and the number of collective contracts shot up. The Ministry of Labour and Social Security and ACFTU held a joint conference, through the national tripartite consultation mechanism, which decided to make the development of a collective consultation system their central task. The Collective Contract Provision was published in 2004. By the end of 2007, further progress had been made and the number of collective contracts reached 975,000, covering 1,704,000 enterprises.

The international financial crisis in 2008 disrupted the growth of the Chinese economy. In the same year, the introduction of the Labour Contract Law and the Labour Dispute Mediation and Arbitration Law substantially improved protection of labour rights and provided procedures for resolving disputes through arbitration or judicial process.

Labour disputes rose sharply. In 2008, 693,000 labour dispute cases were submitted to arbitration, involving 1.21 million people. These included 22,000 collective labour disputes, which was an increase of 69 per cent over the previous year (China Statistical Yearbook, 2010). In the summer of 2010 there was a wave of strikes in the Pearl River delta, the Yangtze River delta and the Dalian Development Zone. Within just two months, 73 factories went on strike in Dalian with nearly 70,000 workers involved. The Nanhai Honda strike of that year attracted worldwide attention.

In response to the financial crisis, a series of national macro-economic policy adjustments had been made to alter the balance between economic development and social stability. The central mission of the 12th Five-Year Plan was intended to expand domestic demand and increase people's income. It set out that collective consultation over wages would provide an important means of adjusting income distribution as required at the macro policy level. In May 2010, ACFTU, the Ministry of Human Resources and Social Security (as it had become) and the Chinese Enterprise Confederation/Chinese Enterprise Directors Association issued what was called a Rainbow Plan. This called for the full implementation of the collective contract system, with a target coverage rate of 80 per cent or more of enterprises by 2011. In 2014, the labour relations tripartite body just mentioned issued plans for advancing the collective contract system further, placing particular emphasis on improving the quality and effectiveness of collective consultation.

The Characteristics of Government-Dominated Collective Consultation

The Procedure of Consultation

National policy towards collective consultation has two main objectives. One is the effective day-to-day conduct of collective negotiations at the local level; the other is continued expansion of collective contracts. To make everyday practice more effective, the ACFTU has called on local unions to learn from each other's experience. Examples of good practice were: a series of monthly activities supporting collective consultation on wages in Hebei province; a programme for training in negotiation skills in Tianjin; and the provision of a group of experts for advice on collective consultation in Liaoning province.

In order to expand collective contract coverage, since 2008 the ACFTU, the Ministry of Human Resources and Social Security and the Chinese Enterprise Confederation/Chinese Enterprise Directors

Association have issued many advisory documents. These included guidance on the rights and obligations of trade unions on collective consultation on wages, and advice on providing instruction in collective consultation. They included training programmes for collective consultation instructors and guidance on initiating regional and sectoral collective consultation. In the Rainbow Plan, for example, the ACFTU proposed to implement collective consultation in three years from 2010 in all the various sorts of enterprise in which trade unions had been established. The coverage of collective contracts was to exceed 60 per cent by the end of 2010 and (as mentioned above) to exceed 80 per cent by the end of 2011.[1] The ACFTU's target for 2014–2018 was to establish collective consultation in more than 80 per cent of enterprises where a trade union already exists, and in more than 90 per cent of enterprises with 100 or more employees.

Local government spared no effort to push forward collective consultation. Action included placing it in the outline of the 12th Five-Year Plan, setting up an instruction team in collective consultation on wages, issuing local laws and policy documents supporting it and putting collective consultation targets into the government performance appraisal system. To achieve the national strategic target, local government and unions also set their own targets. There has been significant progress. In Guangdong province, for example, in line with targets proposed by the Guangdong Federation of Trade Unions, collective consultation had been established in at least 60 per cent of enterprises by the end of 2011, 70 per cent by the end of 2012, and 80 per cent at the end of 2013.[2]

The first step for a trade union in initiating collective consultation is to make a formal wage claim. The Labour Law and Collective Contract Provisions give an enterprise's union the right to make such a claim. But management faces no legal obligation to respond. The act of making a claim places pressure on the enterprise to establish collective consultation and to sign a collective wage contract. In some enterprises, however, a trade union has not been established or, if it has, it does not have the confidence to make a formal claim. In this case, the local union would send the wage claim to management as the agent of the enterprise union. Local unions also often cooperate with government departments, drawing on their administrative power to put pressure on enterprises to respond with a wage offer.

---

[1] Website of Ministry of Human Resources and Social Security, www.mohrss.gov.cn/.
[2] Guangdong Zheng Zhengqu Chutai Gongzi Jitixieshang Xiangguan Guiding (Guangdong province issues regulations about wage collective consultation), *Nanfang Ribao*, (*Nanfang Daily*), 25th September 2011.

When collective consultation activity is supported by the government's performance evaluation system, its advancement is not just a trade union objective, but becomes a common responsibility for both union and local government. In practice, the unions usually choose to work with government, augmenting their authority with administrative power, and thereby increasing the rate of signing collective contracts. In these circumstances, the negotiating team is led by the leader of the Party committee or the chairman of the union, and team members include staff of the Department of Human Resources and Social Security, the Federation of Industry and Commerce, the Enterprise Confederation, the Department of Tax and Finance and other administrative departments. An additional resource is the use of law enforcement inspectors to place pressure on any enterprise that refuses to engage in collective consultation.

Relevant information is a key issue for collective consultation at enterprise level. With incorrect data, or an absence of any data, it is hard to establish the basis for a wage increase. In order to provide a framework for negotiations, the government publishes a range of statistics on economic development, earnings data and approved wage guide-lines. The reality of collective consultation at enterprise level, however, is that the main influence is that of the wage guide-lines that have been set. Most enterprises try to get a wage increase agreed around the middle of the distribution of those prevailing in local enterprises. There is, in practice, a marked similarity in the level of wage increases within any particular locality at any one time. This is partly because the emergence of large wage differentials between different enterprises nearby would affect the stability of labour relations by encouraging workers to move between enterprises and raising labour turnover.

There are additional ways in which external pressure can be put on enterprises which fail to engage. Collective consultation on wages has been included in the annual inspection system for enterprises. Inspection failure can result in fines and the issue of an official notice of criticism. As a condition of their holding an operating licence, the Industry and Commerce Department can require enterprises to establish a collective consultation system for wages. This happened, for example, in Qinghai province. Furthermore, the tax department can refuse to implement its pre-tax salary deduction policy for a company which has failed to establish collective consultation. This happened in the city of Dalian. Chief executives of enterprises that have failed to establish a collective contract system may not be awarded honorary titles above city-level; they may be denied candidacy to be representatives at the National People's Congress or members of the Chinese People's Political Consultative Conference (Wen, 2013).

There are also positive rewards to encourage collective consultation on wages. In the Tianjin Economic Development Area, for example, the government established a special money prize for outstanding contributions to developing wage growth procedures. The Area management committee give enterprises money rewards equivalent to 15 per cent of the wage increase, up to a maximum of RMB 1 million. In 2012, 33 companies shared more than RMB 12 million from these wage growth awards.[3]

The Role of the Parties in Consultation

The role of government in labour relations in most countries is classified as acting as a third party (Bean, 1994; Leat, 2001; Taylor et al., 2003). This third party role in collective bargaining has two main aspects. The government makes the procedural rules for collective bargaining by enacting laws and regulations. Secondly, the government may step in to assist the settlement of collective disputes by conciliating and mediating as a neutral third party.

In the Chinese model of collective conciliation, however, because the state is dominant, the government role is in part one of leadership and it cannot be separated from the exercise of administrative power. Several administrative departments are typically involved in collective consultation, from the initiation of the process, through participation in and supervision of it, through to overseeing the signing of a collective contract. If an enterprise refuses to accept collective consultation, or the resulting collective contract, the game changes. In classic collective bargaining, the key power relationship is between labour and capital. When the government becomes an actor in collective consultation, one player of the game is the enterprise, and the other player is the combination of government and the unions. The role of government is transformed from being a third party to being a central player.

Trade unions in China have what has been termed 'double attributes'. They not only play the role of the workers' representative, but also that of the government representative. The union's behaviour in collective consultation reflects this. The role of the union moves from being a bridge between management and workers to becoming an agent of the government. When a dispute arises during the collective consultation process, the trade union may initially act as a third party conciliator between management and workers. But underlying this, where the state is

---

[3] *Zhongguoqingnianbao* (*China Youth News*), Qiye Zhanggongzi Zhengfu lai Jiangli (Government to reward enterprises for wage increase), 05 February 2013.

dominant, the trade union can cast off the constraint that it lacks law enforcement ability by, in effect, borrowing the government's administrative power. While this greatly enhances the power of unions, at the same time it also strengthens the tendency for them to become administrative agents of government.

Employers have a built-in advantage in terms of their power over workers in the employment relationship. In China, in order to attract foreign investment, local government has traditionally turned a blind eye when employers have chosen low labour cost strategies that imply low wages. Employers have often taken advantage of this, preferring to make quick and convenient unilateral decisions on wages and working conditions so long as they are not seen to be violating the legal minima. Hiding behind the argument that wages should be determined by the market, most employers are not willing to negotiate with their workers. In some circumstances, employers may be willing to act together to negotiate over wages, but the motivating force is not to give workers equal negotiating rights, but to prevent escalating competition over wages between employers themselves. Wages can be stabilised through a collective agreement covering many employers who have formed an alliance and some form of employer organisation. This is the basis of the local sectoral collective agreements that will be discussed later.

Collective consultation when the state is dominant typically eliminates any role for workers themselves; they become passive actors. Its introduction in a top-down way tends to stall when it reaches enterprise level, having no more substance than a signed collective agreement. The enterprise-based workers' congress and any union advisory function becomes a mere formality. Some enterprises neglect to follow any democratic process with workers before signing a collective agreement. Their workers are effectively excluded and kept in the dark.

In short, Chinese collective consultation is not really a contest between labour and capital. The initiative and pressure to force employers to accept collective consultation come from the exercise of administrative power, rather than from worker solidarity. The resulting relationship between the actors, summarised in Figure 7.1, is very distinctive to China.

The Effectiveness of Collective Consultation

Collective consultation with legal collective contracts started in China in the early 1990s. When the Labour Law was introduced in 1992, 81,904 enterprises had collective agreements (Zheng, 1993: 160). Since the Labour Law and the Collective Contract Provision of 1994, the number

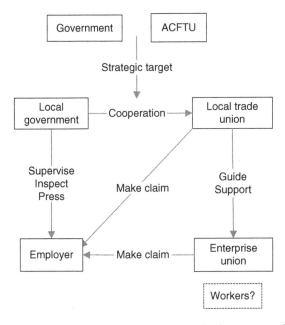

Figure 7.1 Interaction among actors in the process of collective consultation

of collective contracts, and the number of enterprises and employees involved, steadily increased. By 1996, as a result of government pressure, the number of collective contracts reached 114,526, which was a 118 per cent increase over the previous year (Zhang, 1997: 169). The rapid growth in collective consultation after that is shown in Figure 7.2. By the end of 2013, the Department of Human Resources and Social Security recorded 1.55 million collective contracts, involving 157 million employees.

The apparently impressive system of collective contracts does not, however, reflect the real nature of collective bargaining. Since the government pays more attention to the appearance of collective consultation than to the negotiation process, the strategy to promote collective consultation is essentially one of managing numbers (Wu, 2012). Collective consultation is formalistic. The pure formality of the contract text is often self-evident, and many contracts are vacuous, vague or simply a copy of legal material (Warner and Ng, 1999). From a legal point of view, there is a lack of commitment to ensure any bargaining process between capital and labour, or to involve union members who might participate in the devising or drafting of the

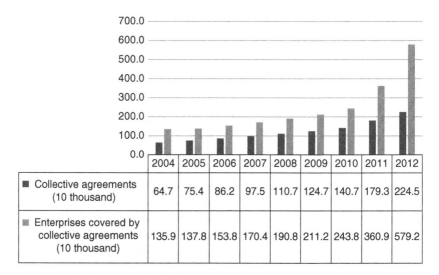

	2004	2005	2006	2007	2008	2009	2010	2011	2012
■ Collective agreements (10 thousand)	64.7	75.4	86.2	97.5	110.7	124.7	140.7	179.3	224.5
▨ Enterprises covered by collective agreements (10 thousand)	135.9	137.8	153.8	170.4	190.8	211.2	243.8	360.9	579.2

Figure 7.2 The number of general collective agreements and of enterprises covered, 2004–2012
Source: Statistical bulletin of the organisation and development of trade unions (2004–2012)

contract. The employers' reluctance to introduce any substantive details ensures that contracts are superficial and standardised. They often use model contracts, sent down from government. Such contracts have consequently failed to promote the union as an effective channel through which workers can express their demands and grievances (Clarke *et al.*, 2004).

The essence of collective bargaining lies in managing the conflict of interest between employers and employees. In practice, however, the power of enterprise management is such that it decides most labour standards unilaterally. The union at enterprise level is so dependent on management that it cannot engage it with any significant power that would give reality to collective bargaining. The promotion of collective consultation has in practice become focussed on the act of signing a collective contract. As soon as it is signed, the enthusiasm of government and the unions for it disappears. There is no institutionalised mechanism to supervise the implementation of the collective contract at enterprise level. Trade unions and the government are not given the duty of implementation and any supervision that occurs is by superficial checks.

The view that collective consultation does not have deep roots was supported by the findings of a nationwide survey of local officials in human resources and social security departments that was conducted by researchers of the Institute of Labour Studies at Renmin University in 2013, described in Chapter 6. The view that collective consultation was promoted by government authority rather than by worker or management pressure was agreed with by 82 per cent of respondents, with fewer than 6 per cent disagreeing. The current implementation of collective contracts was considered unsatisfactory by 39 per cent of them as against 16 per cent who considered it satisfactory. The principal shortcomings of the way it was implemented were seen by respondents to be negative attitudes held by enterprise management, lack of interest shown by government and its formalistic nature.

The Challenge to Collective Consultation since 2010

Changing Workforce Aspirations

Standing behind the contemporary challenge to collective consultation is the new generation of migrant workers. This was acknowledged as a government policy issue in 2010. Attention was drawn to migrant workers born in the 1980s or 1990s who, by comparison with their parents, had less farming experience and a higher level of education. They were seen to be very different in terms of the environment they had grown up in, their socialisation and in their aspirations for personal mobility, identity and careers (Ding, 2009). Their consumption patterns, information technology skills, social networking and expectations were hugely different from the older generation (Wang, 2001; Guo and Huang, 2014; Lu and Pan, 2014). They were familiar with ideas about human rights, freedom and equality (Xiong, 2014). They had more self-awareness, and were more concerned about the dignity of their work and about the right to control their own destiny and defend their legal rights (Cai et al., 2009; Yuan, 2013). The second generation of migrant workers, thanks to their personal experience of anger, pain and exclusion, combined with their use of social media and technology, have more concern with rights and class consciousness and are more willing to take collective action than their parents' generation (Leung and Pun 2009; Pun and Lu 2010).

The economic aspirations of the new generation are different. They are less willing than the previous generation to accept low wages. Most are reluctant to return to the countryside and wish to integrate into urban society. At the political level, while the older generation only seek economic benefits through work, the new generation not only desire economic returns, but also seek to participate in decisions in their enterprise.

They are more likely to take action to express their wishes instead of remaining silent (Chen, 2011). This was illustrated in the 2010 strikes. Striking Nanhai Honda workers explicitly put forward demands which included better pay, promotion prospects and reform of the enterprise union. The core appeal of workers in the Dalian Development Zone strikes was also about wage growth, reflecting their wish to share the achievements of economic development. These changes in consciousness suggest that the new generation of workers will continue to pursue greater bargaining rights, and this is likely to have a substantial impact on collective consultation.

Changes to Collective Consultation Caused by Strike Action

This rise in workers' economic aspirations is reflected in an increase in the proportion of disputes that are concerned with interests rather than rights, discussed in Chapters 2 and 9. Although in most of the workplaces where strikes broke out in 2010 the workers' pay was significantly higher than the local minimum wage, its level was considered to be low. Workers called for higher wages and better welfare, and peace was restored only when wages were increased. The fundamental nature of the conflict was that it was over a dispute of interest (Chang and Brown, 2013). China's basic labour laws do provide minimum individual substantive rights, but workers aspired for something better. In the absence of any procedure to resolve grievances over disputes of interest in advance, there is likely to be increasing resort to strike action.

The increased use of strikes is having a substantial impact on attitudes towards collective consultation. Most strikes are eventually resolved by collective consultation. As a result, spontaneous strikes have become a tacit mechanism to initiate collective negotiations on issues of interest (Li, 2011b). The procedural sequence is, however, in marked contrast with that in the Western market economies. Whereas collective bargaining in those countries commences with formal talks before strike action, and the strikes are last resort when there is a deadlock, in China strikes occur first and are typically followed by collective consultation in search of a solution.

In considering the increased use of strikes, it is useful to distinguish two sources of worker power: association power and structural power. Association power arises from the workers' collective organisation. Structural power comes from workers' position in the economic system (Arrighi and Silver, 1984; Wright, 2000). Structural power can be further divided into that based on the market-place and that based on the workplace. Structural bargaining power deriving directly from the market-place arises from the scarcity of required skills. Structural bargaining power exercised within the workplace depends upon the strategic position of workers within the production process (Wright, 1997). Let us consider these in turn.

For Chinese workers, the associational power arising from spontaneous strike action is quite different from that arising from their being members of the official union. There are numerous instances of workers' engaging in spontaneous strike action without initial use of the official union – the strikes at Honda and Yuyuan in 2010 were examples. They mobilised collective action by using internet communications and they enhanced their bargaining power by drawing in outside expertise. There was a chain-reaction of strikes to other enterprises which amplified the unofficial associational power of the workers.

The market basis of structural bargaining power has been evident since about 2004 when a shortage of migrant workers became increasingly apparent. This first arose on the east coast of China, then in the Yangtze River delta region and later in Anhui, Henan, Shaanxi and other mid-western areas. It was evident that rural areas were no longer an apparently inexhaustible source of labour; there was a growing shortage of migrant workers (Guo, 2014). Official statistics suggested that in 2012 the total size of the working age population actually fell by 3.45 million, and that this decline will continue as a result of demographic changes in China's age structure.

The workplace basis of structural bargaining power depends on how far the position in which workers are situated, in either the production process or the supply chain, will provide them with potential leverage if their ceasing work causes consequential disruption. The modern auto industry has high dependence on extended supply chains involving many hundred component suppliers. Problems with any one supplier can quickly affect the whole industry. For example, the gearbox assembly shop strike in Nanhai Honda took place in a key position in the workplace. Its closure prevented other production, within Honda and beyond. Other enterprises within the corporation that had to close down as a consequence included Guangzhou Honda, at an estimated cost of RMB 230 million, and Dongfeng Honda at a cost of more than RMB 100 million (Lin, 2011).

Collective consultation that has been initiated by strike action is fundamentally different from that arising from government pressure. Table 7.1 summarises this difference. Formal collective consultation is usually the result of top-down guidance from government or from a higher level in the trade union. By contrast, it is the pressure placed directly on the employer by labour that causes the employer to become

Table 7.1 *Different characteristics of collective consultation arising from government direction and from strike action*

	Government directed collective consultation	Collective consultation initiated by strike action
Role		
A. Government	Participant in formal ritual	Third party in a negotiation
B. Trade Unions	Agent of government	Mediator
C. Employers	Actor in a consultation	Negotiating actors
D. Workers	Passive actors	Engaged actors
Bargaining process		
A. Initiator	State/Unions	Strikes
B. Government's strategy	Target management	Mediation of settlement
C. Trade union strategy	Performance evaluation	Coordination
D. Source of bargaining power	Administrative power	Workers' collective power
E. Attitude of Management	Resistance or reluctant compliance	Passive participation

involved in collective consultation initiated by strikes. In the former, top-down mode, the union typically does not consult the workers effectively and is unable to represent their interests as workers perceive them. It is the unity of workers and their collective power that is the basis of the collective consultation initiated by strikes, so workers are necessarily more involved. In addition, formal collective consultation lacks any true sense of bargaining, in terms of a power-related negotiation. The outcome may be called a 'collective agreement', but it is usually little more than a copy of legal minimum standards. By contrast, when collective consultation is triggered by a strike, wages are usually the core issue, and the outcome of the negotiation is usually significantly higher than the legal minimum.

Current Developments in Collective Consultation

Adjustments of Government Labour Policy

Since the 17th CPC National Congress in 2007, social construction has become a part of normal political discourse in China. The 12th Five-Year Plan promised that citizens' income would be doubled by 2020, and that the minimum wage would increase by more than 13 per cent every year. At the same time the Plan encouraged collective consultation on wages by ordaining that pay should be decided jointly by employers and workers. Reflecting these policies, there was a surge of labour legislation, most notably the Labour Contract Law (2008), the Labour Dispute Mediation and Arbitration Law (2008), the Employment Promotion Law (2008) and the Social Insurance Law (2010). As a part of this, collective consultation was encouraged as an important way of coordinating labour relations.

The 2010 strike wave played a major part in giving a sense of urgency to building the collective consultation system. It now came to be seen as the solution to strikes, and as the best means of restoring production. The experience of collective consultation in response to strikes suggested strongly that workers needed some sort of regular and institutionalised channels for the expression of their interests. This suggested that there would have to be reforms to the existing system of collective consultation. The strikes pushed the ACFTU and the government to make the reform and improvement of collective consultation an urgent policy priority. The ACFTU's 2011–2013 work plan for promoting collective consultation on wages was published in January 2011. It involved a policy document which urged the top 500 international companies in China to establish collective consultation on wages. Local government also revised regulations. A number of provinces issued Party and government documents intended to develop the collective consultation system further. These documents have, for example, clarified the procedural role of local government mediators in bringing change to labour relations, and also in getting disorderly collective action back onto the rails through institutionalised collective consultation. The minimum wage standards of provinces also rose in real terms, in clear response to the demands for higher wages.

Trade Union Reforms

The strikes could be interpreted as a reaction to the long-standing imbalance of Chinese labour relations, as well as a consequence of official union silence with regard to labour grievances. Worker demands for union restructuring had been a repeated theme of many of the 2010 strikes, for example at Nanhai Honda, Ohm Electronics Shenzhen and Panyu Sumida electronics. The strikes forced the union to reconsider its position and its role in the collective consultation process and raised questions about the introduction of democratic reforms. The strikes were an important stimulus for union reform (Clarke and Pringle, 2009).

There was a wave of union elections at the enterprise level. In 2012, there were 163 direct elections for enterprise trade unions in Shenzhen, which received widespread public attention (Tusi and Carver, 2006). In 2014, the Guangdong Federation of Trade Unions announced their intention over the following five years to use democratic elections for enterprise trade unions all over Guangdong province. Elections were seen to be a way of allowing workers to choose people who would represent their interests (Chen and Zhang, 2004). They enhance the credibility of the trade union in the eyes of both the workers and management, which increases their capacity to engage in collective negotiation. In 2011, Nanhai Honda workers elected through direct elections a new union vice-president and 20 workshop group union leaders who then played a significant role in their second collective consultation. They were able to gather workers' ideas on a broad basis and to keep in close contact with workers. This meant that the collective consultation held the attention of all the employees and encouraged their personal commitment. In those enterprises which implemented union elections, collective consultation over wages took on a completely new appearance. Unions involved in collective consultation finally acquired a degree of independence and representativeness (Wen, 2014).

The election of negotiating representatives through bottom-up elections strengthened the bargaining power of the trade union by winning the workers' commitment and involvement (Shi, 2012; Wen, 2014; Zhou *et al.*, 2016). This provided a basis for mobilising bargaining pressure because it enabled consultation procedures to reflect worker interests better. One major outcome was that collective consultation over wages resulted in the linking of the size of wage increases to the business performance of individual enterprises, rather than to an externally determined norm. During the second Nanhai Honda collective consultation, the union proposed a common goal, that by 2013 the wage of front-line workers could reach RMB 3500, which would be comparable with FAW Volkswagen, the main rival. This strategy led to a collective agreement which increased wages and bonus by an average of RMB 611.

There are, however, also major difficulties arising from the lack of disclosure of suitable information for collective consultation. Union sources of information for collective negotiations are largely confined to the consumer price index and the average annual growth of industrial wages. There are no data available relating to individual enterprises, so that union negotiators are forced to rely on little that is more substantial than personal experience and impressions.

The Development of Sectoral Collective Consultation

Sectoral collective consultation on wages in China dates from 1995. It has experienced three stages: the initial exploratory stage (1995–2005), a period of rapid advance (2006–2008) and a stage of mature development (2009 to the present). In 1996, in response to the rapid development of small private enterprises, unions in Suzhou, Changzhou and elsewhere in Jiangsu province began to try out sectoral collective consultation on wages in some industries. The legal basis for these sectoral developments came from the official policy statements *Guidance for trade unions participating in the collective negotiation of salaries* (1998), *Trial measures for collective consultation on wages* (2000) and *Collective contract provisions* (2004). In 2006, the Ministry of Labour and Social Security, the ACFTU and the China Enterprise Confederation/China Entrepreneurs Association jointly issued their *Opinions on the implementation of regional and sectoral collective consultation*. Article 53 of the 2008 Labour Contract Law explicitly stipulated that, below the level of the county, trade union and enterprise representatives could sign a sectoral or regional collective contract in construction, mining, catering services and other industries.

An important innovation since 2009 has been the strength of the government's commitment to sectoral collective consultation. In 2009 the ACFTU published a directive promoting local collective consultation based upon individual industries or sectors. In 2011, the ACFTU formulated a working plan entitled *Going deep into the development of collective wage consultation*, which put forward regional and sectoral collective consultation as one of the current key priorities. Since then, a large number of sectoral collective wage consultations have been established. Typical examples have been the security industry in Beijing, the taxi industry in Shanghai, mining in Shanxi, the sheet metal industry in Jiangsu, catering in Wuhan, the machinery industry in Dalian, energy-saving lamps in Zhejiang, coal-mining in Henan, Jiangsu, Wuhan and Shenyang, and the hotel industry in Hainan. In October 2014, the ACFTU developed this further in a plan to deepen collective consultation over the period from 2014 to 2018. This has determined that the main direction of future advance will be based on collective negotiation on a sectoral basis. It is significant that collective bargaining developed historically in Western market economies on a sectoral basis. As discussed in Chapter 1, the fact that pay rises tend to follow profitability within the contours of product markets means that sectoral agreements fit well with the economic constraints and organisational possibilities of both employers and trade unions.

The route to this was not smooth. After the Trade Union Law was amended in 2001, it became possible to organise workers into union structures and to establish collective consultation above the level of the enterprise. At first, the ACFTU focussed on establishing unions at street and community level. After that, the organising activity moved to establishing regional collective contracts. However, the effect of these initial efforts at geographical organisation was very unsatisfactory. The main reason was that there was extreme differentiation of interests between employers who were operating across very diverse product markets within given localities. In addition, fierce competition for suitably skilled labour in the markets for particular products seriously hindered the establishment of employer associations.

Of landmark significance in promoting sectoral collective consultation had been the Wenling woollen sweater industry. As discussed in Chapter 5, in 2003 the employer association of the woollen sweater industry in Wenling in Jiangsu province signed a sectoral wage collective agreement on behalf of the manufacturers. After extended collective consultation, elected worker representatives and the employer representatives determined the wage rates and increases in an agreement for the whole sector. The Wenling model of sectoral collective consultation has been widely followed. Although evaluations differ for this experience, it had important new characteristics by comparison with previous Chinese collective negotiation (Xu, 2005; Cai, 2009; Li, 2011a; Wen, 2011; Lee et al., 2016).

The initiator of Wenling sectoral collective consultation had been the employers' side, rather than the Party or local government. Employers wanted to achieve a single wage structure to avoid disorderly competition between themselves and in order to reduce high labour turnover and eliminate the then high level of labour disputes. There is strong seasonality in sweater demand which meant that at peak production times the employers used higher pay to recruit skilled workers. In an effort to prevent frequent job-hopping, they often used unscrupulous methods such as with-holding wages, which escalated conflict.[4] In protest, in August 2002 workers petitioned the labour bureau.[5] The employers formed an association in 2002 and the matching industrial trade union was formed in 2003. It showed the potential for employers, when faced with high labour turnover and labour disputes, to get organised and to participate in collective consultation at the sectoral level.

A more recent example of sectoral collective consultation is the catering industry in Wuhan, Hubei province. In 2011 a collective contract for catering was successfully signed, after nearly three years of planning and many rounds of negotiations, covering 40,000 catering enterprises and 450,000 employees (*Guanzhou Daily*, 3 May 2011). Its origins lay in labour shortages and low wages which had been evident since 2007 (Xie and Guo, 2011).

---

[4] Interview with the chairman of Woollen Sweater Industry Association, 17 July 2012.
[5] Interview with the deputy director of Wenling Human Resources and Social Security Bureau, 17 July 2012.

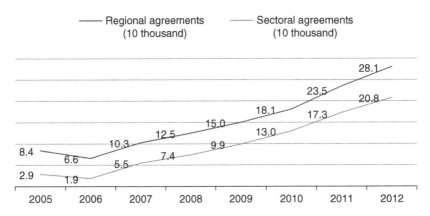

Figure 7.3 Regional and sectoral collective agreements, 2005–2012
Source: Statistical bulletin of trade union organisation (2005–2012)

The low entry threshold into catering tends to depress wages and in Wuhan it was one of the lowest paying industries and had 20 per cent annual labour turnover. The Wuhan Catering Industry Association, founded in 2003 and containing more than 400 large- and medium-sized catering enterprises in the city, represented the employers. The Wuhan Trade Union of the Catering Industry was not founded until 2012 so initially the higher level ACFTU trade union acted in the negotiation process for the catering industry. The resulting collective agreement raised pay in the catering industry 30 per cent higher than the minimum wage standard in Wuhan.

Under official encouragement, the number of sectoral and regional collective contracts has continued to increase (see Figure 7.3). Regional collective consultation mainly takes place in the very local area of districts, streets, villages, towns and industrial parks where small-sized enterprises cannot conduct the collective consultation by themselves. There is no typical model of regional collective consultation. By the end of 2012, the number of regional collective contracts reached 281,000, covering 2.88 million enterprises and 81.29 million workers all over China. But sectoral collective contracts on wages have a more formal structure and, according to the Chinese trade union statistical yearbook, by the end of September 2013, their number had reached 240,000, covering 1.43 million enterprises and 43.52 million workers.

There are constraints on the growth of Chinese sectoral collective consultation. First, the institutional infrastructure is often inadequate. The development of sectoral trade unions is seriously lagging which may result in the sectoral employer association having no union body with which to negotiate. Secondly, sectoral collective consultation is characterised by being dominated by the state. The negotiation and implementation of the contract of the Wuhan catering collective consultation, for example, was inseparable from the local government and municipal federation of trade unions (Xie and Guo, 2011). It is a kind of Party and government-led wage bargaining (Chan and Hui, 2013). Completing a successful sectoral collective consultation requires the setting up of a collective wage consultation system at many enterprises within the sector (Wu, 2012). Third, some sectoral collective contracts do no more than copy legal minimum standards. For example, the Wuqing artificial flower industry collective agreement did no more than set out that the wage of the workers in artificial flowers cannot be below the minimum wage. Sectoral collective consultation does not suit all circumstances, and its benefits for the workers concerned differ greatly with circumstances.

Conclusion

There have been two forces driving the development of collective consultation in China. On the one hand, there have been the government's efforts to build a civil society from the top downwards. On the other hand, there has been bottom-up labour unrest driven by the new generation of migrant workers. Both are responses to the fact that in any market economy the power of labour and capital are inherently unbalanced. The fact that Chinese institutions regulating employment have been so dominated by government means that they are very different from the sort of collective bargaining that developed in Western market economies. The union in China has been an extension of government; collective agreements have generally reflected government policy rather than the collective power and wishes of the workers. Insofar as the profits of the new market economy have been shared with the workers, it has been the result of direct government intervention. For this reason, in China it has been appropriate to refer to 'collective consultation' rather than 'collective bargaining'.

Collective consultation has, however, been adapting to changing circumstances. A new generation of workers seeks to share the prosperity of the enterprises they work in. They also seek more influence over how their work is managed. They have been encouraged by the increased scarcity of labour as migration from the countryside dries up. They are also aware that a different sort of collective consultation has been developing as a way of resolving spontaneous strikes. This has involved the union as mediator and the workers more directly through their elected representatives. The official trade union has also been successful recently in working with employer organisations to establish sectoral collective consultation. This has stabilised the labour market for many employers as well as enhancing pay and job security for workers. It has reduced the dependence of both employers and the workers on the authority of the government. The slowing of economic growth in China will create new problems for labour relations. But it is likely that collective consultation will continue to develop in ways that will help to build civil society in China.

References

Arrighi, G. and Silver, B. (1984), 'Labor movements and capital migration: The US and Western Europe in world-historical perspective', in C. Bergquist (ed.), *Labor in the Capitalist World-Economy*, Beverly Hills, CA: Sage.

Bean, R. (1994), *Comparative Industrial Relations*. 2nd ed., Abingdon: Routledge.

Brown, R. C. (2006), 'China collective contract provisions: Can collective negotiations embody collective Bargaining?' *Duke Journal of Comparative and International Law*, 16, 35–78.

Cai, F. (2009), 'Xieshangminzhu zai zhonguo yujing xia de gongneng yu kongjian', [The function and space of the deliberative democracy in the context of China]. Lilun Daokan (Journal of Socialist Theory Guide). No.9.

Cai, H., Li, C. and Feng, J. (2009), 'Liyishouxun nongmingong de liyi kangzheng xingwei yanjiu', [Behavioural research on the interests and benefit loss of migrant worker], Shehuixue Yanjiu (Sociological Studies), 1.

Chan, K. C. and Hui, S. I. (2013), 'The development of collective bargaining in China: From "collective bargaining by riot" to "party-state led wage bargaining"', *China Quarterly*, 217, 221–242.

Chang, K. and Brown, W. (2013), 'The transition from individual to collective labour relations in China', *Industrial Relations Journal*, 44(2), 102–121.

Chen, F. (2011), 'Bagongchao yu gongren jiti quanli de jianggou', [The strikes and construction of workers' collective rights], Ershiyi shiji (The twenty-first century), 124.

Chen, S. and Zhang, M. (2004), 'Zhongguo difang gonghui gaige yu jiceng gonghui zhixuan', [Chinese local trade union reform and the direct election of trade unions], Xueshujie (Academic Forum), 6.

Cheng, Y. (2004), 'Jiti tanpan zhidu zai woguo mianlin de wenti jiqi jiejue', [Problems and solutions: collective bargaining in China], Zhongguo Renmin Daxue Xuebao (Journal of Renmin University), 2, 136–142.

Clarke, S., Lee, C-H. and Li, Q. (2004). 'Collective consultation and industrial relations in China', *British Journal of Industrial Relations*, 42(2), 235–254.

Clarke, S. and Pringle, T. (2009), 'Can party-led trade unions represent their members?' *Post-Communist Economies*, 21(1), 85–101.

Ding, Z. (2009), 'Woguo xinshengdai nongmingong de tezheng fenxi', [The analysis of the characteristics of Chinese new generation of migrant workers]. Lanzhou xuekan (Lanzhou Academic Journal), 7.

Guo, Y. and Huang B. (2014), 'Xinshiqi gongren zhuangkuang de shehuixue niaokan', [A sociological bird's eye view on the state of the workers in the new period], Shehui, (Chinese Journal of Sociology), 4.

Guo, Zh.(2014), 'Woguo renkou chengzhenhua de pouxi', [The present situation of population urbanisation in China], Shehuixue Yanjiu (Sociological Studies), 1.

Leat, M. (2001), *Exploring Employee Relations*, Oxford: Butterworth-Heinemann.

Lee, C-H., Brown, W. and Wen, X. (2016), 'What sort of collective bargaining is emerging in China?' *British Journal of Industrial Relations*, 54(1), 214–236.

Leung, P. N. and Pun N. (2009), 'The radicalization of the new working class: The collective actions of migrant workers in South China', *Third World Quarterly*, 30(3), 551–565.

Li, B. (2011a), 'Wenlingshi hangye gongzijitixieshang de xingzhi yu zhidu jizhi yanjiu', [Study of the nature and process of Wenling's collective consultation of industrial wages], Wenzhoudaxue Xuebao (Journal of Wenzhou University), 24, 6.

Li, Q. (2003), 'Gaige yu xiu fu', [Reform and amendment: study of contemporary Chinese state-owned enterprise labour relations], Beijing: Zhongguo laodong shehui baozhang chubanshe (China Labour and Social Security Publishing House).

Li, Q. (2011b), 'Qindong jititanpan de qianjizhi', [A tacit mechanism to initiate collective negotiations], Zhongguo Renliziyuan Kaifa (Human Resource Development of China), 2.

Lin, Y. (2011), 'Zhongguo gongren jitixingdong kaocha baogao', [Investigation report on Chinese workers' collective action], Tianjinshi gonghui guanli ganbu xueyuan xuebao, (Journal of Tianjin Trade Union Administrators' College), 4.

Lu, H. and Pan, Y. (2014), 'Dangdai zhongguo dierdai nongmingong de shenfen rentong, qinggan yu jiti xiongdong', [Identity, emotions, and collective action of the second generation of migrant workers in contemporary China], Shehui (Chinese Journal of Sociology), 4.

Pun, N. and Lu H. (2010). 'Unfinished proletarianization: Self, anger and class action of the second generation of peasant workers in reformed China', *Modern China*, 36(5), 493–519.

Qiao, J. (2010), 'Laodongzhe quntixingshijian de fazhan he tedian', [Development and characteristics of labour mass incidents], Zhongguo gaige (China Reform), 7.

Shi, X. (2012), 'Gongren jitixingdong, gonghui zhuxi zhixuan yu gongzi jitixieshang', [Workers' collective actions, direct election of union president and wage collective consultation], Lilun yu Gaige (Theory and Reform), 5.

Statistical Yearbooks, zhongguo gonghui nianjian, Beijing.

Taylor, B., Chang, K. and Li, Q. (2003), *Industrial Relations in China*, Northampton: Edward Elgar.

Tusi, A. and Carver, A. (2006), 'Collective contracts in the Shenzhen economic zone in China, *The International Journal of Comparative Labour Law and Industrial Relations*, 22(4), 469–506.

Wang, Ch. (2001), 'Xinshengdai nongcun liudong renkou de shehui rentong yu chengxiang ronghe de guanxi', [The relationship between social identity and urban integration of the new generation of rural floating population], Shenhuixue Yanjiu. (Sociological Research), 3.

Warner, M. and Ng S-H. (1999), 'Collective contracts in Chinese enterprises: A new brand of collective bargaining under market socialism?' *British Journal of Industrial Relations*, 37(2), 295–314.

Wen, X. (2011), 'Jititanpan de neibuguojia jizhi', [The internal state mechanism in collective bargaining: evidence from the collective bargaining in the Wenling sweater industry]. Shehui (Chinese Journal of Sociology), 31.

Wen, X. (2013), 'Jiti hetong gongzuo zhong de xingzheng moshi yiji gonghui moshi', [The administration mode and the union dilemma in the collective contract system], Zhongguo dangzheng ganbu luntan (Chinese Cadres Tribune), 5.

Wen, X. (2014), 'Gonghui zhixuan: guangdong shijian de jingyan yu jiaoxun', [Direct election of the trade union: practical experience and lessons from Guangdong], Kaifang Shidai (Open Times), 5.

Wright, E. O. (1997), *Class Counts: Comparative Studies in Class Analysis*, Cambridge: Cambridge University Press.

Wright, E. O. (2000), 'Working-class power, capitalist-class interests and class compromise', *American Journal of Sociology*, 105(4), 957–1002.

Wu, Q. (2012), 'Jiti xieshang yu guojiazhudaoxia de laodongguanxi zhili', [Collective consultation and the governance of labour relations under state dominance: the strategies and practice of index management], Shehuixue yanjiu (Sociological Studies), 3, 66–89.

Xie, Y. and Guo, Y. (2011), 'Wuhanshi canyin hangye gongzi jitixieshang diaocha', [A survey of collective consultation on wages in the catering industry in Wuhan]. Zhongguo laodongguanxi xueyuan xubao (Journal of China Institute of Industrial Relations), 25, 6.

Xie, Y. (2012), 'Bie jiang gongzi jitixieshang zuocheng zhengfu he gonghui de ziyuzile', [Don't make wage bargaining a playground for government and union], *Zhongguo gongren* (Chinese Workers), 1.

Xu, X. (2005), 'Ziran zhuangtai de gongzi jitixieshang', [Wage collective consultation under natural conditions], Tianjinshi gonghui guanli ganbu xuyuan xuebao (Journal of Tianjin Trade Union Administrators' College), 13, 3.

Yuan, B. (2013), 'Xinshengdai nongmingong de canyu yishi yu quanli biaoda', [Participation consciousness and right expression of the new generation of migrant workers], Chongqing shehui kexue (Chongqing Social Sciences), 4.

Zhang, G. (1997), 'Zhongguo gonghui tongji nianjian', [Chinese Trade Unions Statistical Yearbook], Zhongguo shehui chubanshe (China Society Press).

Zheng, W. (1993), 'Zhongguo gonghui tongji n ianjian', [Chinese Trade Unions Statistical Yearbook], Zhongguo shehui chubanshe (China Society Press).

Zhou, L., Li, M. and Yang, T. (2016), 'Gonghuizhixuan ruhe tisheng yuangong gonghuichengnuo', [How do trade unions promote employees' commitment to the union?], Zhongguo renli ziyuan kaifa (Human Resources Development of China), 7.

8   The Challenges Faced by Employee Participation

Zhan Jing

Introduction

Industrial democracy and employee participation have never disappeared from view. They have been discussed from the time of syndicalism and the social labour movement of the late 1800s to more recent debates of Marxism, economic democracy, management studies and industrial sociology (Xie and He, 2008). In essence, the purpose of employee participation is to stabilise labour relations through mobilising commitment by extending employees' democratic rights and their economic interests in management. Contrary to the zero-sum logic of labour confrontation, it is based on the positive-sum aim of achieving 'win-win' solutions.

The development of employee participation in China can be traced back to well before the opening up of markets. The government had long emphasised the principle of socialist labour sovereignty, and enterprises had given it considerable attention. Workers' congresses, which involved both management and worker supervisors, were the main form of democratic management. At that time, whether or not workers appreciated that they were owners of the enterprise, it was a fundamental aspect of ideology that the enterprise was committed to their interests.

Since the opening up of the economy, the Chinese government has been concerned with how to enhance the incentives for workers and, so far as worker well-being is concerned, with the consequent constraints on management. The governance structure of state-owned enterprises had always been designed to support their operational efficiency, but more recent changes in emphasis have tended to weaken the workers' willingness to become involved in the organisation's management (Qi, 2005). The weakness of democratic management cannot be ignored in private enterprises either. Two factors contribute to this. They had no tradition of democratic management and, because they were wholly dependent on the market, they focussed on profit maximisation.

The tendency for capital to speak louder than labour has had a negative impact on the development of employee participation.

Despite earlier government guidance, private enterprises had done relatively little about employee participation. When legislative proposals appeared in 2010 that required democratic participation at the local level, opposition came to a head. In September 2010, during the discussion of regulations on democratic management in Guangdong province, the Chinese Manufacturers' Association of Hong Kong and the Chinese Chamber of Commerce, which represent enterprises with heavy Hong Kong investment, expressed their opposition in the press. They objected to collective consultation on wages and to proposals for worker directors. It was claimed that many Hong Kong companies would withdraw their capital if these regulations were passed.

Whatever the objections of private sector employers, as a result of economic and social development, the relative strength of capital and labour has been changing. The number of labour disputes is growing. In 2012 the labour dispute mediation and arbitration system dealt with 1.512 million cases, which was a 6.4 per cent increase over the previous year. In the summer of 2010 a series of spontaneous strikes broke out in the Pearl River Delta, Yangtze River Delta, Dalian Development Zone and the Beijing-Tianjin region. Within just two months there were 73 strikes in Dalian alone, involving 70,000 workers. China's labour relations are shifting from individual to collective (Chang, 2013).

Against this background, both central and local government have become more focussed on the potential of employee participation to encourage peaceful adjustment. Since 2007, more than 20 provinces and cities have issued local regulations to encourage it. In 2012, a joint instruction on 'enterprise democratic management' was issued by the Commission for Inspection on Disciplinary Matters of the Central Committee of the CPC, the Ministry of Organisation, the All-China Federation of Trade Unions (ACFTU) and three other departments. It was the first time that a group of departments had released regulations on the subject. These emphasised the importance of guaranteeing workers the freedom to speak out and also the important role of the workers' congress. They encouraged openness in factory affairs and the use of employee directors and supervisors as a basis for stable labour relations. In February 2015, in a policy statement entitled *Strengthening the building of socialist deliberative democracy*, the Central Committee of the CPC repeated its view that the workers' congress remains the basic form of a company's democratic management system, but added that it needs to be improved.

In this chapter we discuss the challenges facing the use of employee participation in the reform of Chinese labour relations, and how they are being met. The second part discusses the evolution of employee participation. We describe its main forms and its basic features in the third part. In the fourth part, the emphasis will be on the roles in these procedures expected of employees and unions, as the key participants. Finally, we discuss the prospects for employee participation in China.

The Evolution of Employee Participation

The Meaning of Employee Participation

The concept of employee participation became popular in Western industrial countries in the later twentieth century. In 1967, the International Labour Organization defined it as the 'participation of union representatives and employees in a company's management', specifying that employees should be actively involved in decision-making as participants rather than as passive spectators. It required that there should be some mechanism whereby employees would have a direct influence on their organisation's decision making. It was preferable that the entirety of ordinary employees should take part in the company's management, either directly or indirectly, according to specified rules (Chang, 2005).

There are three essential requirements for employee participation. First, ordinary employees, who would otherwise passively follow managers' instructions, should be given rights and opportunities to participate by their enterprise's owner or senior management. Second, these rights should be based on clear regulations and procedures. It is difficult for employees to feel a sense of participation unless they are given very specific ways of being practically involved. The rules of employee participation should as far as possible specify the activities and procedures that require employee involvement. Third, employee participation must have specified scope and limits. Its scope is the range of issues for which workers are entitled to participate and the organisational level at which they may do so. These rights are not unlimited. They do not imply that employees should be involved in every aspect of company management. Workers and managers still have different duties even where there is the highest level of worker participation. However wide the scope of participation, and even if it is accompanied by some changes in managerial roles, it cannot replace all the traditional roles of management (Cohen, 1988). The forms of employee participation covered in this chapter take a fairly moderate form, somewhere between the extremes of autocratic management on the one hand and workers acting as managers themselves on the other.

The Historical Development of Employee Participation

The development of employee participation in China can be divided into three periods. The first was from the foundation of the People's Republic of China in 1949 to the dawn of reform and opening up of the economy in the 1970s. In September 1949, Article 32 of *The Chinese people's political consultative conference programme* stipulated that state-owned enterprises should allow their staff to participate in management. After 1949, the enterprise management system of those geographical areas that had been initially liberated was extended and it became the unified national system. The early forms of employee participation in state-owned enterprises were mainly 'workers' representatives meetings', 'plant management committees' and 'workers' congresses'.

After completing the socialist transformation of the society, China started to implement the 'one-man leadership' system, which followed the example of enterprises in the former Soviet Union. This system met the technical requirements necessary for modernisation, but it weakened the scope for workers' democratic management. Some enterprises paid so much attention to the factory manager's authority and leadership that they abolished the worker representatives' role in the management committee, which effectively eliminated democratic participation.

At the 8th National People's Congress, in September 1956, the CPC decided to implement the principle of collective leadership by the Party committee in all enterprises. By specifying that overall leadership would be both by the factory directors or managers as well as by the workers' congress, it meant that they were to be led by the Party committee. In its policy statement, entitled *Several important issues on the working class*, in April 1957, the CPC called for the expansion of democracy and for rights of workers' participation in enterprise management. This involved giving workers the opportunity to supervise their company's management. During the period of socialist reconstruction, with the backing of central government, Chinese companies developed some unique democratic participation systems. The one that was most representative was described by Chairman Mao in 1960 as the 'two participation, one reformation, three combination' system. This summarised the idea that Party cadres should participate in work, workers should participate in management, that they should reform any unreasonable rules and regulations, and that cadres, workers and technicians should all work in combination. It was officially approved in 1961 under the title of the 'industry seventy points'. Chairman Mao called it the 'Ansteel constitution'. This was a clear reaction to the Soviet Union's 'Masteel constitution', which had emphasised, by contrast, the authority of the leading manager and a small number of experts, who provided clear financial incentives and very limited worker involvement. As a result of the Ansteel innovations, it was also made clear that workers' congresses should come under the leadership of the appropriate enterprise Party committee.

The second phase of China's participation arrangements was from the start of economic reforms in the late 1970s to the opening up of the economy in the 1990s. This was a time of transformation and development. Employee participation went into a crucial transition, against the background of reform both of the economic system and of state-owned enterprises. At this stage, the Party proposed to expand the autonomy of enterprises, giving them the right to manage their own financial accounts (Zhang, 2008). Starting in May 1979, the Capital Iron and Steel Company and seven other companies proceeded to increase the authority of their enterprise management. The factory director, under the leadership of the Party committee, was to take full responsibility for personnel management, employee rewards and punishment, and the workers' congress system(Lu, 2013). In 1980, in its report on *Expanding autonomy in pilot enterprises*, the National Economic Council insisted that these pilot enterprises must establish and promote the workers' congress system.

For a long time the Chinese government had used administrative orders as a substitute for laws, but this was no longer suitable for measures aimed at reforming the economic system. As a result, new laws were enacted in 1986 and 1988 on workers' congress regulations and on factory directors' working rules in publicly owned enterprises. These laws confirmed that employees could participate in management through workers' congresses and other arrangements. China's employee participation was now clearly established in law (Wang, 2011).

The third phase of change of China's employee participation system takes us from the 1990s to the present. It is widely accepted that at the start of this period the then existing participation arrangements – whether workers' congresses or staff representatives on supervisory boards – were often little more than formalities. The legislation of the 1980s had tended to worsen this position. Some idea of the inherent difficulties comes from a consideration of how the enterprise leadership should be appointed. The theoretical position had been that the enterprise was owned by those who work there. Under this, the employees and the workers' congress were entitled to decide who should lead the enterprise. But the laws of the 1980s implied a contrary theoretical position, that enterprises are the property of the whole country, so that it was the government which had the legal right to decide who should be their directors. This provoked controversy over who held supreme authority in enterprises; was it the government department, the workers' congress or the management committee?

In order to resolve this, and to assist the reform of state-owned enterprises, in December 1993 the fifth meeting of the 8th NPC Standing Committee enacted a new company law. This set out two principles. The first one affirmed adherence to the workers' congress system. The second principle introduced a worker representation system on boards of directors and supervisory boards. This provided a more explicit legal basis for employee participation. The boards of directors and boards of supervisors of all incorporated enterprises which were either solely or mainly funded by the state must have workers' representatives on them. These were called employee directors and employee supervisors. Not only did this conform with the practices common in some developed countries, it also added greater substance to employee participation in China.

Viewed as a whole, Chinese company law has inherited provisions for workers' congresses as well as acquiring these new company laws defining the appropriate institutions for enterprise management. At first sight it might appear that three new institutions – the shareholder conference, the board of directors and the supervisory committee – had replaced the three old institutions of the Party committee, the workers' congress and the trade union. However, company law did not distinguish clearly between the legal definitions of the three new institutions and workers' congresses. Legal guidance on the role of the workers' congress is ambiguous (Zhang, 2003). This has contributed to some confusion between the three new institutions and the three old ones. There have even been legal disputes around this. Legal innovation in the later 1980s and 1990s had concentrated on the establishment of modern enterprises. It focussed on central issues such as the regulation of shareholding, only touching lightly on employee participation.

The Current Employee Participation System

As the reform of the market system deepened, Chinese society aspired to new values, such as more democratic processes and more diverse forms of enterprise. At the same time, companies faced increasing competitive pressure in their markets. These changes brought new challenges for the existing system of employee participation. During the establishment of the modern enterprise system, the status of state-owned employees had been steadily diminished and the basis of employee participation was threatened.

At the same time, the number of labour disputes rose. In 2012, there were 640,000 individual labour dispute cases around the country. These cases were now more complex than previously and both the number of collective disputes and the typical number of workers involved in them had been growing. It would be impossible to ignore the implications of this for enterprise development and social stability. Meanwhile, as the quality of life improves, the new generation of workers are becoming more concerned about their rights and interests than ever before. They also have greater confidence and more ambition to pursue them.

The three key parties – enterprises, workers and government – all appreciate the urgency and the importance of stable labour relations for themselves and for society. This is a precondition for the future development of employee participation. In 2015, the CPC Central Committee and State Council reaffirmed the importance of workers' congresses as the basic form of the democratic management. It called for the setting up of regional or industrial (or sectoral) workers' congresses in places where there were local concentrations of small- and medium-sized enterprises. At the same time, emphasis was placed on the routine provision of relevant information to workers on their workplaces, using innovative techniques such as management open days, workers' question and answer sessions, and mail access to general management. The State Council also reaffirmed the importance of worker directors and the worker supervisor system. Compared with the earlier *Regulations on enterprise democratic management* of 2012, this 2015 statement has made provision for some employee participation forms which are more in line with current enterprise practice. It was a confirmation of enterprises' own attempts at building an employee participation system.

The Chinese government is currently putting considerable effort into building employee participation and encouraging the development of democratic management. Key Party Council policy statements include ones on requirements for democratic management at enterprise level, on strengthening socialist deliberative democracy and on the building of harmonious labour relations. These apply to all the different forms of ownership, emphasising that non-public enterprises should also implement systems of democratic management, despite their very different origins from state-owned enterprises. We consider state-owned enterprises first.

Employee Participation in State-Owned Enterprises

A combination of legal requirements provides three ways for the staff of state-owned enterprises to participate in the management of their company. The traditional way is to keep informed through the trade union, using its general membership meetings and the workers' congress. The second way is by electing worker directors or supervisors as representatives on decision-making and supervisory institutions. The third is by holding shares, so that staff can participate in managing the company both as shareholders and employees. Generally speaking, most have all of these, reflecting the deep traditions of employee participation and especially of the workers' congress system in Chinese state-owned enterprises (Liu, 2007).

The deepening of reform of state-owned enterprises has undoubtedly strengthened the authority of their managers. As a consequence, it has weakened employee participation based on the workers' congress. There are four particular problems. The first arises from their double principal-agent relationship. The second is their legacy from the past. The third is the challenge that worker participation poses to managerial authority in an increasingly market-oriented economy. The fourth arises from the tension between state control and local experimentation.

First, the development of employee participation has been damaged by what is effectively a double principal-agent relationship for state-owned enterprises. The government and society as a whole, as the ultimate owners, form the first layer of principal-agent relationship. But since the entire society cannot overcome the unavoidable problems arising from, for example, information barriers and agency costs, the choice of enterprise leaders is naturally entrusted to government. By appointing these leaders, the government creates the second layer of principal-agent relationship in state-owned enterprises (Liu, 2007). In any principal-agent relationship the principal has to be very clear about the form of the relationship and what the agent can deliver. However, in this case of production processes which are owned by the whole people, members of the wider society are barely aware of their having this principal role. They acquired it not through conscious choice but as a result of the change in their social system. Even employees, who collectively may technically be 'the principal', do not in practice have normal rights of ownership of and benefit from their enterprise. Far from assisting employee participation, this characteristic of state-owned enterprises of, in effect, doubling the principal-agent problem, tends on the contrary to impede it.

The second major challenge to employee participation in state-owned enterprises comes from the legacy of their past. The transition from a planned economy to a market economy in China was carried out gradually. Unavoidably there was a high degree of path dependency; that is, institutional inertia from the past direction of travel constrained the choice of future directions. But the nature of this path dependency was not simply passive and unintended. There may be a deliberate adherence to the old system. At the individual level, people with vested interests may not want to break away from the traditional institutional arrangements. More generally, historical traditions and local culture tend to strengthen the stickiness of the behaviour, beliefs and social structures that influence the development of notions of participation. This constrains the flexibility with which a new system can emerge from the old.

The typical employee involvement system of state-owned enterprises is currently the workers' congress. All other systems, whatever form they take, derive from this. Although the relationships between the parties and the circumstances in which they work together have changed substantially under exposure to markets, in practice there has been little change in the way in which workers' congresses and trade unions function. The biggest challenge to successful innovation of employee participation in state-owned enterprises is that the over-simple act of transplanting the old structures has resulted in their roles and institutions being inappropriate to their new environment.

Employee participation is a decentralisation of authority, so there is an inverse relationship between employee participation and managerial authority. The deeper the employee participation, by implication, the weaker the control of the managers. A third challenge arises from this. The central purpose of China's reform of state-owned enterprises is to strengthen their economic function of pursuit of profit. That goal has given state-owned enterprises an increasingly autonomous management. Those managers have increased their control over the employees. This heightens the perceived status divide between them. The result is a tendency to squeeze out any opportunities for employee involvement.

There is an interaction between central government policy and previous employee participation systems that tend to reflect local circumstances. This gives rise to a fourth issue. How individual state-owned enterprises choose to implement employee participation is heavily constrained by the stated policies of government. They cannot choose independently the approach that might feel most suitable in the light of their past experience. But also the versions of the approved systems that they end up choosing may not be as satisfactory as if they had designed them themselves. There are some forms of employee participation – such as self-managing teams, the use of employee opinion surveys, suggestion boxes and bulletin boards – that might have been thought better for a particular enterprise, which they may be prevented from using. It can be very unsatisfactory that the spontaneous ideas of an enterprise for participation are forced to take second place to the procedures required by government policy (Wu and Cui, 2013).

Employee Participation in Private Enterprises

The *Regulations on enterprise democratic management* were issued in 2012. These crossed the boundary of ownership and made it clear that private enterprises should also implement democratic management. Employee participation was seen to be an effective vehicle by which the trade union could safeguard worker rights at a time when both the number of private enterprises and the level of collective labour conflict had been growing (Yang and Zhang, 2013; Zhou and Wang, 2015). It was also becoming apparent to many private enterprises themselves that there was a growing need to promote employee participation. The new generation of industrial workers is more individualistic. They are better educated and better informed about their legal rights than the previous generation. They also have a different attitude to work, being less responsive to rigorous discipline and authoritarian management with its emphasis on unquestioning obedience (Wen, 2013). Some private companies were already exploring new methods of improving productivity and had found that employee participation had positive effects in winning staff enthusiasm and promoting efficiency (Rosenberg and Rosenstein, 1980; Cotton *et al.*, 1988; Cooke, 1994; Guthrie, 2001; Kaufman, 2003; Wagner, 2008; Mueller, 2011).

What influences the form of employee participation that they choose? It is the attitude of the individual private sector employers that is first and foremost the key to their implementing employee participation, whether in response to government prompting or to pressure from employees. As the owners of the production capital, private sector employers unavoidably dominate labour relations and can choose whether or not to empower their employees with rights of participation. What matters is not the theoretical or legal rights, it is the practicalities of arrangements for involvement of employees. It is difficult to achieve effective employee participation if employers do not have a positive attitude towards it. A superficially correct system can be negated by hostile management strategies.

A wide range of methods of employee participation appears to be in use and none has yet emerged as dominant. Evidence on this comes from a study of 247 employers in both state-owned and private enterprises conducted in Hunan Province in 2008, before the 2012 legislation (Xie, 2009). This survey, summarised in Table 8.1, indicated the ranking of the incidence of the different arrangements by state-owned,

Table 8.1 *Ranking of the use of different forms of employee participation*

Ranking type of company	Total ranking	State-owned enterprises	Private enterprises	Foreign-owned enterprises	Others
Providing views directly to the supervisor	1	1	1	1	1
Providing reasoned proposals to the enterprise management	2	3	2	2	2
Democratic discussion meetings	5	5	6	5	5
Employee share ownership	8	11	6	8	6
Autonomous work teams	11	10	7	7	9
Collective consultation	12	11	10	10	10
Employee representation on the board of directors and/or supervisors	10	9	8	10	7
Workers' congress through trade unions	3	2	5	3	3
Gathering of employees' opinions by methods such as suggestion boxes or bulletin boards	4	6	3	2	4
Disclosure of information on company affairs	9	8	9	9	8
Grass-roots opinion polls	6	7	4	4	4
Employee appraisal of management	7	4	7	6	4

Data source: Xie Yuhua, 'Industrial democracy and employee participation in China: the difference between stated-owned enterprises, non-public enterprises and foreign enterprises – a survey from Hunan province', *Comparison of Economic and Social Systems*, 2009(1): 129–135 private and foreign-owned enterprises. What is notable is how little difference there is in the rankings between the different ownership categories. The survey suggests that most of the private enterprises which implement employee participation systems had not made any radical innovations. Although they did change the names of the institutions, using terms such as 'democratic discussion council', or 'democratic talkfest', the basic forms derive from the traditions of state-owned enterprises. Before the 2012 legislation, different circumstances appear to have allowed private sector enterprises to adopt more diverse approaches, with no unified model emerging.

The adoption of employee participation in private enterprises is very uneven. This appears to reflect the individual styles of employers and the pressures placed on them by local government. In the present author's case studies, of four foreign-owned enterprises in Tianjin in 2015, it was found that some do have comprehensive employee participation systems. Some of these were pushed enthusiastically by top managers or by human resource managers without challenging the position of the trade unions. At the Tianjin Fujitsu Ten Group, for example, the human resources department and trade union had set up their own separate channels of employee participation and they encouraged the staff to speak out and put forward their proposals through the two channels. By drawing on both, the human resources department and the trade union had effective cooperation on employee participation. By contrast, there were also some private enterprises that completely failed to establish the legally required procedures or failed to do so adequately. Many procedures just met the government's formal requirements but had no actual effect for the employees.

Workers' democratic participation in the private sector is much more about trying to achieve effective rights than is the case in the state-owned sector. Labour relations in private enterprises are dominated by the employers because they are the owners. If workers have democratic participation, they can use it to fight for and expand their rights in the company. This kind of participation, in effect, sets up democratic employee participation to challenge aspects of the authority of employers. As owner of the capital assets, the private employer's natural instinct is to resist and reject employee participation. But for private enterprise employees, democratic participation can be seen as not only their social and political right as Chinese citizens, but also as the economic right of labour as a factor of production. Effective participation in the private sector is, however, unavoidably made more difficult by the imbalance of power and the lack of any participative tradition.

Worker and Trade Union Perspectives

The Behaviour of Workers in Employee Participation

The discussion so far has been mostly about the company perspective on employee participation. What is the perspective of the workers? Employee participation is a process of converting legal rights into power or influence at work. When the rights given by law are seen to match and potentially advance employees' interests, the law may potentially be effective (Liu, 2007). But for the law to work, it needs to meet two criteria. The first is that the workers believe that the law is in general concerned with their own perceived interests. The second criterion is that they believe that the interests served by the outcomes of the particular issues that are being decided also conform with their own interests. This is necessary for them to be willing to get personally involved with the detail of making participation work (Li and Wu, 2010). This is essential because effective industrial democracy needs workers to become actively involved.

An example where employees felt rewarded by participation and were committed to it comes from a case reported in Zhejiang province. This concerns the Chuan Hua cooperation's employee participation scheme. They had established a workers' congress in 1995. Since 2000, this workers' congress was judged to have solved a range of problems. These included: the integration of the workers' internal endowment insurance scheme with their social endowment insurance schemes; over-crowding of the staff dormitory; provision of married quarters for employees; improvement of bathrooms and of air-conditioning and provision of parking facilities for the employees' living area. Employees trusted the workers' congress and they were reportedly enthusiastic about participation (*Workers' Daily*, 29 November 2010).

In the author's own survey in 2007, of 751 workers in 67 companies in Beijing, Luoyang, Nanjing and three other cities, it was workers with better education and more legal knowledge than the average who played leading roles in participation. Some workers said that it helped them to fulfil their potential at work and that 'we don't want to be nobody, or just carry on being managed forever'. In interviews with the more active employees, most of them appeared to identify with the observation: 'When something inappropriate happens, and when you are a part of it, how can you ignore it?' We can conclude that if both the process and the results meet the employees' economic and non-economic needs, they are likely to participate in management (Zhan, 2008).

In practice there is a hard constraint on the benefits and satisfaction that workers can get from participation. This is the extent to which the employers will tolerate it, a constraint that is dependent upon the power relationship they have with the workers. At present, there is generally a deep gap between the two sides, so that the employees' involvement is controlled by the employers. Thus, in reality, far from providing substantial benefits, employee participation tends to be somewhat tepid, with little evidence of initiative. In the survey carried out in 2007 of 751 workers just mentioned, a question was included on the number of suggestions made by employees in the previous year. The results showed that only 31 per cent had put forward one or more suggestions, while 40 per cent had never made any proposals. In another question, about the degree of attention the employer paid to staff proposals for improved management, only 23 per cent thought they were 'valued' or 'seriously valued'. Their difficulty in getting a response from management may help explain why employees chose not to be actively involved.

The Role of Trade Unions in Employees' Involvement

The exercise of democratic management rights is a form of organised employee behaviour. Achieving the goal of democratic participation requires a broad mass base and full representation. Trade unions are in principle the most competent vehicles for this role (Liu, 2007). In practice, however, trade unions often use their network of resources to prevent employee participation from detracting from their own influence. Union officials try to protect their own power and to be both the advocate and organiser of employee participation.

In China, trade unions are legally restricted as member organisations; although they are connected to the workers, they are to some extent separated from them (You, 2010). It has been observed that union officials have not always supported the interests of the workers, that they have sometimes been slow to reflect and represent those interests, and that they have preferred to follow the commands and interests of government rather than the wishes of workers (Deng, 1950). The ambivalent role of trade unions in democratic management has been a major obstacle to the development of employee participation. What may be worse is that this position of unions has been openly questioned by workers at the grass-roots. When union officials are seen to be unable to organise employee participation, workers are likely to bypass them and to develop other ways to express their voice.

An extreme case of union failure happened in July 2009, when some workers of Jilin Tonghua Iron and Steel Co took action against the Jianlong Group Holdings Tonghua Steel Group and mass incidents broke out. On the morning of 23 July, some of the leaders of Jilin State-owned Assets Supervision and Administration Commission (SASAC) and some Jianlong executives tried to convene a meeting to put things right. They were surrounded by about 100 employees. The SASAC's leaders and Jianlong executives tried their best to explain the situation to the workers but it was of little use. Next day the plant was surrounded by more than 3000 workers and shut down. The arrival of Jianlong executives escalated the crisis to the extraordinary point when Chen Guojun, the general manager of Jianlong, was beaten to death by the protesters.

Trade union involvement can be directed to be far more constructive. Less than a month after the Tonghua incident, in August 2009, workers' mass incidents also broke out at Linzhou Iron and Steel Co in Puyang, Henan, in response to enterprise restructuring. Nearly 3000 workers gathered at the management office, claiming compensation for what they considered unreasonable problems arising from the restructuring. In response, the Henan provincial Party committee and the provincial government jointly made six proposals. These included respecting the wishes of the workers by suspending the restructuring work. They proposed making decisions jointly with the workers' congress on what policy to adopt after the suspension, and also making joint decisions on employees' benefits. Xu Guangchun, the then secretary of Henan provincial Party committee, declared that, from now on, all the restructuring of enterprises would be invalid unless it had been approved by workers' congresses and had passed the official test of risk assessment for social stability. One observer commented that 'If trade unions cannot truly represent workers or protect their interests, acting as no more than mediators, even possibly controlled and dominated by the employers, then it becomes easy for the employers to formulate and push resolutions through workers' congresses that will infringe the workers' interests' (Xu, 2010). It could provoke even greater conflict between labour and capital, including mass incidents, if the union was not perceived by the workers to be acting in their interests in the workers' congress.

The Prospects for Employee Participation in China

The strike wave of 2010 started in Suzhou, moving from the Yangtze River Delta to the Zhujiang River Delta. In May, the Nanhai Honda Strike occurred, which was followed by successive strikes in Zhongshan, Foshan and Shenzhen. After July, the strikes moved to the Dalian Development Zone, involving 73 enterprises. Compared with strikes four or five years earlier, substantially greater collective consciousness and capacity for collective action was evident in 2010. These events influenced workers' perceptions of what was possible.

The promotion of enterprise democracy has been encouraged by government and by support from some private sector employers. But more fundamental to its development is the commitment to it of the workers. As the economy develops, workers' aspirations become more complex. They shift from being concerned with meeting their short-term economic needs to a wider concern with the exercise of power at the workplace and greater freedom in the conduct of work. Workers ask for equality, respect and more satisfaction from work. Accompanying this is a tendency for them to develop a greater awareness of collective rights and organisation. This growing awareness can displace a superficial democracy based on passive participation and can lay the foundations for a more substantial representative democracy at the workplace.

It was already evident that many forms of democratic management were emerging in the early 2000s. At that time a three-year study of local experience by Feng suggested that one form of democratic management largely perpetuated premarket traditions. Another relied on close co-operation with the local Party organisation. Some forms were relatively independent of the traditional system. Others were unstable and their prospects were difficult to predict. From these case studies it was concluded that, although the class structure of participants had changed a lot compared with traditional state-owned enterprises, the basic role of the worker's congress and trade union largely continued to underlie the new forms because of their deep roots (Feng, 2005, 2012).

Some years later, in 2015, the present author studied foreign-owned and joint venture enterprises. Some had responded to collective pressures from employees to develop a form of participation which relied upon close co-operation between the human resource department and the enterprise trade union. At the Tianjin Fujitsu Ten Group, as mentioned earlier, the human resources department was involved with developing twin channels of communication, establishing consultation procedures and providing resources. The trade union was responsible for telling workers what was being done, for training the worker representatives and general motivation. The two acted together to collect employees' opinions and suggestions and to encourage substantial participation. The trade union chairman commented that 'the issues we are concerned about are usually the same at any one time. Although we collect opinions through the different channels, the improvements discussed are the same. The union supervises their implementation and ensures that employee opinions are taken seriously.'

A slightly different case was provided by the Tianjin Ai Xin Corporation. In its relationship with the enterprise trade union, the human resource department was in a more dominant position. The union leadership in Ai Xin said that 'the trade union mainly supports the work of the human resource department and explains it to the workers. If there are changes in the enterprise, our duty is to safeguard the workers' right to know what has happened.' The human resources department managed the procedures of worker participation by arranging the timing and topics of collective discussions.

The influence of the type of corporate ownership on employee participation may be weakening. Earlier research had emphasised this relationship, suggesting that different forms of ownership influenced the extent of participation, the scope of the issues covered, its effectiveness and its development (Chen, 2001; Lei, 2009; Xie, 2009; Wu and Cui, 2013). But more recent research casts doubt on whether this effect is still as strong. One study found only small differences in the choice of participation systems between state, private and foreign-owned enterprises (Xie, 2009). The present author's study of 67 enterprises in 2008 reached a similar conclusion. While workers' congresses were, as expected, almost universal in state-owned enterprises, elsewhere it found that the proportion that had workers' congresses was 40 per cent for the private enterprises, 67 per cent for the collective enterprises and 50 per cent for the foreign-owned enterprises. Considering the weak basis and slight tradition of employee participation in non-state-owned enterprises, these differences are not substantial (Zhan, 2008).

In our pilot investigation of 2005, we interviewed 14 employees in 3 non-state-owned enterprises and found that almost 85 per cent of the interviewees had no awareness at all of participation systems such as workers' congresses. A later investigation by the author in 2015 reinforced the finding just mentioned that the difference in employee participation between non-state-owned enterprises and state-owned enterprises has gradually narrowed. The interviewees (both workers and managers) were more familiar with the forms of employee participation and cared about their right of participation. Based on these surveys, we conclude that ownership is no longer the decisive factor influencing the establishment of employee participation.

The use of the workers' congress may have substantial scope for further development, especially in state-owned enterprises. The author's 2015 study also identified adapted forms of worker congresses in private enterprises. Many of them had some features of the workers' congress system in the way they were developing enterprise democracy, including their working principles and organisation structure, although the names given to them were often very different. Of particular importance is that the way they are operated has become more flexible and their effectiveness has been enhanced. For instance, Tianjin Fujitsu Ten Group established a system of 'serious discussions' in July 2014. In these, as a manager described it: 'The general manager, deputy general manager and managing director listen to employees' opinions face to face, in order to improve the working environment. The "serious discussion" generally takes the form of a symposium and working lunch, and it can be divided into a special session for departments and special session for employees. It is attended by any employee selected from each department, including technicians, workers and dispatched workers. Topics and problems that employees are interested in are discussed at the meeting. Sometimes we will also choose some topics' (Zhan, 2015).

The 'serious discussion' system was also adopted by the Tianjin Ai Xin Corporation. Its human resources department said that 'members present at the meeting are selected from each department, and we will also choose some representative employees. For instance, we selected an employee who is a soldier's wife as a representative to show that we are not nationally biased as a Japanese-owned enterprise. The proportion of male workers to female workers is 80 per cent, but male workers only account for 60 per cent at the serious discussion, since we want to give female workers full right of expression.'

Conclusion

Employee participation in China has been built on long experience of workers' congresses in state-owned enterprises. The opening up of the economy to market forces has greatly increased the divergence of interests between the managers and the workers whom they manage in both the state-owned and private sectors. This has made new demands on employee participation. The Chinese government is actively encouraging it, in parallel with its efforts to encourage and build collective consultation.

Although the state-owned enterprises are still firmly entrenched in the workers' congress system, they are likely to develop more diversified forms of participation in response to their increasingly dominant market environment. In the non-state enterprises, although the tradition of workers congresses remains very evident, there is experimentation with participation systems with more diverse and flexible forms. Growing demand from employees, and increased recognition of its potential by government and by enterprises, is likely to encourage the further development of employee participation in China.

References

Chang, K. (2005), 'Laodongguanxi xue', [Labour relations], Beijing: Zhongguo laodongshehuibaozhang chubanshe.

Chang, K. (2013), 'Laodongguanxi de jitihua zhuanxing yu zhengfu laogongzhengce de wanshan', [The collective transformation of labour relations and the improvement of government labour policy], Zhongguo shehuikexue, 6, 91–108.

Chen, X. (2001), 'Gongsi zhigongcanyuzhidu yanjiu', [Research on the system of employee participation in companies], Xiamen daxue shuoshilunwen.

Cohen, J. (1988), 'Lun min zhu', [On democracy], (Nie C. and Zhu X. Trans.), Beijing: Shangwu yinshuguan.

Cooke, W. N. (1994), 'Employee participation programs, group-based incentives, and company performance: A union-nonunion comparison', *Industrial and Labor Relations Review*, 47(4), 594–609.

Cotton, J. L., Vollrath, D. A., Froggatt, K. L., Lengnick-Hall, M. L. and Jennings, K. R. (1988), 'Employee participation: Diverse forms and different outcomes', *The Academy of Management Review*, 13(1), 8–22.

Deng, Z. (1950), 'Zai zhongnanzonggonghui chouweikuodahuishang de baogao', [Report on the meeting of the preparatory committee of the south trade union, in the selected documents of socialist trade union study], Beijing: Zhonggong dangshi chubanshe, 1992.

Feng, T. (2005), 'Guojia, qiye, zhigong, gonghui zhijianguanxi de liangxingtiaozheng', [A case study of employee participation in the reform of state-owned enterprises], in Feng, T. (ed.), *op.cit.*, 90–146.

Feng, T. (2012), 'Zhongguo zhigongdaibiaodahuizhidu zonglun', [The system of workers' congress in China], in Rudolf Traub-Merz and Kinglun Ngok (ed.), Zhongguo chanyeminzhu [Industrial democracy in China with additional studies on Germany, South-Korea and Vietnam], Beijing: Zhongguo shehuikexue chubanshe, 163–173.

Guthrie, J. P. (2001). 'High-involvement work practices, turnovers, and productivity: Evidence from New-Zealand', *The Academy of Management Journal*, 44(1), 180–190.

Kaufman, B. E. (2003), 'High-level employee involvement at Delta Air Lines', *Human Resource Management*, 42(2), 175–190.

Lei, X. (2009), 'Qiye yuangongcanyu de zuzhiyingxiangyinsu jiqi shizhengyanjiu', [An empirical study of organisational influences on employee participation in enterprises], Hunan: Daxue shuoshilunwen.

Li, H. and Wu, J. (2010), 'Zuzhituanjieguochengzhong de yuangongcanyu', [Employee participation in the process of organisational unity], Beijing: Zhongguo shehuikexue chubanshe.

Liu, Y. (2007), 'Zhigongminzhucanyu lilun yu shijian', [The theory and practice of the democratic management], Beijing: Zhongguo laodongshehuibaozhang chubanshe.

Lu, M. (2013), 'Guoyougangtieqiye gongzuochangsuozhong de yuangongcanyu he yuangongshengyin', [Employee participation and voices in the workplaces of state-owned steel enterprises]. Zhongguo renliziyuankaifa, 96–104.

Mueller, S. (2011), 'Worker councils and firm profits revisited', *British Journal of Industrial Relations*, 49(1), 27–43.

Qi, H. (2005), 'Neibuzhigongcanyu qiyezhilijiegou de yiyi', [On the significance of internal employee participation in the corporate governance structure], Shangye shidai, 34–35.

Rosenberg, R. D. and Rosenstein E. (1980). 'Participation and productivity: An empirical study', *Industrial and Labor Relations Review*, 33(3), 355–367.

Wagner, J. (2008), 'German works councils and productivity', *Applied Economics Letters*, 15(3), 727–730.

Wang, S. (2011), 'Gongrenzhengzhi de luoji jiqi biange', [Logic and reform of workers' politics: Research on employees' representative congresses], Fudan: Daxue boshilunwen.

Wen, X. (2013), 'Qiye renliziyuanguanli de tiaozhan yu laodongguanxiguanlitixi jianshe', [The challenge of human resource management in enterprises and the construction of labor relation management system], Zhongguo renliziyuan-kaifa, 11, 81–86.

Wu, S. and Cui, X. (2013), 'Yuangong de jianjiecanyu he zhijiecanyu', [Indirect and direct employee participation: Theoretical background and research prospects], Xiandai: guanli kexue, 4, 9–11.

Xie, Y. (2009), 'Zhongguogongyeminzhu he yuangongcanyuzhidu ji gongneng', [A comparison of industrial democracy, employee participation systems and their functions in state-owned enterprises, civil enterprises and foreign-funded enterprises – a survey in Hunan], Jingji shehuitizhi bijiao, 1, 129–135.

Xie, Y. and He, B. (2008), 'Zhongguogongyeminzhu he yuangongcanyu yanjiushuping', [Industrial democracy and employee participation: An eternal topic], Shehuizhuyi yanjiu, 3, 86–93.

Xu, X. (2010), 'Zhongguogonghui de shuangchong juesedingwei', [The dual role of Chinese trade unions], Renwen zazhi, 6, 151–160.

Yang, Q. and Zhang, W. (2013), 'Woguo siyingqiye laozimaodunchongtu de yuanyin tanxi', [Analysis on the reasons for labour conflict in private enterprises in China]. Zhengzhoudaxue xuebao, 11, 10–14.

You, Z. (2010), '60nianlai zhongguogonghui de sanci dagaige', [Three big reforms of Chinese trade unions since 1960], Shehuixue yanjiu, 4, 76–105.

Zhan, J. (2008), 'Qiye minzhucanyudongli yanjiu', [Research on the power of enterprise employee participation], Beijing: Shoudu jingjimaoyidaxue chubanshe.

Zhang, D. (2008), 'Zhongguo guoyouqiyegaige de zhidubianqian yanjiu', [Research on the institutional change of China's state-owned enterprises reform], Fudan daxue boshilunwen.

Zhang, Y. (2003), 'Zhongguo zhigongdaibiaodahuizhi yu zhigongcanyumoshi', [An analysis of the political science on the Chinese workers' congress system and the employee participation model]. Beijing xingzhengxueyuan xuebao, 1, 27–33.

Zhou, X. and Wang, M. (2015), 'Zhongguolaozichongtu de xianzhuang, tezheng yu jiejuecuoshi', [The status, characteristics and countermeasures of labour conflict in China]. Xueshu yanjiu, 4, 72–77.

9   Strikes
Rights and Resolution

Meng Quan

'Strike' is a very sensitive word in China. For the most part the Chinese government has intentionally avoided its use, preferring expressions such as 'stopping work' or 'slacking-off' during the 2010 strike wave. Since then, however, particularly in Guangdong province, striking has become the most common way by which workers seek to protect their interests. Strikes have certainly not diminished in number since the advent of the market economy.

Two aspects of strikes are the focus of the following analysis. The first is that the strike can be regarded as a key notion that links concepts of workers' interests and of workers' power which have not yet been clearly defined in China (Kelly, 1998: 4–12). The second is that both the traditional study of strikes in the Western world (Jackson, 1987; Hyman, 1989; Edwards, 1995; Lyddon, 2008) and more recent research by contemporary scholars of China (Chan, 2011; Chen and Meng, 2013; Friedman, 2012, 2013; Meng and Lu, 2013; Tu, 2013) indicate that the relationship between the strike and the institutionalisation of the right to strike has become a central focus of concern. What has been the historical development of strikes and of their institutionalisation in China? If strike action still cannot be protected by labour law, what logic underlies workers' action at the micro level? What is distinctive about the practice of conflict resolution in China when compared to the Western world?

In answering these questions, this chapter will trace the influence of strikes on labour law and on the institutionalisation of rights to strike. It will explore interest relations and power relations and discuss the practical feasibility of strike resolution. The first section will briefly review the recent history of Chinese strikes, developing the discussion of a lack of a right to strike. The second section will focus on the logic of workers' taking strike action and consider the implications for workers' power and for their labour consciousness. The process of strike resolution and the relationship between strikes and collective negotiations will be discussed

184

in the third section. The chapter concludes with a critical perspective on reforming the treatment of strikes.

Strikes since Market Reform

The Shift from Changing Worker Identity to Collective Protests

With exposure to markets, the identity of workers in state-owned enterprises (SOEs) changed from being the masters to being the employees. Similarly, the identity of vast numbers of peasants now became that of rural migrant workers. The new identities, deeply embedded in the market economy, rendered both vulnerable to the demands of capitalism, and resulted in the violation of their rights and interests (Xu, 2009: 77; Gallagher *et al.*, 2011: 3–7).

The collective protests of workers who were laid-off from SOEs can, for the most part, be attributed to their subsequent employment at little better than subsistence wages. They were protesting at having to yield to increasing poverty, injustice and insecurity. Gradually they also lost confidence in obtaining relief from the state. This drove them to resistance. Although their individual actions were generally powerless, they still organised many large-scale protests in an effort to recover the rights lost by privatisation (Lee, 1998; Liu, 2005). News coverage referred to most of these actions as 'collective events' rather than strikes.

Besides those laid-off, the workers who still held their positions were faced with challenges from corporate reform of ownership or the bankruptcy of their employer. Their main grievances focussed on job security and compensation; they called for the punishment of employers for corruption. Such strikes can hardly be regarded as typical of a market economy. Rather, their collective resistance is best seen as a protest that was entangled with the traditions and customs of SOEs (Wu, 2010). Strike action was merely a part of their wider protest. These workers pinned their hopes on their idea of a 'moral economy'. Their demands were closely related to the rights and regulations of the era of the command economy. Such action was still characterised by spontaneity; it was unorganised and was constrained within the factory. As Chen (2003) argued, it only took the form of 'contentious gatherings'. Workers' grievances sometimes extended beyond their immediate discontent to complain about uneven treatment of their interests and about abuses of managerial prerogative. There were even attempts to get rid of despotic management, sometimes when it was sheltered by official power relationships.

Even though workers realised that the market economy was irreversible, they still made use of previous institutional arrangements (such as workers' congresses) and of socialist cultural inheritances from the command economy such as public ownership, their identities as the masters and the view of their factory as a home. In so doing, they sometimes achieved the power from solidarity by which their voices could be expressed and concessions could be achieved (Tong, 2006). It is noteworthy that most of these collective actions in recent years have occurred within single factories, without their expanding to any wider coalition. Two large strikes, for example, successively occurred in July and September 2009 in response to changes of ownership at the Tonghua Steel Manufacturing Company in Tonghua City, Jilin Province, and at the Linzhou Steel Manufacturing Factory in Puyang City, Henan Province.

The collective resistance of these 'peasant workers' continued in the 1990s. After 1990, price inflation reached 20 per cent but, because there was an excess supply of labour, the workers received either no pay rise or even pay cuts. Consequently, in September 1993, a spontaneously organised strike wave erupted in Zhuhai City in Guangdong Province (Leung, 1998). In 1994, a strike launched by female workers in Wanbaozhi Mada, a Japanese investment electronics manufacturing factory, almost triggered a strike wave in the Dalian Development Zone. That was averted when the regional government forced all foreign investment firms to increase wages (Meng, 2012).

The character of strikes changed with the twenty-first century. From 2002 to 2005, according to published statistics, there were 70 strikes in the Pearl River Delta. Of these, 35 were in 2005 (Chan *et al.*, 2010). During this period peasant workers became the main source of collective resistance. Their chief grievances focussed on the non-payment of wage arrears, and on demands for the amelioration of harsh working conditions and for the shortening of working hours. There was also a strike wave that hit 18 companies in the Dalian Development Zone between July and October 2005, involving almost 30,000 workers who were discontented with their low wages (Chen, 2010). The period between 2006 and 2009 was influenced by rising international resource prices and the strengthening value of the RMB. To this was added the world economic recession which undermined the Chinese economy later in 2008. Shrinkage of manufacturing industry led to bankruptcies, closures and serious redundancies. Workers organised strikes to defend interests which they felt had been violated by many employers.

The year 2010 witnessed strike waves and large-scale strikes across some coastal areas, including the Pearl River Delta, the Yangtze River

Delta and the Bohai Area. The immediate reason why workers were so militant was that they were not satisfied with what they perceived to be the unfair treatment of particular groups within their enterprises. There was also a rise in the cost of urban living which they were unable to afford. It has been argued that most of the collective labour disputes in 2010 were interest oriented rather than concerned with legal rights (Chang, 2013).

Peasant workers, and in particular the younger generation of them, were starting to demand a share of profits from the enterprise. They did this by asking for pay rises on the grounds that company profits were growing. They built solidarity both within and outside the factory on the basis of their kinship and classmate relationships (Wang and Meng, 2013). They adopted more effective strategies by mobilising novel resources such as the mass media and the law, as well as drawing in trade unions and making broader emotional appeals (Lyddon *et al.*, 2015). A number of studies have shed light on the strikes of this period. Some analyse the rationale of the workers' behaviour, the foundations of their solidarity and the mechanism of the strike wave (Chan and Hui, 2012). Others study the tactics of the state (Meng, 2014), the employers' counter-movement against the regional institutionalisation of collective bargaining (Hui and Chan, 2014), union reforms in collective negotiation and direct elections (Li, 2014; Wen, 2014), as well as the possibility of legalisation of the right to strike (Chang and Cooke, 2015; Chen, 2015).

As the economic downturn developed in China, many enterprises were confronted with the prospect of ceasing production, of merging and of movement elsewhere. Increasingly since about 2013 there have been fewer calls by workers for wage increases or for sharing profits with the company. Rather, their demands have focussed more on wage arrears, social insurance, job security and dismissal compensation. Although there are still no useful published statistics on strike behaviour, according to research based on 1132 cases of strikes in 2014, this change in the nature of workers' claims has been substantial (Li and Duan, 2015). But despite the general trend, there were still some cases where workers called for a pay rise, better welfare and the re-organising of workplace trade unions. In some instances, workers' demands for grass-roots involvement in organising directly challenged the union officials who were responsible for collective negotiations and union elections (Wang and Shi, 2014; Wang, 2015). A case study of a dock workers' strike after local union reforms in 2013 provides evidence of a continuing demand for the sharing of profits (Cao and Meng, 2017).

This sketch of the history of Chinese strikes since the introduction of market reforms shows how the change in identity of both urban workers in

SOEs and of peasant workers from the rural areas has resulted from their becoming deeply embedded into capitalist employment relations. Faced with the potential for capital's exploitation and violation of their rights and interests, and with the consequences of more flexible employment, there has been an increasing tendency for workers to resort to strikes. It has been an expression of rising discontent, of resistance to the power of capital and even to the authority of management. Before 2010, the state used suppression and coordinated action at times to cope with strikes. But the authorities involved could hardly claim that they had any legal basis for doing so. Many enterprises chose to define workers' collective resistance as illegal action. There is an ambivalent attitude towards strikes that stems in part from an institutional vacuum in China. Fundamental questions have been raised about whether the uncertain status of the right to strike is itself a source of labour problems. That is partly a consequence of the removal of the right from the Constitution and of inconsistent regulations on strikes in contemporary labour law. To this we now turn.

The Progression from Removing the Right to Strike to Regulating Strike Action

The path followed by the right to strike in China has been in a different direction from in the Western world, where it went from the emergence of labour movements to the institutionalisation of rights to strike (Hyman, 1975: 151–155). In China it has been a progression from the cancellation of any rights to the limited regulation of strikes. Since the right was removed from the Constitution relatively recently in 1982, the state is unlikely to restore it in the near future, even though strikes have become commonplace. Strikes remain in limbo in Chinese legislation. There is a disjunction between the strike as a reality and its legal status at the national level.

The right to strike was a fundamental civil right, embodied in both the 1975 and 1978 Constitutions. It was eliminated in 1982 and is not a fundamental right in the current version of the Constitution (Lyddon et al., 2015). It has been argued that it should be reinstated because it has not been possible in its absence for the government to legislate adequately on the regulation of strikes, despite the fact that they have become a common phenomenon (Chang and Cooke, 2015). Currently there are almost no protections for workers engaged in strike action at the national level (Chang, 2005). At the regional level, however, there are a number of regulations regarding strikes.

In 2004, the General Office of CPC Central Committee published *Suggestions about Actively Preventing and Appropriately Addressing Collective*

Events, by which the central government aimed to prevent and cope with any collective events ascribed to internal conflict among citizens. Under this policy, a strike was defined as a 'people's internal conflict'. The government proposed four steps to deal with such collective events, called the 'four early principles'. These were: early finding, early reporting, early controlling and early resolution. In practice, however, the relevant government agency usually learns about collective labour disputes after they occur and only then can it start on the resolution process.

The state began to change its strategy towards labour movements after 2004 by reinforcing individual labour policy. Two important laws were enacted in 2008: the Labour Contract Law and the Labour Dispute Mediation and Arbitration Law (Chen, 2015). According to official statistics, the number of individual labour disputes increased sharply in 2008, and then slightly abated but with a similar number of workers involved. More and more workers mobilised legal resources to defend their rights (Gallagher, 2006). When their interests were jeopardised, recourse to the law became their first choice. Arbitration or litigation offered a less risky option than the alternatives. With its concern with social stability, the state preferred workers to apply for legal redress (Burstein, 1991). However, recourse to the law has its own problems. The implementation of the law is undermined by the complex procedures involved, and by its high cost. In addition, it is weakened by the priority given by central government to economic development and social stability and also by regional governments prioritising economic targets. The inconsistency between strong rhetoric and weak enforcement resulted in workers finding that resorting to the law was constantly failing to help them. This encouraged some to take more radical collective action (Xie, 2010).

The increasing use of strikes prompted more discussion of their legitimacy. Particular attention was given to how to interpret Article 27 of the Trade Union Law. This states that 'if a stoppage or slacking-off occurs in an enterprise or public organisation, the trade union should represent the workers in order to negotiate with the relevant counterpart in the enterprise or public organisation, expressing workers' opinions and demands, and proposing the solution'. There is, however, no clear definition of stoppage and slacking-off. It was usually only when workers' interests were seriously impaired that their strike action would be accommodated by the law. But there is also no clear definition of whether a strike is legal or illegal.

The rules may, paradoxically, permit the trade union to support the workers if they wish to leave an inadequate workplace, but they provide no option for the union to support a strike. The absence of a definition of a strike and of its conduct and procedures has led to the present lack of substantial protection on strikes (Tu, 2013). Some scholars have argued that there is no essential difference between holding a strike and having a stoppage or slacking-off. Article 27 obliged the trade union to represent workers after their industrial action in order to propose solutions to the company, and to satisfy workers' reasonable appeals. This suggests that the legitimacy of a right to strike has at least been partly confirmed. The Article also requires the involvement of the trade union in representing its membership during the strike (Liu, 2011: 516–517). In the long run, however, the workers' right to strike cannot fully be protected and appropriately regulated unless the fundamental concepts are clarified.

Besides regulations in the national Trade Union Law, there are rules in some regional regulations, such as Article 52 and Article 53 in *Promoting Harmonious Labour Relations Regulations in Shenzhen Special Economic Zone*. These suggest dual regulation, including both protective and restrictive constraints. Article 52 is *de facto* an extension of the Article 27 of the Trade Union Law. The objective of Article 53 is to maintain social stability. In addition, Articles 28 and 29 in Chapter 4 of the Collective Consultation Regulation of Shenzhen Special Economic Zone (which is, at time of writing, in preparation for publication) specify how to cope with stoppages, slacking-off and factory closure, by means of collective consultation and mediation. But this prospective regulation cannot over-rule Article 27 of the Trade Union Law (Zhai, 2012).

The Guangdong Corporate Collective Consultation Regulation was once considered a sign of progress in legislation by some commentators. But the relevant rules regarding strikes indicate that its intention is actually more restrictive, or even intended to provide a method of control within Guangdong, which is the place where strikes have been most frequent. For instance, Article 36 of this regulation specifies that the police are able to get involved in a labour dispute. Article 24 sets out that during the period of collective consultation, workers are not entitled to disobey on issues of labour discipline. Actions such as obstructing the entry and exit of the company are banned. Workers are prohibited from stopping people entering the factory, or from preventing goods moving outside the factory. They are prohibited from sabotage or disrupting production, or from disturbing public order. As Chen (2014) has commented, all these rules demonstrate the prioritisation by the government of social stability and control over the orderly conduct of strikes.

Neither the Trade Union Law nor regional laws have properly addressed the issue of strikes. But this may be a case where doing nothing may be better than doing little. The current rules relating to strikes at least can be used by the government to provide practical institutional means to resolve strikes. In effect, this limited regulation on strikes has resulted in blurring the institutional context. It is a context in which workers' collective resistance poses challenges to the inadequacy of the law. What is the logic of workers' action under these incomplete provisions?

The Underlying Logic of Strike Action since 2010

The Awakening of Labour Consciousness

Despite the lack of support from the law, strikes by the new generation of peasant workers in coastal areas are posing a threat to existing labour institutions. This is forcing the government and employers to seek new approaches to strike resolution. The reason why this generation has become more active than their predecessors stems from their social experiences and from perceptions shaped by their urban lifestyle (Chan, 2013). They have become aware of the potential of solidarity and protest.

The social circumstances that the new generation of migrant workers find themselves in are awkwardly divided between the countryside and the city (Tsinghua University, 2012: 110–128). Most of them started their lives and schooling in urban areas, typically accompanying their parents as they moved from one city to another. They became more adapted to the city rather than any rural hometown (Xiong, 2012). When they became assembly line workers, their strong expectation was to become urbanised. Not only are they the producers of consumption goods, they are also the consumers, a part of the consumption culture.

The institutional environment in which they find themselves is substantially better than in the early period of market reform, when their predecessors first worked in urban settings. In particular, the Labour Contract Law and the Labour Dispute Mediation and Arbitration Law not only offer workers a safer employment environment, but they also have heightened workers' awareness of the improvements in their individual rights. As Gallagher's research (2011: 226–228) shows, the coverage of labour contracts and pensions in 2010 was substantially higher than in 2005. Workers' consciousness of the individual rights embodied in the Labour Contract Law has been improved, which has encouraged them to spark labour disputes. For example, studies of strikes that erupted from 2011 to 2014 have demonstrated an increasing concern of peasant workers with receiving compensation for dismissal arising from company mergers, in accordance with the Labour Contract Law (Li and Dai, 2014: 82–83).

The emergence of labour non-government organisations (NGOs) has been another important factor driving the development of labour consciousness. Although there has been some criticism of labour NGOs both for commercialisation and for being incorporated by the government (Lee and Shen, 2011), there can be little doubt that they are having a positive effect on legal training and on the mobilising of workers. It appears that those labour NGOs which are focussed on defending workers' collective rights and interests have made a substantial contribution to inspiring workers and to nurturing their activists and organising collective action (Wang *et al.*, 2015). Labour NGOs appear to have become a catalyst in raising workers' consciousness.

A number of factors have contributed to the greater activism of the new generation. They had a better education than their predecessors. The duration of their full-time education was found to be an average of 10.7 years, two years more than the previous generation. The majority of them graduated from high school, technical school, colleges and even university (Tsinghua University, 2012: 90). Education has been a crucial factor in providing them with an understanding of labour law. It has also enabled them to use modern information technologies in building solidarity (Wang, 2011). The experience of urbanisation appears to have displaced the orthodox values of rural collectivism with values of individualism and personal independence. This may have encouraged a sense of injustice associated with their paradoxical identity as neither peasants nor workers (Pun and Lu, 2010).

The change in the new generation's self-perception appears to have encouraged them to be more adaptable to their changing environment, a necessary prerequisite for developing a collective consciousness. This raises the question of how they might press for and defend their rights and interests, drawing on the collective strength that their emerging consciousness might provide. Evidence from case studies sheds light on the logic underlying their collective action.

Solidarity and the Underlying Logic of Strike Action

What underlies the new generation of workers' evident solidarity in strike activity? Evidence comes from research carried out since 2010 by researchers adopting different disciplinary perspectives (Li, 2012; Wang, 2012; Meng and Lu, 2013; Friedman, 2014). There have been three broad approaches to understanding the roots of worker solidarity: solidarity formed in the process of production; solidarity arising from worker life-styles and solidarity that is reinforced by the experience of collective action. Li (2012), for example, observed that solidarity based upon family connections was partially defused by informal institutions of the workplace. Wang (2012) demonstrated the pivotal role in constructing solidarity of worker relations that were established as colleagues and previously as classmates. But evidence suggests that the most powerful source of solidarity comes from the experience of strike action. Two studies by the present author, one of the 2010 strike waves in automobile manufacturing factories across Guangdong Province and one in the Dalian Development Zone, will be used to shed light on this.

A critical feature of strikes for the new generation of workers lies in their evident capacity to maintain solidarity in the face of opposition from both the employer and the government (Kelly, 1998). Our cases emphasise the importance of three facets of workers' solidarity: the power the workers can generate, the external resources they can mobilise and their capacity to build a common identity.

Structural and Associational Power Workers' bargaining power is, in general, strongly influenced by the extent to which they create value in production and play a critical role in the continuity of operation of the longer chain of production. Silver (2003) argued that the effective mobilisation of this 'structural' power is crucially important in increasing workers' advantage in bargaining with the employer. Workers may be aware of this even when they are at the bottom of a production chain. This is particularly significant in the type of production management model found in Japanese-owned enterprises, such as 'just-in-time', 'lean production', or 'total quality management', which may render the whole global production chain susceptible to fracture once any critical link is threatened (Zhang, 2015). Workers facing an employer who is reluctant to make a concession in a pay bargain may come to realise that, should they resort to a strike, this structural power would amplify the potential economic loss of the employer. This might coerce the employer to compromise. In both Guangdong and Dalian, workers were acutely aware of this.

The effectiveness of workers' structural power may, however, be limited if it is not also backed by the 'associational' power that comes from workers' forming broader coalitions (Chen, 2009). It should be noted that, for Chinese workers, the notion of associational power is not the same as in Western theory because the official Chinese union, as a matter of policy, will not take the lead in organising a strike. It may be better to use the term 'collective' power which reflects the capacity of workers to organise informal groupings to get the maximum bargaining advantage from their structural power. For example, if there are relatively few workers taking strike action, it may be quite easy for the employer to find replacements for their positions in the factory. The deskilling of production degrades their function in the assembly line, rendering them easily replaceable. But once a large number of workers are involved in a strike, it ceases to be feasible for employers to attempt to undermine the workers' structural power by replacing them. For the strikes in Guangdong and the Dalian Development Zone, given the prevailing labour market conditions, there were hundreds, or even thousands of workers maintaining collective resistance in any one factory. The fact that there was a strike wave, encompassing many factories locally, served to magnify the impact of collective power. It is extremely difficult for any company to recruit such numbers of replacements.

The Mobilisation of External Resources   Quite apart from the resources that workers can mobilise to build solidarity within their enterprise, there are important external resources. These include the mass media, the help of outside experts, the use of mobile phones and the internet. During the strike episodes at the Nanhai Honda factory in Guangdong in 2010, for example, the mass media became, in effect, the stage on which the strikers could mobilise public opinion and support. Both national and international media became focussed on the events. Among the journalists whom the present author observed gathered outside the factory during the dispute were representatives of Reuters, Caixin, Sina and Asia Weekly. The striking workers' mobilisation of mass media was based on mutual interaction. On the one side, the journalist concentrated on the progression of events, pursuing newsworthy stories. They seized the opportunity to talk to the strikers about the issues and progress of negotiations. On the other side, the workers were able to use the journalists proactively to manage the release of news to arouse public attention. This fed back to reinforce solidarity. Drawing on interviews with established academic experts, the media were able to write commentary to augment their descriptive articles. On reading these, the workers would become more confident in their own collective actions, finding that their actions had been supported by independent experts. The journalists also enabled the strikers to find more resources outside the factory (Bu, 2010).

The resources in most constant use by the striking workers were mobile phones and the Internet. The new generation of peasant workers have, to a large extent, accepted the urban culture of facility with information and communication technology. Their lives are firmly embedded in the era of the Internet (Qiu, 2014). As part of the process of mobilisation before the strike, the workers established a chat group on the Internet through which they could freely discuss the issues. Many effective strategies were decided this way.

When workers could not communicate freely in traditional ways, the Internet provided a safer space. As well as this interaction on the Internet, they were able to use it to acquire necessary technical information about labour law and other relevant issues, which helped to shape their strategies. The Internet has become the main channel for the workers' voice. In Nanhai Honda, for example, a 'public letter' co-signed by 16 strike leaders was disseminated via the Internet, which proved to be important in winning public understanding and support. Two other Japanese-owned corporations in the automobile sector also provide examples where workers took advantage of the Internet to acquire and disseminate information about their strike.

The use made of social media depends upon the nature of kinship, schooling and workplace networks in a particular location. During the strike wave in the Dalian Development Zone, where many firms are clustered within one industrial area, it was possible for workers to receive relevant information rapidly because most of them lived in the same industrial neighbourhood. Many worked in factories in the same sector, which led them to have friendship bonds between factories. Many had social relationships based on their communities, classmates and relatives that predated their employment. Their mobile phones became the tools with which their friendships could help them both cope with work problems and build solidarity.

Building Collective Identity In the absence of the union as an organising force, workers' resources are generally inadequate to achieve their objectives. For each strike, fragmented groups of workers have to build a common identity for effective collaboration and building agreement (Kelly, 1998). In the case of the Honda workers, their identity was built by developing a consensus on their common interest by constructing and disseminating a culture of solidarity (Fantasia, 1988). This is illustrated by a poem authored by a Nanhai Honda worker:

Honda in our eyes once looked like paradise; Honda in our minds once looked like a bank. But it seems like a prison since we arrived; we'd be better off looking after cows and sheep at home. Everyone told me that Honda is wonderful; each of us wanted to work there. But we spend the money which we earn in the factory; there is almost no cash left for sending home. Everyone says there is a high wage in Honda, but I am not able to afford toothpaste. Everyone says there is good food in Honda, but I can find nothing but vegetables. Pressure on us increases year by year; we are worked like a monkey over eight hours. We may get overtime pay; but we only get criticism. Our heads are kept down in front of the boss; our heads are shaking when we get our wages. Our worries are not just at the end of every month; our worries are constant without better expectations for the future (Interview with workers, 13 August 2010)

Symbols of a common culture like this were shared and spread in chat groups because common pressures, such as high living costs and low wages, were suffered by all Honda workers. A commitment to a sense of shared interest is the precondition for workers' sense of identity. But this is not sufficient to ensure that all workers are willing to take part in collective action in pursuit of their economic interest. Each of them must evaluate the potential cost, such as the risk of job loss, employer punishments and government sanctions. Another element which can reinforce the workers' mutual commitment is their emotional mobilisation.

Emotion is an important adhesive to sustain solidarity. When workers in Nanhai Honda communicated in their chat group, for example, they were fiercely critical of the Japanese employer and of Japanese and Chinese management. Their criticism was passionate. This has been described as 'indignation leading to outrage and steadfast will' (Gamson, 1992: 32). Grumbling is also a normal way in which workers vent their emotion. In Nansha Company, before the strike, workers complained about the low wages which made them unable to make ends meet. They criticised the inequity between their contribution and their income. They decried the absence of any sense of belonging. Workers in the Dalian Development Zone were similar in expressing their anger and complaints when chatting together. A consequence of this venting of emotion can be a contagion of discontent which can intensify to a point where a small loss of temper may trigger a mass response. A worker described the effect as 'Everyone exploded as a result of a tiny spark because there had been discontent for a long time' (Interview at Danson, Guangzhou, 13 May 2011).

Workers can achieve a common sense of identity through a consensus on their interests, bolstered by a contagious surge of emotion. Besides workers' sharing their specific demands and having a common focus of their emotional hostility, there are two further bases for a common identity. One is a shared sense of injustice amongst workers arising from their similar experiences, both inside and outside their workplaces. The other is that the workers directly attribute the cause of their sense of injustice to the same object, namely the employer and management whom they are challenging. A common view on these points underlies the workers sharing a rational understanding of the injustice they face. They agree on the evidence of injustice. Expressing a shared emotional response reinforces their mutual commitment to the sense of injustice. In this way, workers develop common views, which paves the way for a sense of common identity.

This is the foundation for solidarity. All these factors combine to develop a shared consciousness and a resolve to join in collective action. But this is still not sufficient to lead to action. Workers will only take part in action if they perceive that there is an effective strategy to follow. They will only accept the possibility of a strike to be effective if they are convinced by the broader strategy surrounding it. If they are persuaded that they can achieve their objectives, they will be willing to take collective action, fully aware of the risks involved (McAdam, 1988).

The Strategies of Strikes

The strategies of protest that have been employed by the new generation of peasant workers in Guangdong and Dalian are quite different from those of their predecessors. The older generation more often chose to use parades, demonstrations, the blocking of streets and sit-ins to make their protest. By contrast, the younger workers' protest behaviour is generally confined within the factory area, and takes the form of walking around and waiting. The workers' strategic choice is contingent upon their analysis, arrived at through private communication, of the advantages and risks. Their objective has been to lower the risk of a strike while at the same time to raise the probability of its success if it cannot be avoided.

Another strategy to reduce risk is the boosting of workers' morale. On the Nanhai Honda workers' chat-line, for example, they shared legal knowledge as to what was necessary for legitimising proposed strike action in the face of the employers' stigmatising their resistance as illegal actions. This was also necessary to win the support of the mass media for the strike. By spreading information to all participating workers, those whose support was wavering could be encouraged to take part. Chinese patriotism was often used as symbolic discourse to raise workers' morale, especially in Japanese-owned enterprises. Workers' leaders in Nanhai Honda, for example, organised group singing of patriotic songs to exacerbate hostile attitudes towards the Japanese managers. In company TST in Dalian, workers even shouted 'Sack the Japanese personnel managers!' Denied the legitimacy of the support of the official trade union in organising and mobilising, workers are thrown back on such slogans to sustain strike action by stirring up emotion.

Studies of the 2010 strike waves suggest that most of the strikers thought that solidarity was the most important condition for success

(Gray and Jang, 2014). This solidarity was dependent upon their power resources, on the external resources they could recruit and on building a common sense of identity. It was necessary to sustain a sense of solidarity over the whole duration of the industrial conflict. The most effective strategies enhance the chance of success in the strike, while lowering potential risks.

It is not only the workers' organisation that determines the outcomes of strikes. Should the regional government suppress their protest, it might be fruitless. It is notable that the regional governments of both Guangdong and the Dalian Development Zone addressed strikes in a relatively accommodative way. They facilitated the resumption of production by implementing collective negotiation. There is no latent mechanism whereby a strike automatically initiates collective negotiations (Li, 2011).

Strike Resolution

Two Models of the Role of Government in Strike Resolution

Some analyses of the 2010 strikes suggest that the most effective means of resolving the disputes was by initiating collective negotiation (Chang, 2013). But not all those strikes were addressed by collective negotiation. There are marked differences between local governments. Two very different cases were in Tianjin and Suzhou. There the regional governments suppressed the industrial action by using police force. The government put pressure on both the workers and the employers to cease their confrontation. Compelled to stop the strike, the workers quickly resumed production, and were persuaded to deal with the conflict through legal procedures. Both settlements were still upheld three years later in 2014 (CLB, 2015: 25–29). The author's case studies in four regions suggest that the process of strike resolution varies according to the different political resources that the government can rely on. One can identify four categories (See Table 9.1).

The strategy employed by the government in both Guangdong and the Dalian Development Zone was one of mediation. Neither local government got directly involved in the dispute, preferring to set out the broad principles for strike resolution. The trade union, as the only legitimate representative organisation, intervened in both cases in a mediating role, resolving the strike by means of collective negotiation. By contrast, both the governments in Suzhou and in Tianjin directly intervened in the labour dispute, forcing the workers to stop their strike.

Table 9.1 *A strike resolution model of different regional governments*

		Strategies	
Model of strike resolution		Mediation/accommodation	Suppression/coercion
Political resources	Institutional arrangement	Guangdong: Mediation using existing institutions	Suzhou: Suppression using the existing institutions
	State intervention capacity	Dalian Development Zone: Mediation using the intervention capacity of the trade union	Tianjin: Suppression using the intervention capacity of the state administration

What were the differences in the political resources deployed by the four governments? Both Guangdong and Suzhou governments mobilised their existing institutions of collective negotiation through which the conflict could be actively resolved between workers and management. Despite adopting different strategies, they relied on the resources provided by labour law. By contrast, in the Dalian Development Zone and Tianjin, the governments relied on being able to influence outcomes more informally by being embedded deep in the local society. This reliance on the capacity of government to penetrate social life has been the traditional way in which the Chinese government has coped with collective action. In the case of Dalian, there is a powerful workplace trade union network which has managed to penetrate into every factory and was able to coordinate the resolution of labour disputes. The instrument of intervention was different in Tianjin. There a community administrative network was mobilised to guide workers in order to maintain stability and government control.

Despite these differences in the governance models in the four areas, what they have in common is that the regional government has to strike a balance between the economic development, social stability and the legitimacy of the government. In terms of the economy, local government is mainly concerned with priorities such as industrial modernisation, economic order and the flow of tax revenue. As regards the societal aspect, local government places more emphasis upon the necessity of quickly addressing labour disputes in order to ensure social stability. So far as the legitimacy of the government in the eyes of the people is concerned, both the governments in Guangdong and in the Dalian Development Zone drew on the legitimacy of the trade union to represent workers' interests via collective negotiation. But for Suzhou and Tianjin, even though both governments intervened using civil powers in the labour dispute, they still insisted on forcing the employers to make the concession of a pay rise to the aggrieved workers. The local governments all drew on their authority to impose a compromise. By doing this they prevented the disputes from exacerbating tensions between the workers and government, and they also mitigated the workers' discontents. Though they took different forms, all four of these models of strike resolution were based on an underlying pursuit of compromise.

The Representativeness of the Trade Union

Of the different routes to strike resolution we have just described, the institutionally more stable are those offering an accommodation between workers and employers through mediation. When there is a militant labour dispute, it is generally considered preferable to achieve compromise through collective negotiation rather than through public confrontation. But the effective implementation of collective negotiation is dependent upon the capacity of the union to organise the workers. This requires the union not only to enable them to elect representatives but also to defend workers' rights and interests in the subsequent collective negotiation. One difficulty is that, because it is a part of the local administrative bureaucracy, the regional trade union's objectives, strategies and actions are confined within the scope which the government determines (Chen, 2009). As a result, the extent to which an election facilitated by the workplace union can be perceived to be democratic in terms of its procedure, when there is active interference by the regional union, is subject to worker suspicion. The common outcome of what elections there were was that the union chair did not change, and that most of the elected union committee members were from management rather than being front-line workers. Indeed, the activists in the strike did not participate in the elections at all, and frontline workers occupied only a small minority of places on the workplace union committee.

The manner of intervention of the regional trade union in these cases suggests that it is possible for both elections and collective negotiations to remain politically under control. The union can ensure that industrial action can be avoided if it takes part in collective wage negotiations. But at the same time, re-organising the workplace trade union does not necessarily imply that trade union behaviour will then be determined by the workplace activists' involvement in trade union activities. Far from it, in the collective negotiations in both Guangdong and the Dalian Development Zone the regional trade union played dual roles as both leader of the union side and supervisor of the negotiation procedure for the purpose of workplace stability. As part of this process, the workplace union assumed a mediating role between the workers and the employer (Chen, 2010; Meng, 2012).

What is important is that the actions of the union still remain within the constraints that are laid down by the local governments' stated principles for economic and social development. As a result, orderly production can be resumed and maintained. An annual collective negotiation may serve to guarantee industrial peace. In this way, not only does the trade union advance the aspirations of the workers, but it is also successful in becoming, in effect, a functioning extension of government in stabilising society.

Even when the regional and workplace unions do play a mediating role, there may still be further strikes. For example, workers in Shenzhen Yantian International Container Terminal (YICT), having had a strike in 2007, launched a second industrial action in 2013. After the 2010 strike in Nanhai Honda, workers took collective action again in 2012. Such cases reflect one possible consequence when the workplace union extends its controlling function as a mediator. That is that, should the trade union fail to achieve what workers perceive to be effective representativeness, they may finally resort to a strike to defend their interests. The delicate balance pursued by the trade union between the protection of workers' interests and the maintenance of social stability would be broken.

For both sides involved in a strike, collective negotiation offers an effective means of conflict resolution. But although the use of collective negotiation is in practice forced on the parties by workers' collective action, this is not an indication that the right to strike has been institutionalised. It is certainly the case that the relevant official policies regarding collective negotiations are statutory regulations; examples are Regulations on Collective Agreements and also rules on collective consultation that are to be found in different provinces. But, on the other hand, the way that collective negotiation is generally used, whether by the government or by the trade union, in practice has gradually shifted into being a mechanism to prevent strikes. What is more, because the trade union is the mediating agent in this mechanism, this has weakened the extent of participation of common workers in collective consultation.

The result is a paradox. Because the right to collective bargaining is not matched by a right to strike, the apparent effectiveness of collective negotiation has the effect of hindering the possibility of the legalisation of a right to strike. It need not be so. It could be acknowledged that the possibility of a procedure for strikes would have the effect of strengthening collective negotiation providing, that is, that such a procedure were to be legally embedded within the disputes procedures of workplace labour regulations. In this respect, the incongruity of the legal relationship between strikes and collective negotiations in China does not only lie in the practical difficulties it creates for dispute resolution, but also in the failure to take advantage of what are essentially mutually reinforcing rights. Without a legal right to strike, the sustainability of collective negotiation as a means of strike resolution within the workplace must also be in doubt.

Strike Resolution and the Reconstruction of Labour Relations

This chapter has used a historical review of strikes and strike law to point out an institutional gap. It has examined the nature of this gap by exploring the logic lying behind workers' strike action and the practical process of strike resolution since 2010. The right to strike has been removed from the Chinese Constitution. As has been noted, a consequent paradox is that the failure to regulate strikes as a legitimate right has resulted in a gap between the practical resolution of strikes and the strike as a legal right. The fact that workers do strike is having the effect of promoting institutional change. This is reflected in the emergence of functioning strike resolution arrangements which, particularly by involving the trade union, have the effect of often defusing workers' intention to strike. The responses of the government, unions and employers all suggest that these *ad hoc* arrangements to cope with strikes do indeed play a restraining and preventative role in strike resolution. Comparable effects can also be seen in collective wage consultation when carried out with the genuine involvement of workers. Despite this, it is likely that the right to strike still remains remote from legalisation.

It has been argued that, under the principle of government domination, the required method of reforming collective labour relations with the intention of 'diminishing social unrest and defending political stability' is characterised by de-collectivising employment relations (Chen, 2009). As a consequence, strikes constantly pose challenges to the effectiveness of such policies. It is perverse that the effective implementation of collective bargaining in the workplace is in reality being driven by strikes, while, as a consequence, strikes are being restricted by collective bargaining. Putting it another way, collective actions are triggering de-collectivised consequences, through the process of collective bargaining. In effect, the dependence of effective collective bargaining on the use of strikes is being reinforced. This is a paradox that is particular to China.

The heart of the problem lies in a choice between, on the one hand, improving workers' participation in collective bargaining by means of trade union organisation or, on the other hand, strengthening managerial prerogative in the bargaining process. The other crucial issue is whether the trade union should continue to play a restricted role rather than be fully representative of the workers in collective bargaining. As has been noted in other contexts, if the union is not organised in a genuinely representative way, both strikes and collective bargaining may be manipulated by other actors as a game that excludes the workers altogether (Burawoy, 2011).

The Reshaping of Labour Relations

The institutions of the Chinese labour market are undergoing a succession of changes, driven in part by the increasing exposure of the economy to international market forces. What part do strikes play in this transformation? One perspective in industrial sociology would regard strikes as a Polanyian counter-movement against the commercialisation of labour that unavoidably comes with this marketisation. Strikes represent moments of insurgency that play a part in shaping the institutions designed to contain them (Friedman, 2013). But from the perspective of industrial relations, the important outcome of the interplay between the strike and existing institutions is the reshaping of both the interests of and the power relations between different stakeholders. The notion of 'stakeholders' is necessarily broad because strikes are deeply embedded in the wider economic and political relations of a society undergoing the traumas of globalisation. New actors in industrial relations frequently emerge as stakeholders, reflecting the increasing organisational complexity of labour, capital and the state. Notable among them are foreign investors, state agencies, international consumer campaigns, employer associations and labour NGOs (Liu, 2013; Cooke, 2014). How do strikes interact with the interests of the stakeholders?

Strikes interact with the interests of the workers in a distinct way in the Chinese context, because the official union cannot initiate strikes. The result is that there tends to be a marked shift in the nature of the workers' self-perceived interest between the actual time of the strike and afterwards. The workers' involvement in strike action, arising from a process of more-or-less spontaneous grass-roots organising, can be regarded as a major achievement in defending their own interests by mobilising collective power. Conversely, however, should the workers' short-term economic interests be to some degree satisfied, most of them prefer to enjoy their newly won benefits without facing up to the challenges of creating an organisation with the power to build on that over the longer-run. As a consequence, whatever the strike's achievement, workers tend to revert to a focus on short-term economic interests.

Recent years have seen the development of organisational support outside the official union with the establishment of labour NGOs, funded from a variety of sources. These may assist particular instances of collective worker organisation, but they lack any legitimacy in the eyes of the state. A consequence is that they may weaken the effectiveness of worker organisation because the union's mediating role owes so much to its relationship with the state. The danger for those worker organisations that lack a sustainable and independent organisation is that both employers and the state, rather than making temporary concessions in response to strikes, will move to new strategies of control less sympathetic to worker interests. For both trade unions and NGOs there is often a tension between their organisational interest in survival and development on the one hand, and the interests of their membership on the other. Conflicting interests between the organiser and the organised can have a substantial impact on the outcome of a strike.

The interests of the government are of central significance. Both the attitude taken by the employer and its management towards a strike, and the involvement of the trade union and labour NGOs, are strongly influenced by the principles and strategy adopted by the government in addressing labour conflict. How the state judges its own interests, and its relationships with the other actors, will be the major determinant of whether a strike can be an effective method for workers to defend and further their interests or to press for institutional change.

Quite apart from these interactions of different interests, the critical forces reshaping labour relations depend upon power relationships. First and foremost, what matters in a strike is whether workers can mobilise sufficient structural and associational power to counter the power of employers and the state to control events. If they can, there is the possibility that a compromise of interests can be achieved. But this is not enough. A strike wave or a large-scale strike may demonstrate the temporary strength of labour and achieve short-run gains. But whether sustained benefits for the workers can be achieved must remain in doubt so long as labour lacks a stable and independent organisation.

References

Bu L. (2010), 'The Story of Collective Bargaining of Nanhai Honda', (*Nanhai Honda Jiti Tanpan Shimo*), 9 November, www.chineseworkers.com.cn/_d271 079595.htm.

Burawoy, M. (2011), 'The roots of domination: Beyond Bourdieu and Gramsci', *Sociology*, 46(2), 187–206.

Burstein, P. (1991), 'Legal mobilization as a social movement tactic: The struggle for equal employment opportunity', *The American Journal of Sociology*, 96(5), 1201–1225.

Cao, X. and Meng, Q. (2017), 'Dockworkers' resistance and union reform within China's global supply chain', *Globalizations*, 14(2), 272–284.

Chan, C., Pun, N. and Chan, J. (2010), 'The role of the state, labour policy and migrant workers' struggles in globalized China' in P. Bowles and J. Harriss (eds.), *Globalization and Labour in China and India*, Hampshire: Palgrave Macmillan.

Chan, A. (2011), 'Strikes in China's export industries in comparative perspective', *The China Journal*, 65, 27–51.

Chan, C. and E. Hui (2012), 'The dynamics and dilemma of workplace trade union reform in China: The case of the Honda workers' strike', *Journal of Industrial Relations*, 54(5), 653–668.

Chang, K. (2005), 'Bagong quan lifa wenti sikao', [Thinking legislation of the right to strike]. *Xuehai*, 4, 43–55.

Chang, K. (2013), 'Legitimacy and the legal regulation of strikes in China: A case study of the Nanhai Honda strike', *International Journal of Comparative Labour Law and Industrial Relations*, 29(2), 133–144.

Chang, K. and Cooke. F. L. (2015), 'Legislating the right to strike in China: Historical development and prospects', *Journal of Industrial Relations*, 57(3), 440–455.

Chen, B. (2009), 'Laoquan yu fazhan: quanlilun yu gongnenglun de duoyuan fenxi', [*Labour rights and development: multiple analysis upon theories of labour rights and functionalism*], Beijing: Law Publishing House, 233–234.

Chen, F. (2003), 'Between the state and labor: The conflict of Chinese trade unions' dual institutional identity', *The China Quarterly*, 176, 1006–1028.

Chen, F. (2009), 'Union power in China: Source, operation and constraints', *Modern China*, 35(6), 662–689.

Chen, F. (2010), 'Quadripartite interactions of strike settlement in China', *The China Quarterly*, 201, 104–124.

Chen, F. (2015), 'China's road to the construction of labor rights', *Journal of Sociology*, 6, 1–15.

Chen, W. (2014), 'Laozi boyi xia de nanchaner: ping Guangdongsheng qiye jiti hetong tiaoli', [Difficult birth under labour-capital bargaining: comments on the Guangdong Collective Agreement Regulations], submitted to the International Conference of Collective Labour Relations and Collective Negotiation.

CLB (2015), *The Report of China Labour Movement Observation 2013–2014.*

Cooke, F. L. (2014), 'Chinese industrial relations research: in search of a broader analytical framework and representation', *Asian Pacific Journal of Management*, 31, 875–898.

Edwards, P. (1995), 'Strikes and industrial conflict', in Edwards P. (ed.), *Industrial Relations: Theory and Practice in Britain*, Oxford: Blackwell, 434–460

Fantasia, R. (1988), *Cultures of Solidarity: Consciousness, Action and Contemporary American Workers*, Berkeley: University of California Press.

Friedman, E. (2012), 'Getting through the hard times together? Chinese workers and unions respond to the economic crisis', *Journal of Industrial Relations*, 54(5), 459–475.

Friedman, E. (2013) 'Insurgency and institutionalization: The Polanyian countermovement and Chinese labor politics', *Theory and Society*, 42(3), 295–327.

Friedman, E. (2014), *Insurgency Trap: Labor Politics in Post-socialist China*, New York: Cornell University Press.

Gallagher, M. (2006), 'Mobilizing the law in China: "informed disenchantment" and the development of legal consciousness', *Law & Society Review*, 40(4), 783–816.

Gallagher, M. S. (2011), *Contagious Capitalism: Globalisation and the Politics of Labor in China*, Princeton: Princeton University Press.

Gallagher, M. S., Lee, C. K. and Kuruvilla, S. (2011), 'Introduction and Argument', in Kuruvilla, S., C. K. Lee, and M. Gallagher, (eds.), *From Iron Rice Bowl to Informalization: Market Workers, and the State in a Changing China*, New York: Cornell University Press, 1–16.

Gamson, W. (1992), 'The Social Psychology of Collective Action' in A. Morris, and C. Mueller (eds.), *Frontiers in Social Movement Theory*, New Haven: Yale University Press, 53–76.

Gray, K. and Jang Y. (2014), 'Labour unrest in the global political economy: The case of China's 2010 strike wave', *New Political Economy*, http://dx.doi.org/10.1080/13563467.2014.951613.

Hui, E. and Chan, C. K. C. (2014), 'The politics of labour legislation in Southern China: How foreign chambers of commerce and government agencies influence collective bargaining laws', *International Labor Review*, 153(4), 587–607.

Hyman, R. (1975), *Industrial Relations – A Marxist Introduction*, London: Macmillan Press.

Hyman, R. (1989), *Strikes* (4th ed.), London: Macmillan Press.

Jackson, P. M. (1987), *Strikes: Industrial Conflict in Britain, U.S.A. and Australia*, Sussex: Wheatsheaf Books.

Kelly, J. (1998), *Rethinking Industrial Relations: Mobilization, Collectivism and Long Waves*, London: Routledge.

Lee, C.K. (1998), 'The labor politics of market socialism', *Modern China*, 24(1), 3–33.

Lee, C. K. and Shen, Y. (2011), 'The anti-solidarity machine? Labor non-governmental organizations in China', in Kuruvilla, S., Lee, C. K. and Gallagher, M. (eds.), *From Iron Rice Bowl to Informalization: Market Workers, and the State in a Changing China*, New York: Cornell University Press, 173–187.

Leung, W. Y. (1998) 'The Politics of Labour Rebellions in China: 1989–94.' PhD dissertation, University of Hong Kong.

Li, C. (2014), 'Zhongguo laozi jiti duihua butong leixing duibi fenxi: yi guangdong weili', [Comparative analysis of different patterns of collective dialogue between employers and workers: A case study on Guangdong], Zhongguo renli ziyuan kaifa, [*China Human Resource Development*], 5, 111–117.

Li, L. (2012), 'Laoxiang guanxi yu chejian zhengzhi: diyuan tuanjie xingcheng de moshi bijiao', [Villagers' relationship and the politics of regime on the shopfloor: comparative study on patterns of geographical solidarity], in Yuan S. (ed.), Qinghua shehuixue pinglun [*Tsinghua Sociological Review*], (Volume 6)], No. 6. Beijing: sheke wexian chubanshe [Social Science Literature Press], 322–351.

Li, Q. (2011), 'Qindong jiti tanpan de qianjizhi', [The latent mechanism to jnitiate collective negotiation], Zhongguo renli ziyuan kaifa, [*China Human Resource Development*], 2, 82–85.

Li, Q. and C. Dai, (2014), 'Qiye binggou zhongde jiti laodong zhengyi jiqi yingxiang', [Collective labour disputes in company mergers and their impact], [*China Human Resource Development*], 13, 82–87.

Li, Q. and Y. Duan, (2015), 'Zhongguo jiti laodong guanxi hexie yunxing mianlin de tiaozhan yu duice: jiyu xingdongxing jiti laodong zhengyi de fenxi', [Challenges and resolutions to harmony of collective labour relations in China: an analysis of disputes in workers' collective actions], (unpublished).

Liu, A. (2005), 'Xuanze: guoqi biange yu gongren shengcun xingdong', [*Choice: Reform in state-owned enterprises and workers' actions for survival*], Beijing: Sheke wenxian chubanshe [Social Science Literature Press].

Liu, C. (2011), 'Jiti xingdong fa', [Law of Collective Action], Laodong fa [*Labour Law*], Chang, K. (ed.), Beijing: gaodeng jiaoyu chubanshe, [Senior Education Press].

Liu, M. W. (2013), 'China', in Frege, C. and Kelly, J. (eds.), *Comparative Employment Relations in the Global Economy*, London: Routledge, 324–345.

Lyddon, D. (2008), 'Strikes: Industrial conflict under New Labour', in Daniels G. and McIlroy, J. (eds.), *Trade Unions in a Neo-liberal World: British Trade Unions under New Labour*, New York: Routledge, 316–341.

Lyddon, D., Cao, X., Meng, Q. and Lu, J. (2015), 'A strike of "unorganized" workers in a Chinese car factory: The Nanhai Honda event of 2010', *Industrial Relations Journal*, 46 (2), 134–152.

McAdam, D. (1988), 'Micromobilization contexts and recruitment to activism', *International Social Movement Research* 1, 1–10.

Meng, Q. (2012), 'Tanpan youxi zhongde shuoheren: yi DLDA qu gonghui weili', [The mediator in a collective negotiation game: a case study in DLDA], in Shen, Y. (ed), Qinghua shehuixue pinglun [*Tsinghua Sociological Review (Volume 6)*], Beijing: Sheke wenxian chubanshe [Social Science Literature Press], 238–257.

Meng, Q. and Lu, J. (2013), 'Political space in the achievement of collective labor rights: Interaction between regional government and workers' protest', *Journal of Comparative Asian Development*, 12(3), 465–488.

Meng, Q. (2014), 'Suzao jiyu pingheng luoji de huanchong didai: yanhai diqu difang zhengfu zhili laozi chongtu moshi fenxi', [Shaping buffering space based on the logic of balance: Patterns of governance upon labour conflict in coastal regions], *Dongyue luncong* [Dongyu Tribune], (5), 47–54.

Pun, N. and Lu, H. L., (2010), 'Unfinished proletarianization: Self, anger and class action among the second generation of peasant-workers in present-day China', *Modern China*, 36(5), 493–519.

Qiu, L. (2014), 'Gaobie inu: fushikang, shuzi ziben zhuyi yu wangluo laogong dikang', [Farewell internet slave: Foxconn, digital capitalism and workers' protest on the internet], Shehui [*Society*]. (4), 128–139.

Silver, B. (2003), *Forces of Labor: Workers' Movements and Globalization since 1870*, Cambridge: Cambridge University Press.

Tong, X. (2006), 'Yanxu de shehui zhuyi wenhua chuantong: yiqi guoyou qiye gongren jiti xingdong de gean fenxi', [Continuous socialist cultural tradition: a case study on workers' collective action in a SOEs], Shehuixue yanjiu [*Sociological Research*], (1), 59–76.

Tsinghua University, (2012), 'Kunjing yu xingdong: xinshengdai nongmingong yu nongmingong shengchan tizhi de pengzhuang', [Plight and action: the clash between the new generation of peasant workers and peasant workers' regime], in Shen, Y. (ed.), Qinghua shehuixue pinglun [*Tsinghua Sociological Review*], Volume 6, 46–131

Tu, W. (2013), 'Lun woguo chanye xingdong de lifa: jiyu deguo de jingyan', [The legislation of collective action in China: Based on German experience], Zhongguo renli ziyuan kaifa, [*China Human Resource Development*], (1), 100–104.

Wang, J. (2011), 'Hulianwang dongyuan yu daigongchang gongren jiti kangzheng', [The internet mobilisation and workers' collective protest in suppliers' factories], Kaifang shidai [*Open Times*]. (11), 114–128.

Wang, J. (2012), 'Xingongren de shenghuo yu kangzheng zhengzhi: jiyu zhusanjiao jiti kangzheng anli de fenxi', [New labour's life and contentious politics: Analysis of collective protests in the Pearl River Delta], in Shen, Y. (ed.), Qinghua shehuixue pinglun [*Tsinghua Sociological Review*], Volume 6) Beijing: Social Science Literature Press, 190–214.

Wang, J. and Meng, Q. (2013), 'Xinshengdai nongmingong de jiti kangzheng moshi: cong shengchan zhengzhi dao shenghuo zhengzhi', [The patterns of collective protest of the new generation of peasant workers: From politics of production to politics of livelihood], Kaifang shidai [*Open Times*], (1), 165–178.

Wang, J., Meng, Q., Zheng, G. and Shen, Y. (2015), 'Zai zhiduhua yu jijinhua zhijian: zhongguo xinshengdai nongmingong de zuzhihua qushi', [Between institutionalisation and radicalisation: The future of the new generation of peasant workers in organizing in China], Ershiyi shiji [*The 21st Century*], 4.

Wen, X. (2014), 'Gonghui zhixuan: guangdong shijian de jingyan yu jiaoxun', [Union direct election: Experiences and lessons of Guangdong practice], Kaifang shidai [*Open Times*], (5), 54–56.

Wu, Q. (2010), 'Guoqi gaizhi yu chuantong chanye gongren zhuanxing', [*The Reform of SOEs and Transition of Traditional Industrial Workers*], Beijing: Sheke wenxian chubanshe [Social Science Literature Press].

Xie, Y. (2010), 'Cong sifa dongyuan dao jietou kangyi: nongmingong jiti xingdong shibai de zhengzhi yinsu jiqi houguo', [From legal mobilisation to protest on the street: Political causes and consequences of the failure of collective actions launched by peasant workers], Kaifang shidai [*Open Times*], (9), 46–56.

Xiong, Y. (2012), 'Zhengtixing zhili yu zhongguo nongmingong zinu de shehui rongru', [General governance and social integration of peasant workers' children in China], Zhongguo xingzheng guanli [*China Administrative Management*], 5.

Xu, X. (2009), 'Laodongzhe: cong zhurenwong xiang guyong laodongzhe de zhuanbian', [Workers: shift from master to the employed], in Chang, K. and Qiao, J. (eds.), *Chinese Labour Relations Report: Characteristics and Tendency of Labour Relations in Contemporary China*, Beijing: Renmin University, 77–109.

Zhai, Y. (2012), 'Jiti xieshang zhidu goujian de liangdian yu buzu: dui shenzhen jingji tequ jiti xieshang tiaoli (zhengqiu yijian gao) de pingxi', [The pros and cons of Collective consultation regulations: Comments on the *Collective Negotiation Regulation of Shenzhen Economic Special Zone (Draft)*], Makesi zhuyi yu xianshi [*Marxism and Reality*], (2), 186–191.

Zhang, L. (2015), *Inside China's Automobile Factories: The Politics of Labor and Worker Resistance*, Cambridge: Cambridge University Press.

10 Going to Market
Comparing Labour Relations Reform in China, Russia and Vietnam

Tim Pringle

Introduction

We live in interesting times. Following a period of relative tolerance, the Communist Party of China (CPC) has moved to regulate the operational space in which civil society organisations provide legal assistance and collective bargaining guidance to workers in dispute with their employers. These organisations have served as a source of competitive pressure on the All-China Federation of Trade Unions (ACFTU) to improve its representative capacity in the absence of other trade unions. These measures do not appear to have dampened Chinese workers' growing capacity to organise strikes.

In contrast to China, Vietnam had seemed on the cusp of permitting workers to organise outside the Party-led Vietnam Confederation of Labour (VGCL), at least at enterprise level. At present, the VGCL is the only legal trade union permitted. But the Vietnamese government had signed up to the Trans-Pacific Partnership (TPP) trade deal that included a clause on freedom of association. The deal was cancelled by US President Trump in early 2017, but if it had gone ahead, the implications for Vietnam's labour relations would have been significant. On paper at least, TPP granted Vietnamese workers the opportunity to institutionalise the gains they have made by strikes into formal collective agreements negotiated by independently organised unions.

In Russia, it is over two decades since they won the right to organise independently but the results for Russian workers have been modest. The former Party-led trade union re-packaged itself as the Federation of Independent Trade Unions of Russia (FNPR) and has substituted submission to Communist Party leadership for a close alliance with Putin's ruling Mother Russia party. This process of transferring

Thanks as always to Simon Clarke for editorial guidance and intellectual inspiration. Any errors are my own.

allegiance from one ruling party in an authoritarian state to another in a more liberal state has been accompanied by the formal abandonment of class struggle in favour of social partnership. In exchange, the FNPR has benefited from labour laws that privilege its position over the 'alternative' trade unions that emerged during and after the fall of the Soviet Union. Nevertheless, following a period of retreat and atomisation during the first decade of the new century, there are signs that these more militant organisations are gaining in strength in some sectors.

These three very different national experiences provide the basis for this chapter's exploration of the ability of trade unions in formerly command economies to adapt to market conditions. The argument considers three critical aspects of labour relations. First, I look at union (re)organisation during the first phases of transition. Second, I examine the evolving national legal frameworks in which trade unions have to operate. This section is based on the assumption that while labour militancy remains a key driver of trade union reform across all three countries, unions continue to redirect such militancy into juridical channels of resolution whenever possible. I will show that the degree to which this is possible varies considerably. Third, I discuss the evolution of collective bargaining. While the practice is comparatively well-established in Russia, it remains a work in progress in China and Vietnam. Union plurality in Russia generates competition between unions to extract concessions from employers, but this impetus is blunted by a dominant narrative of social partnership. Strikes in China have forced employers to the bargaining table on an irregular basis, often to negotiate terms of closure or relocation. There is scattered evidence of forms of annual collective bargaining being incorporated at firm and even sector – level but this is very far from widespread. In Vietnam, strike waves continue to be a feature of industrial relations but the VGCL has not been able to use them as an opportunity to develop effective collective bargaining despite the opening up of legal opportunities.

Trade Union Organisation in Transition

The transition in each country has been from a command economy in which production was organised to meet targets fixed by central planners, to a partially decentralised market economy. This presented two major and interlinked challenges to trade unions across all three countries: diversification of property rights and union autonomy. Under the command economy, where all enterprises were owned by the 'people' (i.e. the state), trade unions played a directive role that combined often resource-starved welfare provision with the function of organising the workforce to meet output targets fixed in five year plans. Workplace representation of members' rights was subsumed by a culture of production and individual sacrifice to the collective interests of the entire working class – as defined by the Party. While this did not exclude labour protection, it was not based on collective power but rather on the state regulation of employment relations in which the unions played a minimal part. As such, the trade unions were fundamentally different from trade unions in capitalist societies, however much the latter might collaborate with employers and be integrated into corporatist structures of participation (Pringle and Clarke, 2011: 10).

The process of all three countries' re-orientation to a market economy approximately coincided with the ascendancy of neoliberal globalisation following the oil shocks in the 1970s. In 1978, the third plenum of the 11th Central Committee of CPC announced the reform and opening up (*gaige kaifang*) of the economy. In 1985, economic reforms known as *perestroika*, which were instrumentalised by *glasnost* or freedom of speech, were launched in the Soviet Union by Gorbachev. In 1986, the Vietnamese Communist Party announced a process of 'renovation' known as *doi moi*. By 1995, both China and Vietnam had well-established mixed property rights regimes characterised by their respective ruling communist parties as 'socialist market' economies. Both remained one-party states with the capacity to oversee the re-emergence of capitalist labour relations. Both countries' gross domestic product (GDP) and per capita incomes grew substantially, especially China although this was accompanied by significant increases in inequality (Fritzen, 2002: 635; Malesky *et al.*, 2011: 412). The transition process removed enterprises from direct state control and trade unions ceased to be simply agents of state regulation. As property ownership diversified, up to and including private property, Party-led trade unions found themselves mediating the relationship between the labour force and the employer in the private sector. In the state sector, unions made no attempt to challenge the mass redundancies generated by the restructuring and privatisation of state-owned enterprises (Clarke and Pringle, 2009: 91).

In Russia, the pace of transition was much faster and the outcome more traumatic. The soviet administrative-command system of management collapsed into a 'wild market' system characterised by rapid privatisation in which direct state ownership was substituted by a powerful and violent oligarchy made up of former state enterprise directors, crime bosses and adventurers (Pringle and Clarke, 2011: 17). The soviet era All Union Central Council of Trade Unions (VTsSPS) declared independence from the Party-state as early as 1987 in an attempt to distance itself from the more radical aspects of privatisation.

However, neither the independence of the 'traditional' unions nor the new 'alternative' unions that emerged were able to ameliorate the consequent dramatic decline in the living standards of the working class that accompanied and followed in the wake of the fall of the Soviet Union.

Whether mediated gradually via the socialist market economy or brutally imposed by a Chicago-school inspired 'big bang' privatisation, the emergence of capitalist labour relations raised the challenge of what was effectively a new trade union function in a changing environment. This was the representation of members' interests that stood in opposition to capital and frequently to the state. In China, the implications first made their presence felt at the 11th Congress of the ACFTU in 1988. For the first time since 1953, union autonomy was again on the congress agenda provoking significant debate. At the close, the union's national newspaper indicated progress in an editorial calling for 'the establishment of an independent, sovereign trade union with a high degree of democracy and which workers could trust' (*Workers' Daily*, 1988). While 'independent' in this context did not mean separation from the Party, any moves to act in the spirit of the congress discussions were brought to a halt by the student protests in Tiananmen Square, tacitly supported by the union via financial donations. This act of solidarity led to a thorough purge of the organisation in the wake of the violent suppression of the protests.

The question of union organisation next publicly emerged in the years following the 15th Party Congress in 1997 that focussed on economic restructuring of the state sector, hitherto confined to pilot projects. The Party Congress had concluded on the slogan *zhua da fang xiao* (hold on to the large and medium [state enterprises] release the small). This signalled the rolling out of a national programme of state-owned enterprise (SOE) restructuring and phased redundancy that had hitherto been restricted to local-level pilots in cities such as Shanghai and Sichuan (Pringle, 2011: 25). The restructuring – up to and including full privatisation – laid off between 30 and 50 million workers between 1997 and 2002 (Pringle and Leung, 2009) and culminated in a wave of resistance by workers in north east China's heavy industry, who were hit especially hard by the restructuring (Lee, 2007). Added to the ACFTU failure to react in defence of its members' jobs was its seeming inability to establish a presence in the rapidly expanding non-state economy.

Transition had plunged the organisation into crisis. This was eloquently expressed in a speech by the then chair of the ACFTU, Wei Jianxing:

a considerable number of trade union organizations [and branches] have collapsed and their members washed away. But the organization of trade unions in newly established enterprises has simply not happened. At the end of 1999, national trade union membership dropped to eighty-seven million, leaving more than one hundred million workers unorganized. When there is not even a trade union, what is the point of talking about trade unions upholding the legal rights of workers? Or trade unions being the transmission belt between the Party and the masses? Or trade unions being an important social pillar of state power? (Wei, 2000 cited in Human Rights Watch, 2002: 10).

In effect, this broadside laid the groundwork for the ACFTU's recruitment drive in the private sector, especially in foreign-invested enterprises, that followed its 14th Congress in 2003. The congress finally recognised that China's vast number of off-farm workers, officially classified as 'peasant workers' (*nongmin gong*), were part of the working class and could be therefore be organised into the trade unions. This was despite the continued institutional discrimination arising from China's residence-based system of identity cards that privileged urban residents over rural residents.

In Vietnam the 6th Party Congress in 1986 announced *doi moi* (renovation). *Doi moi* was based on three major policies: the opening up of the economy to non-state investment, including foreign direct investment; restructuring of SOEs; and the development of an export-orientated industrialisation strategy. SOE restructuring proceeded with caution, slowed by well-established economic and political links between SOEs and state-owned commercial banks which were reflected in the former's favoured access to loans (Klump and Bonschab 2004: 31). Nevertheless, Vietnam's SOEs came under severe pressure at the end of the 1980s as they faced subsidy cuts in the wake of the withdrawal of Soviet aid. Between 1988 and 1992 almost a third of SOE workers, 800,000 people, predominantly women from smaller SOEs, were laid off. Unlike in China, there was little evidence of resistance (Pringle and Clarke, 2011: 17). As in China, reform fostered discussion on the role of the Party-led trade union, in this case at the very highest levels of power. Former VGCL Chairman Nguyen Van Linh used his position as no less than General Secretary of the Vietnamese Communist Party to argue for 'institutional independence of the VGCL' at the union's 6th National Congress held in 1988. Again, independence should not be interpreted as separation from the Party. His speech enjoyed considerable support from VGCL cadres in attendance (Schweisshelm and Do, 2015). However, these debates abruptly ceased when the regime observed the chaos in the rest of the Communist world in 1989, including democracy protests in China and national strikes in the Soviet Union. Discussion of trade union reform, let alone of independence, was dropped.

Russia's road to market reforms was a much more dramatic process because in 1989 miners' strikes, sparked by competition over state resources, placed huge pressure on the state (Clarke and Kabalina, 1995). After cautiously introducing economic liberalisation in the latter half of the 1980s, Gorbachev had attempted to harness workers' protests and strikes to generate pressure for trade union reform as a manifestation of '*perestroika*' from below. This implied a democratisation of trade union structures that were already weakened by the Law on Cooperatives (1988) that ended the era of the state as sole legal employer. In the coal-mining regions, strike committees representing up to 600,000 strikers had replaced traditional union representation, forcing the state to concede freedom of association in 1990. Nevertheless, despite the emergence of the NPG (or national Independent Miners Union), militants were assimilated into the bureaucratic trade union apparatus, as the much lower impact of the 1991 strike wave demonstrated, (Clarke, Fairbrother and Borisov, 1995). In practice, these events had only a marginal impact on the conduct of the traditional unions in Russia, most of which were affiliated to the FNPR which had been founded in 1990 (Pringle and Clarke, 2011).

More successful alternative unions did, however, spring up in sectors where workers enjoyed a considerable degree of immediate 'structural power' (Silver, 2003). Air-traffic controllers, dock workers and transport workers organised independent trade unions and strike committees that emulated the miners. The most successful was the Federation of Air Traffic Controllers' Unions (FPAD), although success was short-lived and involved a degree of political horse-trading with Gorbachev's successor, Yeltsin. The FPAD had extracted concessions from the Soviet government in 1991 and supported Yeltsin during a putsch in August of the same year. This support was rewarded with a favourable agreement covering air-traffic controllers signed with the state in May 1992 (Pringle and Clarke, 2011: 50). Failure to implement fully the terms of the agreement led the FPAD to issue a strike call in August 1992. In marked contrast to earlier deals, the strike was met with threats from Yeltsin to liquidate the union and seize its assets. The subsequent history of the union has been one of intimidation and repression by both government and employers.

This pattern has dogged the alternative unions and was reinforced, as we shall see, by a new Labour Code passed by the Russian parliament in 2001. Crucially for the FNPR, the new law awarded bargaining rights and the right to call a strike to the representative of the majority of the workforce in a given enterprise or sector; this was nearly always the

FNPR. This made life especially difficult for those alternative unions representing particular sections of the working class or professional groups which had previously deployed strikes or the threat of strikes as a primary form of struggle.

Employment Relations, Trade Unions and the Law

All three countries have made significant efforts to regulate capitalist employment relations by legislation. China's first national labour law was introduced in 1995, the outcome of the consolidation of piecemeal legislation developed via regulations (*tiaoli*), methods (*banfa*) and opinions (*yijian*) issued since the start of the reform era. The law attempted to balance employment creation with the protection of workers. This was in the context of the introduction of fixed-term contracts in both the rapidly developing private sector and SOEs (at least for new hires) – contracts that were replacing the former model of permanent employment. The new law restated the earlier reform of the Trade Union Law (1992) that prohibited freedom of association, restricting union organisation to the ACFTU (Article 7). Article 36 set the working week at 44 hours with a maximum of 36 hours overtime in a given month (Article 41) and stipulated the conditions under which an employee could be dismissed prior to contract expiration (Articles 26–29). Article 30 stated that, where it believes the employing unit has violated the law or regulations in cancelling a contract, the trade union can question the process and must support any legal challenges of the person concerned. The law also consolidated the framework of a dispute resolution system based on mediation, arbitration and the courts (Article 77). Conciliation committees were to be established in all enterprises to facilitate mediation between employers and employees in individual disputes. Failure to reach agreement meant that the dispute could be referred to a tripartite Labour Disputes and Arbitration Committee chaired by an official from the local labour bureau.

Perhaps the most striking feature of China's new Labour Law was its emphasis on individual labour rights. For example, only three articles were devoted to collective contracts, despite the ACFTU lobbying for more emphasis on collective rights. In contrast, as we shall see, the Labour Contract Law that was introduced 15 years later in 2008 devoted an entire chapter to collective contracts. Reflecting the strong state intervention from the pre-reform era, the standards and range of labour rights covered in the law were high in comparison to those of other developing countries. Their practical implementation was an unlikely prospect, however, given weak primary trade unions and the absence of a tradition of collective bargaining. The law was a balancing act. The policy aims of the regulation of the private sector and downsizing of the public sector were balanced against the political risks of social unrest that the substitution of permanent employment with fixed-term contracts carried. The right to strike, which had been deleted from the constitution in 1982, remained a grey area, with no explicit stipulation forbidding strike action and likewise none protecting it. In the event, collective labour disputes throughout the 1990s were met with repressive measures (Chan, 2001).

Unlike in China, Article 7 of Vietnam's national Labour Code (1994) awarded workers the right to strike (Article 7.4). However, this right was qualified by the Trade Union Law (1990) that stipulated that all trade unions must be affiliated to the VGCL and only these legal unions could organise a strike, which they were unlikely to do. Moreover, even if a VGCL union agreed to lead a strike, this could only take place after the grievances had gone through a company level conciliation council or the provincial level Labour Arbitration Council (Article 171). The workers' consequent lack of confidence in the official unions' capacity to represent their rights and interests is illustrated by the complete absence of any examples in which workers have organised strikes via enterprise unions, despite the sustained increase in wildcat strikes (Ly Khanh, 2015: 116).

The Labour Code of 1994 divided contracts into three categories: permanent contracts, contracts of one to three years and contracts for seasonal work over less than one year (Article 27). Article 38 stipulated the conditions in which employers were allowed to dismiss employees, although such a recourse required consultation with the trade unions. The law also included chapters on wages, stipulating that they should not be lower than the minimum wage set by the state (Chapter 6), and on Collective Labour Agreements (Chapter 5) of one to three years in duration (Article 50). These provisions were more detailed than those in China's Labour Law (1994) and explicitly encouraged the setting of labour standards more 'favourable to workers than those of labour legislation' (Article 44). As was the case in China, the Labour Code offered a high degree of protection to Vietnamese workers, but the extent to which employers complied with these high standards in practice was seriously constrained by the absence of strong primary level trade unions. In effect, the disciplining of capital remained the responsibility of the state, a state which, in both China and Vietnam, was focussed on employment creation through foreign investment and the promotion of exports.

This was not the case in Russia. Following a period of economic stagnation in the 1990s, a rise in energy prices supported a partial economic recovery during the first decade of the new century. The recovery has since been seriously constrained by the fallout from the 2008 financial crisis, a fall in oil prices and sanctions by Western countries following the events in Ukraine. Although Russia has attracted foreign investment, the government has not pursued export promotion in manufacturing along Asian lines (Burawoy, 1996). The recession of the nineties, combined with tensions between Yeltsin's government and the traditional FNPR-affiliated unions, alongside a power struggle between the new 'alternative' unions and the FNPR, combined to delay the replacement of the 1972 Soviet Labour Code that had effectively defused labour conflicts during the former era (Pringle and Clarke, 2011: 23). This procrastination was intensified by the attempts of the International Monetary Fund and World Bank to impose draconian neo-liberal inspired revisions to labour legislation that were largely unsuccessful, despite the onslaughts of the 'Chicago boys'. Indeed, some scholars argue that the new Labour Code that finally came into force in 2002 still reflected Soviet era preoccupations with full employment and generating a post-socialist 'Russian labour market model', and that it sits in contrast to the widespread privatisations that characterised Russia's transition period (Vinagradova *et al.*, 2015: 194).

The revised code certainly preserved most of the substantial protective elements of the Soviet Labour Code, such as protection against arbitrary dismissal, the right to a minimum wage and a 40-hour working week, as well as paid leave and detailed health and safety provisions. However, it removed the trade union right to veto management proposals and, as stated above, it awarded bargaining and effective representation rights to the largest trade union in a given enterprise, which was nearly always the traditional FNPR affiliated union. Strikes were prohibited in the emergency services and 'may be prohibited by federal law in the organisations ... directly related to providing vital services to the population (energy supply, heating and heat supply, water supply, gas supply, air, rail, and water transportation, communications and hospitals)'.[1] In 2006, recommendations from the International Labour Organisation (ILO) led to an easing of the technical constraints on the right to strike but 'they did not bring any substantial changes' (Vinagradova *et al.*, 2015: 197).

These Russian labour laws were subject to revisions during the first decade of the new millennium. As capitalist labour relations became more entrenched, class-orientated struggles emerged to challenge capital and

---

[1] See www.tobaccocontrollaws.org/files/live/Russia/Russia%20-%20Labour%20Code.pdf (unofficial translation). Accessed 28 July 2016.

mobilise the state into further reforms of the legal frameworks governing labour relations. Upholding social stability was the common impetus underlining these reforms but their direction has not been uniform. In 2009 the reduction of union influence over management was consolidated further when the Constitutional Court revoked article 374 of the Labour Code (2002) that protected primary trade union leaders from dismissal unless the employer had obtained the agreement of a higher union body (Pringle and Clarke, 2015: 26). Union autonomy was further set back when the Russian Federation's Law on Combating Extremist Activity was used by the courts to judge some union literature extremist and therefore illegal (Pringle, 2015a: 217). More in labour's favour, a new law came into effect in January 2016 prohibiting the practice of 'labour leasing', whereby companies provide personnel to client companies who are responsible for the management and task allocation of the employees even though they still receive wages from the original provider company. Considerably weakening this, the same law formalises the more universal practice of firms employing agency workers via, according to the law, accredited employment companies with a minimum capitalisation of one million roubles (Hellevig *et al.*, 2014: 26).

In China, a sustained increase in strikes encouraged the state to introduce a raft of legislation in 2008 that most scholars agree was an attempt to slow the rate of informalisation and re-balance, even collectivise, employment relations in favour of labour (Kuruvilla *et al.*, 2011: 6). The Labour Contract Law (2008) was introduced after an intense period of public consultation as well as lobbying from academics, civil society organisations and even a submission from the International Trade Union Congress, which has a history of delicate relations with the ACFTU. The new law made written contracts mandatory (article 10), stipulated permanent employment to employees who have served two fixed-term contracts (article 14), and clarified severance pay for those workers whose contracts are not renewed (article 46). Perhaps most significant, it expanded the three clauses on collective contracts in the original labour law into an entire chapter.

An unintended consequence of the Labour Contract Law was that employers have since increased the use of agency (or dispatched) workers, especially in the state sector, in order to avoid the obligation to provide permanent employment (Chan *et al.*, 2015). The Chinese government moved to clamp down on this practice when the Ministry of Human Resources and Social Security issued the Interim Regulations of Labour Dispatch in January 2014. The regulation gave companies just over two years to reduce the proportion of dispatched workers to ten per cent of the workforce with a deadline of March 2016. Labour lawyers do not expect the target to be met, especially as the state sector is the most significant employer of China's 60 million dispatched workers, having seen an increase of 33 million over the preceding three years (*Jingji Guancha bao*, 2011). One Shanghai-based law practitioner considered that 'there are those who sign them on as regular employees, but there would seem to be many more who just do nothing, whether out of ignorance, inefficiency, disregard or lack of fear of consequences because they feel they can resolve problems with their "*guanxi*"'.[2] The practice of employing agency workers is likely to remain widespread, particularly as the Chinese rate of growth slows and the pressure on labour markets eases.

The Labour Disputes and Mediation Law was also rolled out nationally in 2008, resulting in lower costs to workers pursuing grievances through arbitration and a predictable increase in cases going to both arbitration and the courts (Cooney *et al.*, 2013). Such has been the increase that the city level trade unions have been encouraging primary unions to focus on mediation and conciliation procedures to ease pressure on arbitration committees and the courts where 'delays of up to one year were not uncommon' (Gallagher and Dong, 2011: 58).

In Vietnam, strikes were the major impetus behind a revision of Chapter 14 of the Labour Code in 2006 (Do, 2013: 195) pertaining to the settlement of disputes. The issue of strikes and their resolution has historically created tension and vigorous debates between the Ministry of Labour and Social Security (MOLISA) and VGCL. The Ministry were behind an amendment permitting workers in non-unionised workplaces to elect three representatives and to negotiate with employers and even organise strikes. This was a measure that the Ministry proposed to strengthen by extending the right of non-union representatives to conclude collective bargaining agreements thus 'opening the door to freedom of association' (Pringle and Clarke, 2011: 127). MOLISA-sponsored revisions also stated that henceforth disputes were to be distinguished between rights-based and interest-based conflicts in recognition of strikes in which workers' demands went beyond minimum legal requirements – some disputes have elements of both. These substantial revisions had very little impact and did not head off further strike waves, most of which were in unionised companies (Pringle and Clarke, *op. cit.* 127), further underlining the VGCL's inability to prevent collective disputes at workplace level. On the other hand, it has been found that 'work stoppages are more common among unionized workplaces because the presence of a union in the workplace signals to workers that by engaging in a wildcat strike, they

---

[2] See: www.mayerbrown.com/China-Companies-Must-Shed-Dispatch-Workers-04–04–2016/. Accessed 31 July 2016.

may be able to activate the representation and protection roles of official trade unions' (Anner and Liu, 2016: 3). Indeed, after conducting a survey of 3943 foreign-invested enterprises between 2010 and 2012, the authors suggest that 'the role of trade unions in socialist states maybe more nuanced than previously assumed'.

In 2012, the Labour Code was again subject to revisions. MOLISA's victory over VGCL with regard to workers in non-unionised workplaces having the right to elect representatives to bargain with employers was revoked; instead bargaining rights in non-unionised workplaces were transferred to the relevant higher VGCL union. But the revisions also introduced a new chapter devoted to social dialogue. This requires 'the election of worker representatives and worker–management meetings once every three months to discuss production, implementation of collective bargaining agreements, working conditions, and other issues requested by worker representatives' (Anner, 2015: 9).

Another important addition to the legal framework has been the formation of a National Wage Council (NWC) modelled on the Korean Minimum Wage Council and the outcome of guidance from the International Labour Organization (Khanh, 2015: 121). The 1994 Labour Code stipulated that minimum wages should be set following consultations with the VGCL and 'representatives of the employers' (Article 56) – that is, the Vietnam Chamber of Commerce and Industry (VCCI) and the Vietnam Cooperative Alliance (VCA). The NWC is a highly structured body made up of 15 members: five from the VGCL, five from MOLISA and five from the main employers' organisations including VCCI, VCA, the Vietnam Textile and Apparel Association, the Vietnam Leather and Footwear Association, and the Vietnam Association of Small and Medium Enterprises (Khanh, 2015: 122). According to the ILO, the NWC 'marks a transformation from a solely Government-led minimum wage fixing mechanism into a new tripartite body which recognises the importance of workers' and employers' participation' (2013).[3] It was a complementary wage-setting mechanism working alongside collective bargaining according to the then ILO Country Director Sziraczki. Khanh takes the opposite view, noting that the NWC is important precisely because of the absence of strong collective bargaining mechanisms, but that its contribution to minimum wage setting is constrained by the lack of 'legitimate representation characteristic of these social partners' (Khanh, 2015: 121), a direct reference to the absence of freedom of association in Vietnam for both workers and employers.

---

[3] See: www.ilo.org/hanoi/Informationresources/Publicinformation/WCMS_218763/lang–en/index.htm.

This section has provided a comparative summary of the evolution of labour legislation across all three countries. In China and Vietnam, labour unrest, and specifically strikes, were identified as a key driver of reform and of its impact on union representation. Likewise in Russia, the state's fear of social unrest and instability has given rise to a labour market model in which 'the disparity between Russia's overall economic trends and employment trends has been mostly due to labor regulations that make the costs of adjusting the labor force to declining market demand rather high for employers, as well as to state interventions aimed at avoiding mass dismissals fraught with social tensions' (Vinagradova *et al.*, 2015: 194). In other words, employment is privileged but only on the condition of a generally passive trade unionism premised on social partnership.

In the next section, I focus on how unions have fared in these post-socialist frameworks by examining their ability to engage in collective bargaining. In doing so I draw on relevant legal and regulatory interventions placed in the context of the social relations that have influenced the evolution of this crucial instrument of class compromise.

Forms of Collective Bargaining and the Forces of Labour

In China, a form of negotiation known as 'collective consultation' (*jiti xieshang*) has been used by both government and union officials to refer to collective labour relations and contracts throughout the reform period. The term is preferred over 'collective bargaining' (*jiti tanpan*) in order to avoid the connotation of separate and antagonistic interests that remains a politically sensitive issue in China where the one-party state remains in place. This is not the case in Vietnam, despite still being a one-party state. Nor is it the case in Russia where the term 'collective bargaining' is used in both law and by concerned actors, possibly reflecting a more relaxed approach of officials to strikes in Vietnam and the existence of freedom of association in Russia.

In recent years, labour academics researching in China – notably those contributing to this volume – as well as practitioners in labour non-governmental organisations have increasingly referred to 'collective bargaining'. The term is loosely used to describe the rise in various forms of more or less participatory bargaining between employer and workers' representatives, especially since 2010 when it was collective bargaining that arguably resolved an unprecedented 19-day strike in the Nanhai Honda auto parts factory in Guangdong (Lyddon *et al.*, 2015; Chan and Hui, 2012). In Vietnam, there appears to be political tolerance of forms of collective bargaining at a conceptual level – as evidenced by the willingness to sign up to the labour clauses in the now defunct TPP – but little evidence of it in practice. But it is the presence of freedom of association in Russia that dictates that it is here that we find a model of collective bargaining that on paper is closest to the international standards set out in ILO Conventions 87 on Freedom of Association and Protection of the Right to Organise and Convention 98 on the Right to Organise and Collective Bargaining. Legal frameworks in both Vietnam and China do not meet the standards of these core labour rights.

This does not mean that collective bargaining in Russia has made a successful transition from the productionist preoccupations of Soviet era trade unions to an accountable and effective system of collective bargaining. Indeed, Gerasimova and Bolsheva find that 'there are many examples of CLAs [collective labour agreements] that just contain general provisions and the repetition of legal obligations' largely irrelevant to 'fixing real working conditions and wages' (2015: 334–335). According to the ILO, union density in Russia is 28 per cent including membership of the alternative unions, most of which are now united under one confederation, the Confederation of Labour of Russia (KTR). Gerasimova and Bolsheva (2015:331) put total union density slightly higher at 33 per cent but this drops to 25 per cent of total employment if students and pensioners are excluded. The ILO reports collective bargaining coverage of 23 per cent of employees although many of these CLAs are purely formal.

One of the main constraints on collective bargaining in Russia is the absence of partners from the employers' side. This leads to unions at national and regional level concluding bipartite agreements with the government. The same is true for sectoral CLAs and, although such agreements only apply to employers who sign on to them, primary level unions use them as a reference point, a trend that contributes towards CLAs simply duplicating minimum standards. The FNPR has for the most part attempted to improve the quality of CLAs in the sectors where it already has primary unions rather than venture into new private sectors where there is much less union activity. This policy of consolidation has indeed led to some improvement in the quality of CLAs that numbered 155,540 in 2012 as well as 6,781 sectoral and territorial CLAs. These figures do not include a further 1,700 sectoral agreements and 37,000 plant level CLAs signed with non-FNPR unions or 'other representative bodies' (Gerasimova and Bolsheva, 2015: 333). On the other hand, the improvements in CLA quality were undermined by union weaknesses at primary level and the onset of the financial crisis. For example, only three of the 29 agreements in the private sector (oil, chemicals and construction) provided for a minimum wage equal to the subsistence minimum discussed later, nine included recommendations on pay differentials, and eight on the average wage in the industry. Fifteen fixed the proportion of basic pay in the wage, but only four achieved the FNPR goal of setting this at 70 per cent of pay.[4] The global financial crisis of 2008 led to employers in the oil industry refusing to sign agreements and, in six of the 29 private-sector agreements, the specified minimum wage fell below the legal minimum (Pringle, 2015a: 223).

In China, the statistics for trade union membership and collective agreement coverage tell us very little. The top-down union recruitment drive that followed Chairman Wei Jianxing's dressing down of union cadres and the ACFTU's 14th National Conference in 2003 produced a paper membership of over 280 million by 2014.[5] A very large proportion of these members are enrolled in the union via closed shop agreements with employers rather than through organising campaigns directed at workers. The initially clandestine organisation into unions of a small number of Wal-Mart stores did provide an interesting exception but this quickly deteriorated into the top down imposition of a national collective contract (Chan, 2011: 199–216). A more recent summary of the relevant ACFTU statistics between 2003 and 2011 reports that 223.2 million people are covered by general collective agreements out of a membership of 258 million. If we compare this figure with the year of the 14th Congress in 2003, we find an increase in membership of 134.6 million in under a decade and an equally remarkable increase in the number of people covered by general collective agreements of 156.2 million (Lee *et al.*, 2016: 219). Random conversations with migrant workers in industrial districts in China would suggest that even if they are aware of a collective contract, hardly any workers will have participated in the process of concluding it.[6]

In Vietnam union membership stood at 7.9 million across 113,000 primary trade union branches in 2013 and the vast majority of these are in government institutions and SOEs (Schweisshelm, 2015). There is no centralised system of reporting collective agreements in Vietnam rendering it difficult to establish how many workers are covered, although the VGCL does compile its own figures on CLAs signed. A large informal economy in which more than 80 per cent of the economically active population finds work adds to the statistical challenge (Dieu and Dong, 2015: 50). However, the VGCL has invested considerable resources so

---

[4] *Vesti FNPR* 6 (2008): 25, 61–71, cited in Pringle and Clarke, *Challenge of Transition*, 85.
[5] Barnes, T. and Lin, K. 'China's growing labour movement offers hope for workers globally'. http://theconversation.com/chinas-growing-labour-movement-offers-hope-for-workers-globally-39921.
[6] The author conducted just such a random exercise in the Dalian Development Zone in June 2016.

that 'thousands of training courses raising skills in negotiating and signing CLAs were organized for union activists at all levels' (Dieu and Dong, 2015: 52). Some of these involve direct cooperation with international unions such as IndustriALL who are 'operating a union building project in Vietnam, providing training on collective bargaining for shop stewards or workplace union representatives'.[7] The union claimed that in 2011, 65.2 per cent of all enterprises were covered by a CLA: 96.3 per cent in SOEs, 59.2 per cent of private enterprises and 64.6 per cent of FIEs (VGCL, 2011 cited in Dieu and Dong, 2015: 52). Most of these agreements 'simply reproduce legal provisions without bringing any more benefits to the workers than prescribed by law and anyway are not implemented in reality (especially at the private enterprises and FIEs)' (Dieu and Dong, 2015: 52). The VGCL itself admits that only 40 per cent of these CLAs are 'good quality' (VGCL, 2011 cited in Dieu and Dong, 2015: 52) by which it means that the contents include improvements of minimum legal standards.

Minimum Wages

Given the tendency across all three countries for collective agreements to reproduce minimum legal standards, the process of minimum wage setting is important to the scope and development of collective bargaining. Vietnam has four minimum wages but the most important for this chapter are the regional minimum wage levels that apply to all enterprises and the sectoral minimum wages. Prior to the establishment of the NWC, the setting of minimum wage levels was something of a political football between the Vietnamese government, MOLISA and the VGCL. Due to its general lack of progress in collective bargaining, the VGCL has traditionally been inclined to leave regulation of labour relations to MOLISA. This was despite MOLISA's apparent attempts, mentioned earlier, to undermine the trade union by reforms to the Labour Code that appeared to the bypass VGCL's monopoly on representation.

The VGCL has been generally quick to attribute responsibility for strike waves during the 2000s to low minimum wage levels and to government procrastination over increasing them (Pringle and Clarke, 2011: 108). Following a strike wave in 2005, the VGCL began to pressure the government to increase the minimum wage, using tripartite meetings, a media campaign and lobbying the National Assembly and Party Committee. The establishment of the NWC was an attempt to break

---

[7] See: 'Advancing trade unions in Vietnam'. www.industriall-union.org/developing-trade-unions-in-vietnam.

the cycle of strikes, buck passing between government agencies, dramatic wage hikes, and employer dissatisfaction, in favour of systematic tripartite standard-setting and forms of collective bargaining. Article 91 of the revised Labour Code (2012) stipulates that regional minimum wages are set in four separate geographical regions reflecting economic conditions, social factors, government policy and labour market conditions (Dieu and Dong, 2015: 45). However, minimum wages are not sufficient to meet minimum living standards, which give some credence to the VGCL's arguments that economic pressures on workers are the main cause of strikes. A survey conducted by the Vietnam Institute for Workers and Trade Unions found that minimum wages in SOEs across the four regions 'only meet 60–72 per cent of workers' minimum standard of living' (Dieu and Dong, 2015: 46).

In Russia, the gap between minimum subsistence levels and regional minimum wages has led to the FNPR encouraging affiliated unions to ensure that minimum wages at least meet subsistence levels and that CLAs reflect as much. The 2001 Labour Code seemed to indicate that this would be the case by specifying that the minimum wage should be no less than the adult subsistence minimum at a time when 40 per cent of employees earned less than the subsistence minimum. However, this was something of a pyrrhic victory for the FNPR, at least as far as its members are concerned. The union has campaigned for over 15 years for the Federal government to increase the minimum wage to subsistence level, mainly by lobbying at the Russian Tripartite Commission for the Regulation of Social-Labour Relations which was established by Yeltsin in 1999. Unions, employers and the government each have 30 seats on the Commission with three union seats taken by representatives from the 'alternative unions' (Vinagradova *et al.*, 2015: 198). The Commission's General Agreement for the period 2008–2010 seemed to indicate a success for the unions with a decision to bring minimum wages in line with Federal and regional subsistence levels. This did indeed generate a significant rise in 2009 that brought minimum wage levels in 2010 to 4,330 rubles per month, almost double the rate for 2008.[8] Moreover in March 2016, the Russian government announced a 21 per cent rise in the minimum wage to 7,500 rubles per month, but this remains well below the subsistence level of 9,452 rubles. This ongoing pattern of state regulation of wages is really more a reflection of union weakness in an unequal partnership with the state than of successful union lobbying. Despite over a decade of campaigning by FNPR on the issue, the Labour

---

[8] See www.tradingeconomics.com/russia/minimum-wages.

Minister Maxim Topilin estimated that it would take another three years to match the two levels.[9]

In China, minimum wages are set at provincial or equivalent level as stipulated by Article 48 of the Labour Law (1995). They are designed to 'provide the floor to underpin both labour and collective contracts' (Cooney et al., 2013: 80). Minimum Wage Regulations (2004) issued by the MOHRSS in 2003 added specific guidelines on the calculation of minimum wages and also set penalties for employers failing to pay them (Article 13). Despite these regulatory interventions, the implementation of minimum wage levels was far from uniform (Cooney et al., 2013) and the problem was certainly exacerbated by a culture of wage arrears that characterised employment relations during the 1990s and 2000s (Greenfield and Pringle, 2002: 30). In 2013 the State Council issued an *Opinion Concerning Deepening the Reform of the Income Redistribution System* that recommended an increase in minimum wage to at least 40 per cent of average wages.[10] This was hardly new. The 2004 Regulations had also stipulated that each region should set its wage at between 40 and 60 per cent of a given region's average wage. In August 2016, China Labour Bulletin (CLB) reported that in most cities the minimum wage was around 30 per cent and in Beijing was as low as 24 per cent of average wages. Given that average wages in China increased at an annual rate of approximately 10 per cent since 2000[11] – 15 per cent in the private sector where most migrant workers are employed since 2005 (according to the International Monetary Fund)[12] – CLB argues that 'the pay gap between many low-paid workers and those earning the average wage is actually widening in real terms'.[13]

The different politics of the minimum wage in China and Vietnam is illustrated by their contrasting trade union behaviour in terms of strikes. In Shenzhen, south China, the minimum wage was increased by up to a third in 2005 and 2006 in response to strikes, but there was little evidence of the ACFTU playing any part in these decisions. When the local government failed to increase wages in July 2007, workers struck again, forcing the government to raise wages. Again, the ACFTU appeared to have no role. In contrast, at the end of 2005 workers in the south of Vietnam launched strike waves holding out for wages higher than

[9] Russia Raises Minimum Monthly Wage to $110. https://themoscowtimes.com/articles/russia-raises-minimum-monthly-wage-to-110–52290.

[10] See www.gov.cn/zwgk/2013–02/05/content_2327531.htm.

[11] See www.bloomberg.com/news/articles/2016–03–22/china-s-great-wage-boom-seen-subsiding-with-unemployment-rising.

[12] See www.imf.org/external/pubs/ft/dp/2016/apd1601.pdf.

[13] Wage and Employment. www.clb.org.hk/content/wages-and-employment.

the statutory minimum. Press reports, including articles criticising the government's tardiness in the VGCL's *Lao Dong*, raised workers' expectations that minimum wages would be raised in early 2006. When the raise did not materialise, strikes broke out in foreign-invested enterprises (FIEs) and the government increased wages by 40 per cent for workers in FIE factories but held out when workers in domestic enterprises demanded the same. The economic consequences for state funds would have been much heavier because at the time Vietnam had separate minimum wages for foreign and domestic enterprises. Although state reactions to the strikes were similar in both countries – significant hikes in the minimum wage – the attitude of the Party-controlled unions was different. The VGCL adopted an openly critical line of the government's delay in raising the minimum wage whereas the ACFTU appeared to be 'more sensitive to the concerns of local government that increases in the minimum wage will discourage investment, so it is better to make piecemeal concessions to the most aggrieved workers, rather than legislate for a general wage increase' (Pringle and Clarke, 2011: 109).

Strikes and Collective Bargaining

The Labour Code (2001), and specifically its Chapter 61, made legal strikes in Russia virtually impossible. This is reflected in official strike statistics that record a dramatic decline from 17,007 in 1997 to just three recorded strikes in 2013 with a total of 196 participants (Gerasimova, 2014: 261). However, these statistics are restricted to strikes that have gone through all the official procedures and even then Rosstat only records them as strikes if employers report them as such. The Centre for Social and Labour Rights began using data-trawling technology to monitor all forms of workplace disputes in 2008 and presents a set of figures that indicate higher levels of militancy – though still low in comparison with Vietnam and China – recording 102 strikes in 2013 (Gerasimova, 2014: 263). Legal restrictions only partly explain the figures. Trade union reticence to organise strikes in the context of the so-called 'Russian Model' is another significant barrier. For example, employers tend to prefer wage reductions – facilitated by the low basic wage component of Russia's wage system – over redundancies in times of economic downturn. In general, FNPR-affiliated unions do not resist for fear of substituting social partnership with class struggle and consequently incurring government censure, with the result that some workers take individual exit options from companies but mass redundancies are avoided (Vinagradova *et al.*, 2015). Indeed it has been argued that the 'simultaneous use of … instruments (inflationary depreciation of real compensation, cuts in premiums, wage arrears and shrinkage of shadow wages) contained labor costs and made mass downsizing not vitally important' (Gimpelson and Kapeliushnikov, 2011: 10). This 'Russian Model' (Vinagradova *et al.*, 2015) of low strike activity, employment rigidity and wage flexibility is the context for collective bargaining in Russia today.

Given the low incidence of strikes it is not surprising that collective bargaining at national, regional and company levels is framed in terms of social partnership (Gerasimova and Bolsheva, 2015: 332). However, it would be a mistake to assume that social partnership was a model incapable of producing improvements. The improved economic situation from 2000 until the financial crisis of 2008 allowed room for improved CLAs from the perspective of labour. In the booming oil, gas and metallurgy sectors, unions were able to extract concessions from employers and even backed up their collective bargaining strategies with threats of strike action (Pringle and Clarke, 2011: 84). Nevertheless, 'employees themselves do not always consider a strike as the most effective way to settle collective labour disputes' (Gerasimova, 2014: 264) and it is usually the so-called 'alternative' unions that lead the way in this respect.

Events at a Ford car plant illustrate that a more accountable and militant trade unionism can find expression in collective bargaining in Russia, but that it is often reliant on the energy of individual activists and remains difficult to emulate.[14] Two workers at the Vsevolozhsk Ford car factory outside St. Petersburg were inspired to reorganise their plant following a chance exposure to militant Brazilian auto industry unions. One of them was the charismatic Alexei Etmanov, who has since been physically attacked at least twice.[15] Etmanov and fellow activists at the plant were able to persuade a majority of the plant workers to vote for a new union committee, secure bargaining rights and use targeted strike actions to improve the collective agreement with Ford. By connecting with activists in other auto plants, they organised the Inter-regional Trade Union of Motor Industry Workers (MPRA), which elected Etmanov as president. Although efforts to emulate the Vsevolozhsk Ford plant at other St. Petersburg enterprises have not met with the same degree of success, Etmanov claims that at Ford, the new union committee 'concluded one of the best collective agreements … [and] provides wage increases outpacing inflation'.[16] While the MPRA has not challenged

---

[14] See http://web.warwick.ac.uk/russia/ngpa/.
[15] See ITUC: http://survey.ituc-csi.org/Ford-Motors-update-Etmanov-still.html.
[16] See http://sovietrussianow.blogspot.co.uk/2014/03/a-etmanov-do-not-cry-organize.html.

the dominance of traditional trade union practices, the MPRA nevertheless provides an alternative version of trade unionism that hitherto did
not exist in China or Vietnam (Pringle, 2015a: 231).

Whether an implemented TPP agreement and concomitant opportunity for independently organised primary trade unions would have generated similar strike-backed collective bargaining with global capital in
Vietnam was the subject of considerable debate. The country's workforce
is predominantly employed in the informal economy and, while workers
in the formal economy – especially in FIEs – have acquired a reputation
for militancy, some commentators remain confident that the combination
of a large informal economy and the Vietnamese government's capacity to
bypass ILO norms will facilitate the survival of Party-led trade unionism
(Clarke, 2006: 348).[17] Nevertheless, workers in Vietnam have the right to
strike but only if it is organised by the trade union. In the absence of
freedom of association, this means that the VGCL would have to lead
a strike and this is an extremely rare occurrence. These constraints seem
to have only an incidental impact on Vietnamese workers themselves.
The tendency for workers in Vietnam to ignore formal bureaucratic
channels of dispute resolution was documented during the 2000s
(Clarke, 2006; Clarke *et al.*, 2007; Pringle and Clarke, 2011). Clarke
noted that workers are 'interested in securing what they regard as their
legitimate interests by the most effective means at their disposal, and the
most effective means has proved to be the wildcat strike' (Clarke *et al.*,
2007: 561). Between 1995 and May 2005, figures from the VGCL and
Vietnam News show 879 strikes of which 64 per cent were in the foreign-
invested sector, 27 per cent were in the private sector and only 8 per cent
were in the state sector (Clarke, 2006: 348).

As we have seen, the government responded to strikes by raising the
minimum wage but this has not been sufficient to head off the militancy.
Following a major strike wave in 2006, the VGCL began to take collective
bargaining more seriously, issuing a major directive in the same year that
stressed collective agreements should include better-than-minimum benefits for workers. Higher unions were instructed to provide support for
primary unions in collective negotiations and also to explore the possibility of above-workplace agreements with groups of employers. The 10th
Congress of the VGCL in 2008 proposed that, by the end of 2013,
70 per cent of enterprises should have concluded collective agreements
that provide better conditions for workers (Pringle and Clarke, 2011:
101). The 2012 revisions to the Trade Union Law allowed higher trade

---

[17] See http://blogs.soas.ac.uk/lsmd/2015/11/30/will-the-tpp-be-good-for-workers-in-
vietnam/.

unions to organise strikes and conduct collective bargaining in workplaces without trade unions.

None of this has served to stop the strikes. The survey previously cited
of 3943 FIEs carried out over 2010–2012 concluded that 'Vietnam has
experienced one of the greatest strike waves in its contemporary history'
(Anner and Liu, 2016: 5). Khanh (2015: 118) argued that weak
employer-dependent primary trade unions and the consequent weakness
in collective bargaining mechanisms has led to the problem that the actual
wages of the workers are heavily dependent on the minimum wage as
regulated by the government. On the other hand, Do is more optimistic
about the prospects for certain forms of collective bargaining. She argues
that strikes are well-organised and provide an impetus for more effective
collective bargaining, a stated goal of the VGCL. Citing a longitudinal
study of strikes across seven provinces between 2005 and 2015,
Do argues that 'strike waves result from the characteristics of industrial
clusters, coordination among foreign employers, and worker communities inside industrial zones, which together create the basis of informal
pattern bargaining' (Do, 2015).

Pattern bargaining is the term used when a settlement reached with one
employer sets an effective precedent in subsequent negotiations with
other employers. Forms of pattern and sectoral bargaining are beginning
to show up on Vietnam's industrial relations map. Chapter 5 of the
Labour Code (1995) provided for sectoral bargaining and it was priori-
tised through largely unsuccessful pilots in the coal-mining and garment
sectors following a meeting between the VGCL and the Prime Minister in
2007. However, article 91.3 of the Labour Code (2012) appeared to
signal more scope for sector-level agreements by linking them with sectoral minimum wages and stipulating that the latter are 'determined
through sectoral collective bargaining and stated in the sectoral collective
bargaining agreements, but shall not be lower than the regional minimum
wage announced by the Government'.[18] The ILO has supported this
initiative and there are some signs of progress as reported by the
VGCL's *Lao Dong* newspaper in January 2016. A multi-employer agreement covering 700 workers in the tourist sector employed in four companies included a wage rise 3.3 per cent above the minimum wage and
improvements in meal allowances. Placing the agreement in the context
of Vietnam's status 'as a member state of the ILO', the organisation's
Vietnam Country Director Chang-Hee Lee observed that 'this is the first
time trade unions and employers in Viet Nam have successfully

---

[18] See: www.wageindicator.org/main/salary/minimum-wage/vietnam/faqs-minimum-
wages-in-vietnam#header1.

negotiated collective agreements, covering multiple enterprises rather than just one. It is a major innovation in labour relations practices.'[19]

Moving towards meeting standards set in ILO core labour rights on collective bargaining and freedom of association do not appear to be among the goals of the Chinese state although the current situation is not straightforward. Despite being a signatory to the United Nation's International Covenant on Economic, Social and Cultural Rights, the Chinese government entered a reservation on the clause pertaining to freedom of association when it ratified the treaty in 2001. The reservation insisted that Article 8 Clause 1 would only be implemented within the parameters of China's Trade Union Law (2001), Article 10 of which awards a monopoly on organising to the ACFTU. The absence of other trade unions means that there are just two push factors that can serve as impetus for forms of collective bargaining that improve on the system of collective consultation discussed earlier: labour militancy and the state's fear of it. The former is documented in Chapter 9 in this book. With regard to the latter, an important feature of the militancy in recent years has been the willingness of a minority of labour non-governmental organisations to shift the focus of their operations from providing legal assistance to individual workers pursuing grievances through juridical channels of dispute resolution, to training and supporting workers pursuing collective interests via strikes in collective bargaining (Pringle, 2015b; Franceschini, 2016: 18). Disputes often arise over the terms of closure and workers have been anxious to ensure that employers do not leave the closed workplace owing wages, social insurance premiums or contributions to the statutory housing provident fund.

A broad pattern of cooperation between labour NGOs and workers has emerged. It has demonstrated a capacity to bring employers to the bargaining table in what can be called 'closure bargaining'. First, demands are re-organised into a coordinated package that has the support of as many workers as possible in a given workplace. Second, labour NGOs foster solidarity between workers across different sections, shops and departments in the workplace. While many workers have direct experience of short strikes, few are aware of collective bargaining procedures and of the extended solidarity that drawn out negotiations require. Third, workers' representatives who are prepared to act as negotiators with employers are elected. This can be risky as employers will often attempt to bribe or threaten elected reps into making concessions without seeking

---

[19] See: http://vietnamnews.vn/society/281229/collective-bargaining-offers-workers-emplo yers-opportunities-to-progress.html#UemsHaIX9oOrKADY.97.

agreement from the workforce. Fourth, labour NGOs increasingly organise training sessions in collective bargaining skills as a precursor to negotiation.

An example is striking workers at the Taiwan-owned QLT Golf Supplies Factory in Shenzhen, who returned to work in July 2014 following a successful collective bargaining session with their employer. The latter had initially refused to negotiate with 200 striking employees but the threat of the strike spreading to the rest of the 2000-strong workforce and pressure from the local government persuaded QLT management to negotiate. Assisted by a Shenzhen-based labour NGO, the workers elected their own representatives to form a workers' committee at the factory. During the bargaining, management eventually agreed to formalise this into factory-wide elections for a trade union committee. In the context of a threatened relocation, the workers' key demand was for the company to pay arrears in social insurance premiums. Throughout the QLT dispute, workers' militancy informed by labour NGO expertise in collective bargaining was crucial to the outcome. By holding training sessions in collective bargaining for over 60 QLT workers, the labour NGO was able to transform the anger of a divided workforce into negotiable demands that formed the material basis for a stronger solidarity. While it still took a short strike to persuade management to recognise the workers' representatives and to negotiate, the seeds of collective negotiation were put in place with the potential to negotiate the terms of possible relocation or to improve pay and conditions incrementally (Pringle, 2015b: 4–5).

These labour NGOs have stopped short of organising strikes in order to remain within the law, and they have played an important part in the development of collective bargaining in Guangdong. They are following a familiar strategy of using the law, in particular the recent Guangdong *Regulation on Enterprise Collective Consultation and Collective Contracts* (2015). Labour NGOs are consolidating their position by using this cautious attempt by the Guangdong government both to contain labour unrest and to institutionalise collective negotiations. In conjunction with labour militancy, their presence puts pressure on the ACFTU to improve its representative capacity and promote its own pilot projects in collective bargaining (Pringle, 2015b; Lee *et al.*, 2016). It reinforces the view that the government's policy of slowing the rate of informalisation of employment relations (Gallagher *et al.*, 2011: 6) by disciplining capital to signing formal contracts with employees means that 'the new collective bargaining practices are having substantive impacts on wages and other working conditions' (Lee *et al.*, 2016: 232). Going against this view, recent government interventions to regulate[20] – and almost inevitably constrain – the activities of civil society organisations are not likely to encourage workers and potential organisers to familiarise themselves with the skills required for collective bargaining. While the ACFTU is more than capable of bureaucratising initiatives from below and reducing worker participation, the arrest of key labour NGO players is likely to facilitate the repression of strikes rather than their resolution through forms of collective bargaining that may develop into institutionalised practices.

Conclusion

This chapter has compared labour relations in general and trade union roles and performance in particular across three so-called 'post-socialist' countries that are making the transition from command to market economies. I have used three aspects of trade union performance as comparative yardsticks: union (re)organisation; the evolution of national legal frameworks for labour relations; and collective bargaining.

In Russia, alternative trade unions did emerge to challenge the traditional union practices that had been repackaged into social partnership by the FNPR following the fall of the Soviet Union. But the progress of these alternatives was blocked by a new Labour Code. Crucially, the code privileged the FNPR's domination of collective bargaining. A 'Russian Model' of avoiding sudden mass redundancies and using social partnership to gain union agreement for wage cuts at company level has continued to keep union influence at a low level. Neither the state nor capital has hesitated to resort to threats and intimidation when more militant alternative unions are deemed to be stepping too far out of line from the *status quo*.

In Vietnam, the VGCL has not been able to move towards institutionalised collective bargaining despite international support and high levels of strikes and labour militancy. There are some signs of progress in this direction. The prospect of more room for independent union organising will inevitably test the VGCL and its capacity for reform – or perhaps even survival.

In China, a slowing economy and narrowing of space for civil society have not generated a decline in strikes or labour militancy. As capital flows and investment move to the interior of the country in search of lower wages and less militant workforces, the gradual evolution of forms of

---

[20] China's Charity Law came in to effect in September 2016. The Overseas NGO Law will be effective from 1 January 2017.

collective bargaining is at a crucial stage. Will they survive the new environment? Will they be reproduced in adapted forms in massive urban centres of accumulation away from the coasts such as Chongqing, Chengdu and Wuhan? In all three countries, it will be the capacity of workers to pursue collective class-based demands that will continue to drive and influence the outcomes of trade union transitions.

References

Anner, M. (2015), 'Worker resistance in global supply chains: Wildcat strikes, international accords and transnational campaigns', *International Journal of Labour Research*, 7(1–2), 17–34.

Anner, M. and Liu, X. M. (2016), 'Harmonious unions and rebellious workers: A study of wildcat strikes in Vietnam', *ILR Review* 69(1), 3–28.

Burawoy, M. (1996), 'The state and economic involution: Russia through a China lens', *World Development* 24(6), 1105–1117.

Chan, A. (2011), 'Unionizing China's Walmart stores', in Chan, A. (ed.), *Walmart in China*, Ithaca and London: ILR Press, 199–216.

Chan, K. C. and Hui, E. (2012), 'The dynamics and dilemma of workplace trade union reform in China: The case of the Honda workers' strike', *Journal of Industrial Relations* 54(5), 653–668.

Chan. J., Pun, N. and Selden, M. (2015), 'Interns or workers? China's student labor regime', *The Asia-Pacific Journal*, 13(36). Available at: http://apjjf.org/-Mark-Selden–Pun-Ngai–Jenny-Chan/4372/article.pdf (accessed 20 August 2016).

Clarke, S., Fairbrother, P. and Borisov, V. (1995), *The Workers' Movement in Russia*, Cheltenham: Edward Elgar.

Clarke, S. and Kabalina, V. (1995), 'Privatisation and the struggle for control in the Russian enterprise' in Lane, D. (ed.), *Russia in Transition*, London: Longman, 142–58.

Clarke, S. (2006), 'The changing character of strikes in Vietnam', *Post-Communist Economies*, 18(3), 345–361.

Clarke, S., Lee, C. H. and Do, Q. C. (2007), 'From rights to interests: The challenge of industrial relations in Vietnam', *Journal of Industrial Relations*, 49(4), 545–568.

Clarke, S. and Pringle, T. (2009), 'Can Party-led unions represent their members?' *Post-Communist Economies*, 21(1), 85–101.

Cooney, S., Biddulph, S. and Zhu, Y. (2013), *Law and Fair Work in China*, Abingdon: Routledge.

Dieu, Q. D. and Dong, H. T. T. (2015), 'Vietnam' in Klaveren, M., Gregory, D. and Schulten, T. (eds.), *Minimum Wages, Collective Bargaining and Economic Development in Asia and Europe*, Basingstoke: Palgrave Macmillan, 39–58.

Do, Q. C. (2013), 'Enhanced employee participation and the influence from below', *Asia Pacific Journal of Human Resources*, 51, 193–207.

Do, Q. C. (2015), 'Coordination among strikes and prospects for pattern bargaining in Vietnam', *Global Labour Journal*, 234, Available at: http://column

.global-labour-university.org/2016/05/coordination-among-strikes-and.html (accessed 21 August 2016).

Franceschini, I. (2016), 'Revisiting Chinese LNGOs: Some grounds for hope?' *Made in China*, 1(16), Available at: www.chinoiresie.info/PDF/madeinchina-2016_ISSUE1.pdf (accessed 21 August 2016).

Fritzen, S. (2002), 'Growth, inequality and the future of poverty reduction in Vietnam', *Journal of Asian Economics*, 13, 635–657.

Gallagher, M., Lee, C. K. and Kuruvilla, S. (2011), 'Introduction and argument', in Kuruvilla, S., Lee CK. and Gallagher, M. (eds.), '*From Iron Rice Bowl to Informalization: Markets, Workers, and the State in a Changing China*', Ithaca, NY: ILR Press, 1–14.

Gallagher, M. and Dong, B. H. (2011), 'Legislating harmony: Labor law reform in contemporary China', in Kuruvilla, S., Lee, CK. and Gallagher, M. (eds.), *op cit*, 36–60

Gerasimova, E. (2014), 'The resolution of collective labour disputes and the realization of the right to strike in Russia' in Lebedev, V. and Radevich, E. (eds.), *Labour Law in Russia: Recent Developments and New Challenges*. Newcastle-upon-Tyne: Cambridge Scholars Publishing, 259–288.

Gerasimova, E. and Bolsheva, A. (2015), 'The Russian Federation' in Klaveren M, Gregory D and Schulten T (eds.), *op cit.*, 325–343.

Gimpelson, V. and Kapeliushnikov, R. (2011), 'Labor market adjustment: is Russia different?' Institute for the Study of Labor, Available at: http://ftp.iza.org/dp5588.pdf (accessed 19 August 2016).

Greenfield, G. and Pringle, T. (2002), 'The challenges of wage arrears in China', International Labour Organisation', Available at: www.ilo.org/wcmsp5/groups/public/-ed_dialogue/-actrav/documents/publication/wcms_111463.pdf (accessed 17 August 2017).

Hellevig, J., Usov, A. and Katyshev, I. (2014), *Awara Russian Labor Law Guide 2014*, Moscow: Awara Group.

Human Rights Watch (2002), *Paying the Price: Worker Unrest in Northeast China*, Available at: www.hrw.org/reports/2002/chinalbr02/ (accessed 17 August 2016).

Jingji Guancha bao (2011), 'Quanwei baogao cheng "laowu paiqian" da 6000 wan ren quanzong jianyi xiugai "laodong hetongfa" ', [authoritative report claims 'labor dispatch' has reached 60million people, ACFTU suggests revisions to Labor Contract Law], 25 February.

Khanh T. (2015), 'The right to strike in Vietnam's private sector', *Asian Journal of Law and Society*, 2(1), 115–135.

Klump, R. and Bonschab, T. (2004), 'Operationalising pro-poor growth in Vietnam', World Bank, Available at: http://siteresources.worldbank.org/INTPGI/Resources/342674-1115051237044/oppgvietnam.pdf (accessed 17 August 2016).

Kuruvilla, S., Lee, C. K. and Gallagher, M. (2011), *From Iron Rice Bowl to Informalization: Markets, Workers, and the State in a Changing China*. Ithaca, NY: ILR Press.

Lee, C. H., Brown, W. and Wen, X. Y. (2016), 'What sort of collective bargaining is emerging in China?' *British Journal of Industrial Relations*, 54(1), 214–236.

Lee, C. K. (2007), *Against the Law: Labor Protests in China's Rustbelt and Sunbelt*, Berkeley: University of California Press.

Lyddon, D., Cao, X. B., Quan, M. and Lu, J, (2015), 'A strike of "unorganised" workers in a Chinese car factory: the Nanhai Honda event of 2010', *Industrial Relations Journal*, 46(2), 134–152.

Malesky, E., Abrami, R. and Zheng, Y. (2011), 'Institutions and inequality in single party regimes: A comparative analysis of China and Vietnam', *Comparative Politics*, 43(4), 409–427.

Pringle, T. and Leung, A. (2009), 'Causes, implementation and consequences of "xiagang"', In Luk, P. (ed.), *Xiagang: The Sacrifice in the Transformation of Labour Policy in China from State to Market*, Hong Kong: Asia Monitor Resource Centre.

Pringle, T (2011) *Trade Unions in China: The Challenge of Labour Unrest*, Abingdon: Routledge.

Pringle, T. and Clarke, S. (2011), *The Challenge of Transition: Trade Unions in Russia, China and Vietnam*, Basingstoke: Palgrave.

Pringle, T. (2015a), 'Trade union reform in Russia and China: Harmony, partnership and the power from below', Chan, A. (ed.), *Chinese Workers in Comparative Perspective*, Ithaca and London: ILR Press, pp. 201–234.

Pringle, T. (2015b), 'Labour under threat: The rise (and possible fall) of collective bargaining in Guangdong', *International Union Rights*, 22 (4), 3–5.

Schweisshelm, E. (2015), 'Trade unions in Vietnam: changing industrial relations in Vietnam', *Global Labour Column*, Available at: http://column.global-labour-university.org/2014/09/trade-unions-in-transition-changing.html   (accessed 17 August 2016).

Schweisshelm, E. and Do, Q. C. (2015), 'From harmony to conflict: Vietnam's trade union at the threshold of reform', sponsored by Friedrich Ebert Stiftung, Trade Unions in Transition Societies, St. Petersburg, Russia, 7–8 July 2015.

Silver, B. (2003), *Forces of Labour: Workers' Movements and Globalization since 1870*, Cambridge: Cambridge University Press.

Wei, J. X. (2000). 'Renzhen xuexi guanche dang de shiwu ju wu zhong quan hui jingshen. Jin yi bu jiakuai xin jian qiye gonghui zujian bufa', [Conscientiously implement the spirit of the fifth plenary session of the 15th Central Committee: Speed up the organising and establishing of trade unions in new enterprises], www.bjzgh.gov.cn/jianghua/5_jianghua_13.php.

Workers Daily (1988), 'Jianshe duli zizhu, gaodu minzhu, zhigong xinlai de gonghui', [Build an independent, autonomous, democratic trade union trusted by staff and workers], 29 October.

VGCL (2011). *Research Report on Recruiting Trade Union Members, Develop Workplace Union and Collective Negotiation*, Hanoi.

Vinagradova, E., Kozina, I. and Cook, L. J. (2015), 'Labor relations in Russia: Moving to a "market social contract"', *Problems of Post-Communism*, 62, 193–203.

11   Conclusion

William Brown and Chang Kai

What sort of industrial relations is emerging in China? The potential for conflict over employment has been increasing. It is unavoidable as jobs in China become more exposed to markets. Unregulated markets have never on their own balanced the interests of workers with those of employers and investors. Improving and protecting working conditions and job security always requires positive action and is unavoidably a collective issue. The central concern of this book has been with how far institutions are being developed in China to protect workers' interests, to channel their collective responses and to mediate the compromises necessary for stable labour relations.

Despite its integration into global markets, China remains a strongly state-led market economy. The most distinctive feature of its labour relations is the extent of government intervention at all levels. In the previous chapter we saw how much greater this intervention continues to be in China by comparison with Russia and Vietnam, two countries which opened up their markets at much the same time. The building of institutions for regulating labour relations in China has been under way for thirty years, and has been firmly directed from the top down, but the process is far from complete. Although a transition towards collective labour regulation has been initiated, labour relations across the country are still typically autocratically managed and individualised. Even the formal appearance of collective arrangements of recent years belies reality. But to dismiss this policy of collective regulation as superficial would be a mistake. The way that Chinese policy towards employment has progressed has long been through cautious, incremental change. It is typically developed by carefully building on solid research and learning from pilot exercises. As earlier chapters have made clear, the process of achieving change in Chinese labour relations draws not only on legislation, but also on the wider use of political and administrative power and the mobilising of civil society.

The chapters in this book have concentrated on the years since 2008, when the Labour Contract Law completed a solid platform for workers' individual rights. The international financial crisis of that year gave urgency to the use of both collective consultation and statutory minimum wages to raise consumption at home by ensuring that workers got a share of the growing profits of the market sector. The strike wave of 2010 drew attention to the changing aspirations of the newly urbanised work-force and to the collective expression of its discontents. Since then reports of spontaneously organised strikes have become more frequent. At the same time, declining migration from the countryside has led to a tightening labour market and a westward shift of investment within China. After two decades of extraordinarily rapid expansion, the growth rate of the economy has started to fall to more sustainable levels.

The Chinese government has responded to these pressures with increased emphasis on the collective nature of employment. It has strengthened what are, in effect, the recognition rights of the official trade union with a vigorous campaign to extend both trade union membership and collective consultation in the growing private sector. The immediate consequences of so rapid an expansion, in a private sector where managers have typically given their workers no voice, are at best superficial. But it does make clear the official intention that the trade union should be the driving force behind the improvement of workers' terms and conditions of employment. Collective consultation among smaller, locally owned enterprises, competing for scarce labour in the same industries, has been given real substance by the encouragement of sectoral agreements. In an effort to extend employee involvement, the state-sector tradition of enterprise-based workers' congresses is being pressed on the private sector. The direction of policy seems to be clear. It remains to be seen how far employers choose to respond in ways that help their workers. That depends, as is always the case, on the diligence of government in enforcing employment rights and on the capacity of workers to defend and advance their interests at enterprise level. But there can be no doubting that government policy is firmly committed to a collective approach.

The earlier chapters have reflected the lively debate that is underway concerning rights to strike in China. Readers familiar with labour law in other countries will be aware that explicit legal rights to strike are a double-edged weapon from a trade union point of view; narrowly defined, they can be as much a constraint as a freedom. What is more significant is what is happening on the ground. Here there has been a marked change in local government behaviour towards strikes. Work stoppages are no longer automatically classified as threats to social order. Local authorities are increasingly placing the responsibility for settling labour disputes on employers, so long as disputes are confined to the enterprise premises. If the authorities do intervene, they increasingly do so not by taking the employer's side as the enforcers of civil order, but more as independent mediators, if necessary applying pressure to employers to reach a settlement.

The response of private sector employers to market forces in China has in many ways replicated their behaviour in older market economies. As in other countries, the early employers in China's market sector tended to be autocratic managers, relying on the civil authorities to suppress labour unrest. But more recently, although there are great variations between different types of firm, a more self-confident workforce is persuading many employers to adopt a more responsive style of employee management. The employers' response to the government pressure to engage in collective consultation continues generally to be one of resistance or extreme caution, and of maintaining management control over any workplace-based trade union. As in more established market economies, common employer strategies to resist worker solidarity include the employment of student interns and of agency workers, outsourcing of work and the black-listing and dismissal of worker activists.

There is little evidence in China as yet of the sort of formal workplace procedures that would be considered routine for regulating collective conflict in Western economies – procedures for dispute resolution, for grievance settlement and for disciplinary matters. Experience elsewhere suggests that such procedures, with independent mediation and arbitration, are essential for the orderly resolution of collective conflict. Much is spoken in China of harmonious workplace relations, but the maintenance of harmony requires a constant possibility of consultation and of negotiation. It requires procedural rights for worker representatives, and thereby becomes important in connecting workplace activists to the wider trade union. As was observed earlier, procedural rules provide a scaffolding of legitimacy for relations between employers and workers. They are at least as important as rights to strike.

A powerful employer response to labour shortages and increased government intervention in China has been to get organised. To a surprising extent this growth of employer organisations has so far been relatively free from government guidance. But increasing employer involvement in sectoral collective consultation may be indicative that this is changing. The history of industrial relations elsewhere suggests that sectoral institutions with strong legal support provide a robust and economically effective basis for the governance of employment in internationally exposed markets. Whether or not this develops further in China, an important function of employer organisation has already become the lobbying of government on issues of concern such as employment legislation, even to the extent of lobbying against the official trade union.

The expanding of consumer demand within China is now a central part of the country's strategy for both economic development and the maintenance of social harmony. This has added to the authority of the official trade union in ways that trade unions in other countries might envy. The union now plays an important part both in achieving pay increases and in drafting legislation. But because the union is effectively a part of government, its role is very different from that of trade unions in other market economies. It carries a duty to maintain social order as well as to protect and advance the rights of workers. It does not have the legal authority to initiate strikes which elsewhere has been an important option for trade unions.

But that does not mean the union is powerless in defence of worker interests. On the contrary, its proximity to government provides other means of influencing employers. It has for some years played a central role in the development of legislation, notably with the Labour Contracts Law. More recently it took the lead in the regulations introduced to limit employer use of agency workers. As the Chinese economy develops, the union's organisational structure is proving to be adaptable, with the capacity to develop organisations at whatever level allows most effective negotiation with employers. This is one reason why local sectoral agreements have been spreading. Resources are being shifted down within the union to give more support to collective consultation at the local level. Some union officials are being recruited at enterprise level who are not themselves enterprise employees. There have been many cautious experiments with ballots and at least partial elections to give decisions and appointments greater legitimacy in the eyes of workers. When strikes have broken out, union officials, working with local government, have been effective mediators. In response to the tougher demands of markets, the trade union is arguably becoming more distanced from employers in the market sector. It is drawing closer to government. But it is also taking substantial steps to draw closer to the workers.

The need for this is clear. There are in effect two trade union movements in China: the official trade union federation and unofficial enterprise-based activism. Workplace activism is typically short-lived and isolated. But it is often effective, and its organisational sophistication has been increasing. Local trade union officials play an important role on the interface between these two movements, both in preventing labour disputes and in resolving them. The research described in this book has shown that these pressures from below are often managed with considerable skill and pragmatic flexibility by the union. The pressures can be expected to increase. The union has the central role in protecting and improving working conditions. But at a time when government is reducing its direct involvement in workplace employment relations, this will be difficult unless the union can mobilise the energy and commitment of workers at enterprise level.

Any consideration of the emerging industrial relations of China must place it in wider context. Collective bargaining, which contributed so much to improving labour standards worldwide in the twentieth century, is now in general decline. In the market sectors of most developed countries it is diminishing in both coverage and impact. The main exceptions are some countries of Western Europe where trade unions and collective agreements still have substantial legal support. The decline in market sector collective bargaining is even greater in most of the developing world. Without legal support for collective bargaining, it has undoubtedly become very hard to protect labour standards wherever employment is exposed to international competition for products and for investment. In country after country, this has exposed employees to individualised contracts which are typically inferior in terms of job security, pay, conditions and rights.

This is what makes the Chinese position so very remarkable. The world has never seen so great an expansion of a market economy as in China over the past twenty years. But the direction of policy in China has not followed the global trend of allowing businesses to adopt a more autocratic, individualistic approach to labour. On the contrary, government policy has been to build collective employment relations. Chinese employers are being encouraged to develop more independent, but also more collective, ways of reconciling conflicts of interest with workers. The trade union is seeking to augment its official authority through closer links to workers. China's emerging industrial relations has the potential to develop enduring institutions to represent, advance and defend the workers' interests, and to provide the means for compromise in conflict resolution.

The End

Index

Printed in the United States
By Bookmasters